INTELLECTUAL PROPERTY AND COMPETITIVE
STRATEGIES IN THE 21st CENTURY

KLUWER LAW INTERNATIONAL

# Intellectual Property and Competitive Strategies in the 21st Century

## SECOND EDITION

By
## SHAHID ALIKHAN
and
## RAGHUNATH MASHELKAR

Wolters Kluwer

Law & Business

AUSTIN    BOSTON    CHICAGO    NEW YORK    THE NETHERLANDS

*Published by:*
Kluwer Law International
PO Box 316
2400 AH Alphen aan den Rijn
The Netherlands
Website: www.kluwerlaw.com

*Sold and distributed in North, Central and South America by:*
Aspen Publishers, Inc.
7201 McKinney Circle
Frederick, MD 21704
United States of America
Email: customer.care@aspenpubl.com

*Sold and distributed in all other countries by:*
Turpin Distribution Services Ltd.
Stratton Business Park
Pegasus Drive, Biggleswade
Bedfordshire SG18 8TQ
United Kingdom
Email: kluwerlaw@turpin-distribution.com

*Printed on acid-free paper.*

ISBN 978-90-411-2644-3

© 2009 Kluwer Law International BV, The Netherlands

Printed in Great Britain.

# TABLE OF CONTENTS

# PREFACE

That knowledge has played a key role in human progress has long been acknowledged by leaders in all walks of life. It is the vitality of new and original knowledge and of creative expressions of ideas which has brought the role of knowledge, and consequently of the intellectual property system, into the limelight in recent years.

We build on the basis of accumulated knowledge through creative adaptation, innovative interpretation and ingenious insights. Creating an environment which fosters and enhances the use of this improved understanding of ourselves and our environment is a key challenge and a core concern for the state, market and society in many countries.

The modern intellectual property system has become an important tool for harnessing the power of knowledge for development, and this enhanced focus on intellectual property has put this system under intense scrutiny from multiple perspectives worldwide. The dynamics of economic, social, cultural and political factors in a democratic dialogue and consensus-driven environment invariably interface with and shape the future evolution of the intellectual property system.

The authors are internationally well-known authorities on intellectual property matters – Shahid Alikhan, a former Deputy Director General of the World Intellectual Property Organization (WIPO); and Raghunath Mashelkar, an outstanding scientist and dynamic leader of the Council of Scientific and Industrial Research (CSIR) of India. They have, through this book, helped to demystify the subject of intellectual property for a varied audience and have done so with a singular conviction that, if properly managed, the intellectual property system can contribute to the betterment of the human condition in all societies. Their presentation on *Intellectual Property and Competitive Strategies in the 21st Century* is unique in its emphasis on the techno-economic impact of intellectual property rights on enterprise competitiveness. Its coverage of a number of current issues that pose challenges to the intellectual property system is especially timely.

This book deals with a wide array of topics in a lucid, coherent and concise manner, and provides a panoramic view of the pitfalls, challenges and possibilities linked to the intellectual property system as an instrument for socio-economic, cultural and technological development as well as for improving the quality of life of the many people of our planet.


**Kamil Idris**
Ex-Director General
WIPO

# ACKNOWLEDGEMENTS

It is a pleasure to present the second edition of this book. The edition contains a judicious update of the data and analysis. This has been done especially in light of significant advances in the intellectual property arena that have taken place over the past five years in many critical areas that help shape competitive strategies.

This book arose out of our recognition of the need to enhance and increase broad-based awareness of the techno-economic effects of intellectual property rights protection on enterprise competitiveness, national growth and development.

We wish to record our deep gratitude and thanks to the Director General of the World Intellectual Property Organization (WIPO), Dr Kamil Idris, for writing the preface for this book.

A number of WIPO officials and friends have made many suggestions and willingly provided considerable assistance by going through the relevant portions of the text and by providing very useful comments and input, including updating of information. In the latter context, we wish particularly to thank very much Guriqbal Singh Jaiya and Anuradha Madhavan for their enormous help. In the same connection, we equally and profusely thank our other friends in WIPO, including Francis Gurry, Geoffrey Yu, Carlotta Graffigna, Yo Takagi, Kurt Kemper, Sherif Saadallah, Jorgen Blomqvist, Inayeth Syed, Wang Zhengfa, Alejandro Roca, Richard Owens, Wolfgang Starein, Vladmir Yossifov, Li Jiahao, Pushpendra Rai, Edward Kwakwa, Colin Buffam, Marcus Hopperger, Denis Croze, William Guy, Wend Wendland, Irfan Baloch, Monique Ivanovsky, Anil Sinha, Larry Allman, Dimiter Gantchev, Christine Collard and Cecile Muller-Soligon, among others. Our grateful thanks are also due to our friends in the WTO, including the former Director General, Mike Moore, whose addresses, sent to a co-author, we have partially quoted.

Our warm thanks are also due to friends in the government, the private sector and national and international organizations in our country, including S. Narayan, Economic Adviser to the Prime Minister and former Finance Secretary and also Secretary, Industrial Policy and Promotion, Government of India; Raghubir Singh, former Legislative Secretary, Ministry of Law and Justice, Government of India and Secretary of the National Commission to Review the Working of the Constitution; S. Chakravarthy, former Senior Indian Civil Servant and Member, Monopolies and Restrictive Trade Practices Commission; Suresh Chandra, Additional Secretary and Development Commissioner (SSI), Ministry of Small Scale Industries, Government of India; Rajiv Ranjan, Director, Department of Industrial Policy and Promotion, Ministry of Commerce and Industry, Government of India.

Our grateful thanks are also owed to Kiran Karnik, President, National Association of Software and Service Companies (NASSCOM); Arun Agrawal, Secretary-General, World

Association of Small and Medium Enterprises (WASME); V.N. Prasad, Senior Economic Adviser, WASME; Sanjay Tandon, Director General, Indian Performing Rights Society (IPRS); Aditya Trivedi, Secretary, Indian Institute of Intellectual Property Development (IIPD) and Joint Secretary, Federation of Indian Chambers of Commerce and Industry (FICCI).

We wish also to acknowledge with grateful thanks the assistance by way of requested information that was readily provided by our many friends in the international and national non-governmental organizations in other countries such as, among many others, Federico Mayor, former Director General of UNEWSCO; Mithaly Ficsor, former Assistant Director General, WIPO and currently Director, Centre for Information Technology and Intellectual Property, Budapest; Eric H. Smith, President, International Intellectual Property Alliance, Washington, DC; Clive Bradley, former Chief Executive of the British Publishers' Federation, London; Benoit Muller, former Director General, International Publishers Association, Geneva; Denis de Freitas, President of Honour of the British Copyright Council; Geoffrey Adams, Vice President and Janet Ibbotson, Secretary of the British Copyright Council, London; Moira Burnett, Legal Adviser, Legal Department, European Broadcasting Union, Geneva; and Elizabeth Iles, Head of Library Services, International Federation of the Phonographic Industry, London.

The significant contributions also made by the scientists and supporting staff of the National Institute of Science Communication and Information Resources (NISCAIR) – a constituent unit of the Indian Council of Scientific and Industrial Research (CSIR), and by the staff of CSIR are greatly appreciated. In particular, our very special thanks, for their immense help in many ways, are due to V.K. Gupta, Director, NISCAIR; R.K. Gupta, Head of the Intellectual Property Management Division of CSIR; NISCAIR's Editor B.C. Sharma, and scientists M.M.S. Karki, Archana Sharma, N.R. Mankad, B. Subramaniam, and their colleagues Vinod Kumar Sharma, Deepak Sheopuri, and many others who also assisted us readily and painstakingly. Further, our profuse thanks are also due to the staff of the office of the Director General, CSIR headquarters, namely Deputy Secretary S.C. Kalra and his colleagues, Sunil Kumar, N.K. Taneja, V.K. Sharma and Satish Chand, who always provided much help willingly.

Grateful thanks are also due to Arvind Chinchure and Amey Mashelkar of Reliance Innovation Leadership Council in Pune, who provided invaluable help in amending the second edition of this book.

# ABOUT THE AUTHORS

**Shahid Alikhan** is a highly distinguished elder statesman in the field of intellectual property. A former Deputy Director General of the World Intellectual Property Organization (WIPO) and Undersecretary General in the United Nations, he is the author of numerous articles, monographs and books on various aspects of intellectual property rights as they relate to corporate competitiveness and socio-economic development. Now retired, he continues to write, lecture, and conduct seminars in such diverse areas of intellectual property rights as counterfeiting, the Internet, and electronic commerce, for such UN organizations as WIPO, UNESCO and ITC, as well as governmental and non-governmental organizations, and private sector institutions in Europe and in developing countries. He also acts as a representative and senior adviser of the World Association for Small and Medium Enterprises (WASME) on continuing and promoting assistance to single- and medium-sized enterprises (SMEs) worldwide, and serves on the editorial board of the monthly *Journal of Intellectual Property Rights of the National Institute of Science Communication and Information Resources* (NISCAIR) in New Delhi. He is also a member of the Governing Council of the Indian Institute of Intellectual Property Development (IIPD).

**Raghunath Mashelkar**, one of the world's outstanding chemical engineering scientists, has published more than 200 scientific research articles in polymer science and engineering. He is also known for his work on the nexus of intellectual property rights and economic development, particularly in the area of the protection of India's traditional knowledge base. For more than eleven years he was the Director General of the Council of Scientific & Industrial Research (CSIR), the largest chain of industrial research and development institutions in the world. He has also been the Chairman of the Standing Committee on Information Technology of the World Intellectual Property Rights (SCIT), a member of the UK Commission on Intellectual Property Rights (CIPR) and the Vice-Chairman of WHO Commission on IPR, Innovation & Public Health (CIPIH). He is one of only three Indian engineers in the twentieth century to be elected a Fellow of the Royal Society (FRS), London. His academic distinctions include Foreign Associateships of the US National Academies of Science and Engineering, the Third World Academy of Sciences, the UK Royal Academy of Engineering, and the World Academy of Art and Science, US. He has won numerous honours and awards nationally and internationally, including twenty-six honorary doctorates from major universities worldwide.

CHAPTER ONE

# INTRODUCTION TO INTELLECTUAL PROPERTY

*– Nature of the Intellectual Property (IP) System*
*– Rationale for Its Protection*

## 1.1 EMERGENCE OF A KNOWLEDGE DOMINATED CENTURY

Leadership of the world in the twenty-first century will increasingly be in the hands of those who create and harness knowledge. This century, often called the century of knowledge, is indeed the century of the mind. A nation's ability to convert knowledge into wealth and social good through creativity and innovation will determine its future standing in the comity of nations.

The truism that knowledge is power has never been more apt than it is now. Trade and industry are becoming more knowledge driven. For instance, we can see a dramatic change in international trade. While it was formerly dominated by commodities such as iron ore, coffee and unprocessed cotton, it is increasingly moving towards knowledge-intensive goods. High technology goods have doubled their share of world merchandize exports from 11% in 1976 to 22% in 1996, while the share of primary products dropped from 45% to 22%. More than half of the gross domestic product (GDP) of the major Organization of Economic Cooperation and Development (OECD) countries relates to the production and distribution of knowledge.

In today's world, for both individuals and enterprises, confidence in the Intellectual Property (IP) system acts as a powerful stimulus to creativity and innovation. The increasing internationalization of corporate activities and the borderlessness of trade and technology offer new challenges and new opportunities. More specifically: exponential growth of scientific and technical knowledge; increasing demands for new forms of IP protection for hitherto excluded areas and for outputs in new fields of human endeavour; easier access to IP-related information; increasing dominance of the new knowledge economy over the old 'brick and mortar' economy; and complexities linked to IP issues in traditional knowledge, genetic resources and folklore, are trends that pose a great challenge as well as offer opportunities. These will ultimately lead to the establishment of the IP agenda for the twenty-first century.

An understanding of the role of intellectual property rights (IPRs) in the process of innovation and the role of innovation itself in the process of development is crucial. New or original knowledge and the creative expression of ideas provide the basis for creating and sustaining business and enterprise competitiveness. In every enterprise, whether it produces or delivers goods or services, the knowledge component is becoming the predominant element in differentiating it from its competitors. Protecting such new or

1

original knowledge and/or creative expression of ideas has been considered by different competitors in the marketplace as a key to preventing others from free riding on the success and goodwill of individuals or enterprises. Enterprises and businesses need the IP system to protect their manufacturing secrets and other useful information in order to remain ahead of the competition. Issues of generation, identification, valuation, protection and exploitation of IP assets are attracting increasing attention all around the world.

Understanding the importance of the nature and various forms of IP systems and using them optimally as an integral part of business strategy will be of crucial importance for success in the marketplace. Enterprises need to utilize their IP assets effectively to ensure the quality of their products and services and to develop and retain their customers.

## 1.2 NATURE OF THE IP SYSTEM

IP is defined – in an all-pervasive sense in Article 2 (viii) of the Convention Establishing the World Intellectual Property Organization (WIPO), signed in Stockholm on 14 July 1967 – to include the rights relating to literary, artistic and scientific works; performances of performing artists, phonograms, and broadcasts; inventions in all fields of human endeavour; scientific discoveries; industrial designs; trademarks, service marks and commercial names and designations; protection against unfair competition. Significantly, it further specifies: 'and all other rights resulting from intellectual activity in the industrial, scientific, or artistic fields'.

The IP system refers to the entire gamut of IP laws, procedures, practices and institutions responsible for protecting, administering, enforcing, and using intellectual assets for social, cultural and economic progress. While IP laws provide the mechanism for imparting some characteristics of tangible property to intangible assets, the institutions, procedures and practices provide the practical means for creators, innovators, businesses and industry to reap the benefits of intellectual assets if the circumstances are conducive. Intellectual assets are essentially new or original products of the human mind – its creative and innovative output – which manifests itself in various forms including the creative expression of ideas. Depending on the nature of the output, different types of IPRs are made available if the conditions and requirements prescribed in the relevant national or regional laws are fulfilled.

While IPRs are private rights and, in essence, pertain to individuals, in practice, these rights are being exercised more and more by corporate entities such as firms, businesses, corporations and other institutions that can legally hold, exercise and dispose of these rights. It is no wonder that the IP system has become an important instrument of economic and trade policies in many countries worldwide, apart from its role at the enterprise level where the IP strategy of the enterprise is a key component of its growth plan. The protection of IPRs enables countries to participate more actively in international trade as well as influence investment decisions. The importance of and linkage between the protection of IP, competitiveness in international trade and techno-economic growth and development has been a core concern of governments, the private sector and civil society as the IP system is seen as a determining factor in safeguarding the results of technological

2

developments as well as in encouraging, nourishing and sustaining creative expression. Economic progress is becoming increasingly technology driven, in as much as it is accelerated through the use of new, highly sophisticated technologies based on new or original ideas, techniques, processes and creative expression thereof.

Understanding and appreciating the social, cultural and techno-economic foundations of the IP system and its nature and the rationale for its protection is a prerequisite for comprehending its increasing importance and role in formulating national strategies for enhancing competitiveness and accelerating development, and in enterprise level strategy for higher profitability and market exclusivity.

## 1.3 RATIONALE FOR PROTECTION OF IP

The IP system is no longer considered a distinct or self-contained domain, but as an important and effective policy instrument which is relevant to a wide range of cultural, socio-economic and technological concerns. This far-reaching paradigm shift in international trade and commercial policy was brought into sharp focus by the Uruguay Round of trade negotiations, which resulted in the establishment of the World Trade Organization (WTO), requiring Member States to abide by its Agreement on Trade-Related Aspects of Intellectual Property Rights (TRIPS Agreement). The TRIPS Agreement (concluded on 15 April 1994 and effective as of 1 January 1995) lays down the minimum norms and standards for protection of IPRs and more importantly, their effective enforcement, unlike any other international treaty in the field of IP.

The development of skills and competence to manage IPRs at the enterprise, institutional or national level, and to leverage its influence is receiving increasing focus and attention by entrepreneurs, managers, administrators, policy-makers and politicians. Industrial and business activities have to compete not only in local or domestic markets but also in the sub-regional, regional and international marketplace. Developing internationally competitive products and services needs increasingly higher levels of investment in technology. In such a market-oriented situation, industries and businesses will require reasonable incentives and rewards to develop and deploy new and better products and services. These incentives and rewards are provided, among other things, by creating conditions for fair play in the marketplace through a balanced but effective IP protection system. For example, the patent system not only protects inventive processes and/or products of the inventor, whether owned by him or his employer, but also makes available to the public through patent documents the legal, business and technical information contained in these documents once they are published.

To be acceptable, any system of IPRs has to strike a balance, on the one hand, between providing incentives and rewards to the rights holders, and on the other hand, facilitating access to, and widespread diffusion and adoption of the fruits of creativity and innovation. This balance is reflected in Article 27 of the 1948 Universal Declaration of Human Rights, which recognizes both that 'Everyone has the right to the protection of the moral and material interest resulting from any scientific, literary or artistic production of which he is the author', and that 'everyone has the right . . . to share in scientific advancement and its benefits'. Thus, the challenge is to create and fine-tune the balance between the interest of the inventor or creator and that of society in an optimum manner.

In many countries, especially the scientifically advanced developing countries, the potential economic value of IP and the socio-economic benefits of works of the mind have to be fully tapped. The IP system has to be viewed as an important instrument of economic and trade competition. The main objective of IPR protection is to encourage creative activity, thereby providing economic and speedy benefits of such activity for the largest possible number of people. To enable the IP system to play its due role in helping to shape the direction of research and development (R&D) in industries, business establishments, government institutions and universities there is a need for greater emphasis on the development of a highly skilled workforce, as the effective use of emerging modern technologies depends increasingly on the skills of a technocratic workforce.

Various types of IPRs are created through legislation. These are mostly national, but sometimes are created at sub-national or supra-national levels. For each category of rights, certain conditions prescribed in the relevant legislation must be fulfilled for either the registration or the grant of the right. In the case of industrial property rights, registration or grant of rights is administered by an office established by the government concerned, or optional registration in respect of copyright works as provided in some legislations.

There is a growing recognition that the IP system ought to provide a balance of interests between the creators of new knowledge and original creative expressions – who often have to provide and risk large outlays and resources to create and develop the technology – and those that use the technology as an important tool for accelerating economic and industrial development. A report entitled 'Integrating Intellectual Property Rights and Development Policy' by the Commission on Intellectual Property Rights (CIPR) addresses this issue of balance. While mentioning, inter alia, the importance of IPR protection for the more technologically advanced developing countries in obtaining access to protected high technologies through foreign investment or through licensing, the report points out that achieving the right balance in this regard may be difficult for some countries.[1]

On the whole, it may be surmised that both the uncritical enthusiasm and the uninform hostility to the IP system is diminishing. The challenge is to provide objective and credible evidence in support of opposing claims of the different parties to the debate on the usefulness of the IP system as a tool for socio-economic and cultural development.

## 1.4 FORMS OF IP

Historically, the IP system has been divided into two main branches. One branch dealt with industrial property, mostly useful in commerce and industry, comprising:

(a) technological inventions that provide new solutions to technical problems and are registered as patents;

---

[1] Report of the UK CIPR, London, Sep. 2002: <www.iprcommission.org/graphic/documents/final_report.htm>.

(b) utility models also known as 'petty patents' or 'utility innovations';
(c) trademarks for goods and services;
(d) commercial names and designations;
(e) industrial designs or aesthetic creations determining the appearance of industrial products or handicrafts;
(f) geographical indications or indications of source and appellations of origin; and
(g) layout designs of integrated circuits.

A second branch deals with copyright and related rights protecting literary and artistic expression or works of culture, which, in the broadest sense, relate to creative expression of ideas. Copyright provides protection of literary, musical, artistic, photographic and audio-visual works, computer programs, software, multimedia creations, etc., and in many countries, works of applied art. Related rights, neighbouring on copyright, protect the rights of performing artists, producers of phonograms, and broadcasting organizations. The protection of confidential business information of commercial value, often called 'trade secrets' is also an important and distinct form of IP. The protection of breeders' rights in relation to new varieties of plants is another distinct form of IP. An emerging contentious form of IP is that of non-original database rights.

### 1.4.1 Patents and Utility Models

A patent is an exclusive right granted by the government patent or IP office to an inventor to prevent others from making, using, selling, distributing or importing his new product or using his new process. This right is granted for a limited period of time. It is granted if three basic conditions of patentability are met. Generally, the three requirements for patentability are: novelty (new characteristics, which are not prior art, that is, which do not form part of the existing state of the art), inventive step or non-obviousness (knowledge being not obvious to one skilled in the field), and industrial applicability or utility (inventions which are susceptible to industrial application). In respect to legal protection for industrial property, the inventor is required to provide sufficient and full disclosure of an invention in his patent application which, at the appropriate time, is published in an official publication to notify all others who may be interested in its contents.

A patent will have one claim and may have a series of dependent claims which spell out the scope of the invention as to how it is different from, and/or improves upon, prior art.

The disclosure of an invention should be such that a skilled person in the relevant area or art would be able to practice the invention, that is, the invention must be described in the legal and government-prescribed patent application form in sufficient detail to indicate how the technology works. The patent application is published through an official notification, which enables the details of the invention to become accessible to the public. A patent prevents others from making, using, selling or exporting an invention. It is usually granted for twenty years from the date on which the patent application was filed in the relevant government office. Its validity is also limited to the territory wherein the granting patent law applies. There is no world or international patent but each invention, when

5

patented in a number of countries, contributes to a 'family' of patents including the relevant new and useful invention.

Historically, the first patents were granted for mechanical inventions such as the safety pin by Walter Hunt, the zipper by Whitcomb Judson and the locomotive steam engine for rail track by John Ruggles, which were granted patents in 1849, 1893 and 1930, respectively. Next came electrical inventions such as electrical lamps by Thomas Alva Edison in 1879 and still later, chemical inventions such as linear condensation polymers by Dupont in 1937. More recently, the scope of patenting has increased in many ways to include processes and products of genetic engineering (modern biotechnology); computer programs (for example, systems, methods and computer programs for providing financial protection of equity investments); business methods for commercializing goods and services over a global digital network; and electronic methods and systems for controlling and tracking information related to business transactions.

Exploitation of a patented invention without the prior authorization of the patent owner is illegal. No one will spend time, money and efforts on innovation if someone else can copy his or her invention. Patent legislation, however, generally provides for exceptions in the public interest in the form of compulsory licenses. The grounds and conditions for the grant of a compulsory license are specified in national legislation. The grant of such licenses requires that an adequate compensation be paid to the owner of the patent.

The patent system has greatly contributed to the orderly exploitation of inventions in newer and evolving fields of technology. This has proven to be a key factor in encouraging the investment flow into R&D projects generally and into high technology areas in particular. For enterprises investing money, time and manpower in the inventive process, the expenditure involved in the acquisition of a patent will not be wasted; it should be considered as a part of the overhead costs, as it will be an investment towards ensuring future profits for the enterprise.

The number of national patent applications filed, for example, in the year 2005, varied greatly from country to country.[2] Japan topped the list (367,960 from residents and 59,118 from non-residents); next was the United States of America (207,867 and 182,866 respectively), followed by China, the Republic of Korea, the European Patent Office, Germany, Canada, the Russian Federation, Australia, the United Kingdom and India, in that order. Among developing countries, the Republic of Korea took the lead (122,188 from residents and 38,733 from non-residents), followed by China (93,485 and 79,842 respectively). The others countries with the top twenty most impressive number of applications were India, Brazil, Mexico, Singapore and Thailand, in that order.

While the above figures are in respect of patents registered nationally, in the larger context of global competitiveness, it is the US patents that constitute an important factor in the measurement of technological progress. In this regard, it is interesting to compare the grant of US patents to certain developing countries. Table 1 below shows the relevant data.

---

[2] 2007 WIPO Patent Report 'Statistics on Worldwide Patent Activities': <www.wipo.int/freepublications/en/patents/931/wipo_pub_931.pdf>.

Table 1. US Patents Granted to Certain Developing Countries (1990-2005)

|  | *1990* | *1995* | *2000* | *2005* |
|---|---|---|---|---|
| Taiwan | 732 | 1,620 | 4,667 | 5,118 |
| Korea | 225 | 1,161 | 3,314 | 4,352 |
| Hong Kong | 52 | 86 | 179 | 283 |
| Singapore | 12 | 53 | 218 | 346 |
| India | 23 | 37 | 131 | 384 |
| South Africa | 114 | 123 | 111 | 87 |
| Brazil | 41 | 63 | 98 | 77 |
| China | 47 | 62 | 119 | 402 |
| Mexico | 32 | 40 | 76 | 80 |
| Argentina | 17 | 31 | 54 | 24 |
| Malaysia | 3 | 7 | 42 | 88 |
| I. Total of above | 1,298 | 3,283 | 9,009 | 11,241 |
| II Total World | 90,365 | 101,419 | 157,494 | 143,806 |
| III Share of Total (I) in World Total (II) | 1.44 | 3.24 | 5.72 | 7.82 |

Source: US Patent and Trademark Office, <www.uspto.gov>

In addition to patents, some countries provide protection for utility models otherwise known as 'petty patents' or 'utility innovations'. Many technical creations involve a contribution of minor additions to existing technology which may not qualify under the higher criteria of inventiveness required for patenting an invention. These are protected by utility models which are granted for incremental or small innovations for a shorter duration, without having to go through substantive examination. The criteria of inventiveness is lower than for patents and the maximum term of protection for a utility model is shorter than that for a patent, usually ranging from six to ten years, and the procedure for obtaining it is shorter and simpler than that for a patent.

The introduction of utility models can also help boost national R&D of technology. A number of countries, both developed and developing, have provided for protection of utility models. Incidentally, the European Commission had, subsequent to publication of its Green Paper in July 1995, adopted in December 1997, a proposal for a Directive for harmonizing rules for the protection of utility models.

### 1.4.1.1 Patent Documentation as an Information Resource

Patent documentation is a valuable and much sought-after source of technological information. The well-documented disclosure of such information helps promote ideas for further inventions and innovations. It encourages the efforts of other inventors in coming up with even better inventions. Thus, each invention patented and disclosed has a multiplier effect. It is the basis for new technological developments, since patent documents are a source of the state-of-the-art technological and commercial information, helping in further development of new inventions and of creative new technologies.

As competition in international trade becomes more intensive, the value of patent information becomes more obvious to those who are forced to compete in order to maintain and improve their position in the marketplace. Again the economic value of patent information lies primarily in its ability to provide industry and enterprises with technological and market information which could be used to their commercial advantage.

In order to encourage inventive and innovative activity amongst their technical staff, the corporate sector and enterprises as well as research institutions should use the valuable base of information provided through patent documents. Over sixty million patent documents have been published in the world. The number of patent documents indicating detailed information about new inventions published each year is well over one and a half million. The collection and computerization of such patent documents can help avoid costly duplication of effort in R&D of ideas already developed; solve given technical problems; and inform enterprises concerning the products their competitors may have developed or are developing.

The very large number of inventions which are documented and disclosed through patent documents each year worldwide are an excellent and invaluable base for the development of new technologies. It is important to re-emphasize that technology disclosed through patent applications serves to stimulate ideas for further inventions and innovations. It could encourage the efforts of inventors to develop even better inventions or invent 'around' the original.

Certainly not all the several million registered patents in the world can be major technological breakthroughs. A sizeable number encompass mere 'incremental' inventions consisting of small improvements to products and processes that increase their efficiency and marketability. Many of these are improvements which are built around existing patents. Valuable technology is not always high-tech, nor does it always have to come from abroad. Patents cover all kinds of items such as ballpoint pens, clips, locks, electrical switches, computers, motors, improved brake systems for bicycles, spare parts for tractors and so on.

Research institutions and industry should be encouraged to use patent information to obtain the latest inventions in their relevant fields of technology so that they can adapt or adopt them to produce ever more qualitatively superior products. Generation of one's own technologies can be helped through providing various incentives, but most importantly by providing the latest patent information to prospective inventors.

## 1.4.2 Industrial Design

While patents protect the technical solution or innovative technical improvement in a process or a product, the new or original shape and external appearance of a useful object is protected by an industrial design right. Market success and market retention are often determined by the visual appearance of an article that is new or original. Industrial design – which refers to the aesthetic shapes, aspects and characteristics of useful commercial products and outward appearance of an article – is of particular importance in influencing the decision of consumers for a variety of products such as textiles, tobacco, cosmetics, cars, mobile phones, etc. The good industrial design of an article is what makes it attractive and appealing to customers. The perceptible features of goods have an important role in persuading consumers to purchase a particular brand of merchandize. If a design combines functional improvements with aesthetic features, then it might also be protected under patent or utility model protection.

Industrial design protection relates to features of shape, configuration, pattern or ornamentation of any article made by industrial process or handicraft. Generally, an industrial design must be registered in order to be protected under the industrial design law of a country. Both two- and three-dimensional designs can be registered by application to the concerned patent office, or to its design registry, where such a branch exists. The design, as mentioned above, should be new and must not have been published or offered for sale before applying for its registration. Once the industrial design is registered, a registration certificate is issued.

The creator of a design owns the rights to it, unless he or she created the design in the course of employment, in which case the right belongs to the employer. Registration of the design provides the right that excludes others from using the design for making, importing for business, renting, selling or offering for sale or rent any article in context of which the design is registered, and to which the design or a design not differing substantially from it, has been applied. Most countries register industrial designs for a period ranging from ten to twenty-five years. The TRIPS Agreement, in Article 26.3, states that the duration of protection available for industrial design shall amount to at least ten years. Fees are payable for registration and for extension of registration.

An industrial design may be protected as a 'work of art' under copyright law, and under certain circumstances it may be protected under unfair competition law in certain countries. Generally, industrial design protection is limited to the country in which the protection is granted.

Industrial design protection is territorial. Enterprises seeking protection of their industrial design should apply to their national industrial property office in which they require protection. Where regional protection is sought through a single application, this could be filed at the appropriate regional IP office related to a group of countries that are bound through regional agreements for providing registration of industrial designs. Examples of such regional offices include:

(a) the Office for Harmonization in the Internal Market (OHIM) for community designs in the countries of the European Community (EC);
(b) the African Regional Industrial Property Office (ARIPO) for industrial design protection in English speaking African countries;

(c) the Organisation Africaine de la Propriété Intellectuelle (OAPI) for protection in French speaking African countries;
(d) the Benelux Design Office (BDO) for protection in Belgium, the Netherlands and Luxembourg.

Where enterprises desire to register their designs internationally in several countries, the procedures offered by the Hague Agreement concerning the International Deposit of Industrial Designs are to be followed.

According to Article 25.1 of the TRIPS Agreement 'independently created industrial designs' may be protected if they are new or original. In some countries, mainly in Europe, there is an unregistered design right associated with any aspect of the shape or configuration of an article. It is provided for a period of only three years from the time it is first made available to the public. The unregistered design right comes into existence automatically whenever an original design is created, but is generally a weaker form of right.

A registered design right makes it easier for the owner to bring an action for infringement. But registration may be expensive as it requires professional advice, drawing up of detailed specifications and payment of registration and renewal fees. An unregistered design right, on the other hand, becomes automatically available upon its creation and is not subject to any registration procedure.

By introducing a community system of design registration and a community based unregistered design right and harmonizing the European designs law, efforts are being made by the European Commission to simplify the protection of aesthetic designs. The Commission's work has resulted in the enactment of a Directive harmonizing the law of registered designs in the Member States and a Council Regulation that introduces both community-wide registered design rights and community-wide unregistered design rights.

The Regulation for Community Designs was adopted by the Council on 12 December 2001. The unregistered design right became available from 6 March 2002, while the registered design right became available from 2003, once the implementing and fees regulations were adopted by the European Commission and the implementation date was notified. The system introduced by the regulation is administered by the OHIM in Alicante, Spain, which has been receiving applications for registering community designs since the implementing regulations were finalized.

The advent of the Community unregistered design right gives automatic protection to designs which are published within the European Union. Designers should be able to enforce this community unregistered design right in any European country in which a copy of a protected design is discovered. A new Europe-wide registered design system is also contemplated, which will allow a single design application to be filed in order to gain protection for a design in every Member State.

Amongst industrial designs registered in the year 2000, the maximum were in Germany (58,244 from residents and 13,131 from non-residents), followed by China (46,532 and 3,588 respectively). Next were Japan, the Republic of Korea, the United States of America, the United Kingdom, France, Australia, India, Thailand, Switzerland, the Russian Federation and Mexico[3] in that order.

For exploiting an enterprise's exclusivity over its registered designs and also for creating an additional source of revenue, industrial designs are licensed. The designer grants permission to another person to use the design for some mutually agreed purposes.

### 1.4.3 Trademarks

The modern concept of a trademark, developed in parallel with industrial mass production, dates back about two centuries; the enhanced circulation of goods and services has now made it increasingly necessary to use a distinctive mark or name to identify a product, service or enterprise. This serves the interest of the producers, traders and consumers. The development of international trade has led to greater use of trademarks in all countries and in different fields of activity. A trademark serves as a guarantee of quality for consumers. A well-selected trademark is a valuable business asset. Trademarks have an increasingly important role in a country's commerce and trade. Once a trademark has acquired a reputation, it makes it easier to get into new markets, which could stimulate exports. Industrial and business enterprises use trademarks for diversifying their market strategies in their own as well as in other countries. Use of trademarks for ensuring efficient marketing of products requires an in-depth knowledge of trademark law and practice at the national and international levels.

Trademarks are distinctive signs capable of distinguishing and identifying goods or services produced or provided by one enterprise from those of others producing similar goods or services. A trademark is protected on the basis of its use in the marketplace in some countries, and on the basis of registration in others. It is of primary importance in the marketing process:

> Estimates of the value of some of the world's most famous trademarks such as Coca-Cola, Microsoft or IBM, exceed 50 billion dollars each. This is because consumers value trademarks, their reputation, their image and a set of desired qualities they associate with a mark and are willing to pay more for a product bearing a trademark that they recognize and meets their expectations. Therefore, the very ownership of a trademark with a good image and reputation provides a company with a competitive edge over its competitors.[4]

Most countries which protect trademarks on the basis of use also provide for registration of the trademark for more effective protection. Trademarks should not only be inherently distinctive but fit the product or image of the concerned enterprise and have a positive connotation. These could comprise letters, words, drawings, pictures, shapes, labels, etc., used to identify goods and services.

---

3   2000 WIPO report on Industrial Designs (IP/STAT/2000/B): <www.wipo.int/export/sites/www/ipstats/en/statistics/designs/pdf/designs_00.pdf>.
4   <www.wipo.int/trademarks/en/trademarks.html>.

Registration of a trademark provides the owner of the trademark with prima facie proof of its validity, ownership and reputation for the quality of goods or services to which the particular trademark relates. It also gives the owner the exclusive right to prevent third parties who do not have the owner's consent, from using identical or similar signs for goods and services which are either identical or similar to those in respect of which a trademark is registered. According to the TRIPS Agreement (Article 15.4), the nature of the goods or services to which a trademark is to be applied shall in no case form an obstacle to registration of the trademark.

As per Article 6*bis* of the Paris Convention for the Protection of Industrial Property administered by WIPO, member countries, if their legislation so permits, could prohibit the use of a trademark which constitutes a reproduction, imitation or a translation liable to create confusion, of a mark which is considered to be well known in the country of registration and used for identical or similar goods. Again, as per the TRIPS Agreement (Article 16.2), in determining whether a trademark is well known, account should be taken of the knowledge of the trademark in the relevant public sector as well as knowledge obtained via promotion of the trademark's production. Factors for consideration in the determination of well-known marks also include the value associated with the mark concerned.

The registration and subsequent renewal of such registration of a trademark is for a period of not less than seven years. Renewal of trademark registration is permitted for an indefinite period provided the trademark remains in use, although evidence of such use is not required to be produced for the renewal of registration. Thus, normally, the protection of a trademark is not limited in time, provided its registration is renewed.

As for applications filed in the year 2005 for registration of trademarks, the largest number were in China (593,382 for residents, 63,902 for non-residents, and 13,600 for Madrid System) followed by United States of America (224,269, 28,359 and 11,882 respectively). These were followed by a very wide range of countries: Japan, the Republic of Korea, Brazil, Germany, France, Turkey, Mexico, Spain Australia, the Russian Federation, the United Kingdom, Singapore, South Africa, Switzerland, Ukraine, Malaysia, Poland, Romania, New Zealand and Sweden.[5] These figures show that in most developed and developing countries, the number of trademark applications registered by residents is much higher than by non-residents.

### 1.4.4 Collective and Certification Marks

Trademarks typically identify individual enterprises as the originators of marked goods or services. Some countries provide for the registration of collective and certification marks, which are used to indicate the affiliation of enterprises using the mark or which refer to identifiable standards met by the products for which a mark is used. Collective marks are

---

[5] WIPO Report on 'Trademark Applications by Office (1883 to 2006)': <www.wipo.int/ipstats/en/statistics/marks/>.

those used to identify goods or services produced or provided by members of an association, while certification marks are those used to identify products that comply with a set of standards and have been certified by a certifying authority.

Article 7*bis* of Paris Convention for the Protection of Industrial Property requires that Member States of the Paris Union accept for filing and protect collective marks. This provision ensures that collective marks are admitted for registration and protection in countries other than the country where the association owning the collective mark has been established. This means that the fact that the said association has not been established in accordance with the law of the country where protection is sought is no reason for refusing such protection. On the other hand, the Convention expressly mentions the right of each Member State to apply its own conditions of protection and to refuse protection if the collective mark is contrary to the public interest. Moreover, the Paris Convention does not define the term 'collective mark', nor does it specifically address certification marks. Article 7*bis* is among the provisions of the Paris Convention incorporated in the TRIPS Agreement by virtue of its Article 2.1.

The concepts of 'collective mark' and 'certification mark' (in some countries 'guarantee mark') differ from country to country. Depending on the national law, a collective or certification mark may serve to indicate, inter alia, the origin of goods or services and, therefore, may to some extent be suitable for the protection of a geographical indication.

Generally speaking, the main difference between collective and certification marks is that the former may be used only by particular enterprises, for example, members of the association that own the collective mark, while the latter may be used by anybody who complies with the defined standards. Thus, the users of collective marks form a 'club' while, in respect of certification marks, an 'open shop' principle applies.

### 1.4.4.1 Collective Marks

Under the IP law of most countries, there are provisions for the protection of collective marks. These are usually defined as signs that distinguish the geographical origin, material, mode of manufacture or other common characteristics of goods or services of enterprises using the collective mark. The owner may be either an association of which those enterprises are members, a public institution, or a cooperative whose members may use the collective mark to market their products. An internationally known example of a collective mark is INTER-FLORA, used worldwide by a flower ordering service.

A collective mark may be owned by an association which itself does not use the collective mark but whose members may use the collective mark. The members may use the collective mark if they comply with the requirements fixed in the regulations concerning the use of the collective mark. An enterprise entitled to use the collective mark may in addition also use its own trademark. Collective marks provide an effective way of jointly marketing the products of a group of enterprises which might otherwise find it difficult to make their individual marks recognized by consumers and/or distributed by the main retailers.

The regulations concerning the use of a collective mark normally have to be included in an application for the registration of the collective mark and the Trademark Office must be notified of any modifications to the regulations. The laws of some countries contain strict use requirements which may result in cancellation of the registration of the collective mark if it is not continuously used. In several countries, the registration of collective mark may be cancelled if that mark is used contrary to the provisions of the regulations or in a manner which misleads the public. Collective marks, therefore, can play a significant role in the protection of consumers against misleading practices.

### 1.4.4.2 Certification Marks

Quite a number of countries also provide for protection of certification marks. These are given for compliance with defined standards but not confined to any membership. Thus in contrast to collective marks, certification marks are not owned by a collective body such as an association of producers, but by a certification authority. Such authority may be a local governmental entity or a private association which is not itself engaged in production or trade of the products concerned. An important requirement for certification marks is that the entity which applies for registration must be considered competent to certify the products concerned. As an illustrative example, famous certification marks include Woolmark, which certifies that the goods carrying the mark are made entirely of wool. The Woolmark symbol is the registered trade certification mark of the Woolmark Company. It denotes that the products on which it is used are from 100% new wool. Woolmark Company is registered in more than 140 countries and is licensed to manufacture in nearly seventy countries where it can ensure meeting the quality standards.

An important requirement for the registration of a certification mark is that the entity which applies for registration is 'competent to certify' the products concerned. Thus, the owner of a certification mark must be the representative for the products to which the certification mark applies. This is an important safeguard to protect the public against misleading practices.

There are generally three types of certification marks. First of all, there are certification marks which certify that goods or services originate in a specific geographical region. Secondly, there are marks which certify that the goods or services meet certain standards in relation to quality, materials or mode of manufacture, and finally, marks which certify that the performer of the services or the manufacturer of the goods has met certain standards, or belongs to a certain organization or union.

A certification mark does not indicate origin in a single commercial or proprietary source; it does not indicate source in a trademark sense at all. It does not indicate who manufactured the goods or performed the services. On the contrary, identical certification marks are used on the goods and services of many different producers.

The message conveyed by a certification mark, when it is applied to goods or used in connection with services, is that the goods and services have been examined, tested, inspected or in some way checked by a person who is not their producer, by methods determined by the certifier/owner.

The application for the registration of a certification mark is accompanied by regulations which will govern its use. A certification mark may normally be used by anybody whose products comply with its regulatory requirements. The institution that owns the registered certification mark has the right to prohibit the use of that mark by entities whose products do not comply with its regulatory requirements.

### 1.4.5 Trade Names and Trade Secrets

Trade names, or commercial names and designations, are those that identify an enterprise. Most countries protect trade names without the obligation of filing or registration. Protection means that the trade name of one enterprise is not to be used by another, either as a trade name or trademark, and that a name or designation similar to the trade name may not be used by another enterprise.

As far as trade secrets are concerned, traditionally confidential business information of commercial value was not considered to be IP. In fact, even today most countries do not have a specific law for protection of such information, which is often also simply called 'trade secrets'. These generally include information regarding 'a formula, pattern, compilation, program, device, method, technique or process that has commercial value to a business and that wants to keep secret from competitors and customers. . . . Nevertheless, business enterprises may, as a matter of corporate strategy, sometimes choose whether to apply for a patent for a formula or manufacturing process or hold the information secret'.[6] But given the growing importance and enormous potential of such information in providing a competitive edge in the marketplace and protecting the business against future competitors, it is now generally agreed that trade secrets are not just a starting point but also an integral part of the IP system and often one of its most valuable parts.

A trade secret is information that is in fact, or is potentially valuable to its owner, is not known nor readily ascertainable by the public and which its owner has made a reasonable effort to keep secret. A trade secret has costs involved in its development and it is not common knowledge in the industry or business.

Most businesses want to know their competitors' secret of success, including any proprietary information of commercial value. Generally, the value of trade secrets is lost if they are disclosed either wilfully or inadvertently. As trade secrets must be used in business and industry, those who need to know such trade secrets are generally bound by contractual clauses in employment agreements which prohibit disclosure of such secrets during or after leaving the employment. In addition, an ex-employee cannot use trade secrets of the former employer to set up a competing business, or use such secrets while working for a competitor of the former employer. An extremely diverse range of business information may qualify to be trade secrets, provided the employer has made reasonable efforts to keep such information confidential, and has also made it known to all

---

[6]    Michael P. Ryan, *Knowledge Diplomacy: Global Competition and the Politics of Intellectual Property* (Washington, D.C: Brookings Institution Press, 1998), 40: <www.brookings.edu/press/Books/1998/ knowledg.aspx>.

employees concerned that it is so. An enterprise-wide information security and protection is imperative for protection of trade secrets. Companies and enterprises safeguard confidential information of commercial value against accidental or wilful misappropriation, misuse or loss. Secret information and data need proper protection and management for ensuring competitive advantage.

Discovery of trade secrets by fair means, that is, by legitimate reverse engineering, means that the originator has no right to exclude its use by those who discover it in a fair manner. Unfair competition includes such activities as industrial espionage, inducing employees to reveal trade secrets and encouraging defection of technical employees to produce their own versions of a product based on proprietary information.

It is necessary for business enterprises, in respect of their trade secrets, to:

(a) identify them;
(b) develop an effective protection policy through employee education and monitoring compliance;
(c) restrict access to trade secrets to the minimum number of employees concerned;
(d) maintain and ensure their secrecy including computer secrecy, restricting public access to the enterprise's facilities, etc.

Section 7 of the TRIPS Agreement provides for the 'Protection of Undisclosed Information', according to Article 39.2, wherein owners 'shall have the possibility of preventing information lawfully within their control from being disclosed to, acquired by, or used by others without their consent in a manner contrary to honest commercial practices.' The latter is explained to mean practices such as breach of contract, breach of confidence and inducement to breach, and includes the acquisition of undisclosed information by third parties who knew or were grossly negligent in failing to know that such practices were involved in the acquisition.

This article also seeks to prevent use of such information such as '(a) is secret in the sense that it is not . . . generally known among or readily accessible to persons within circles that normally deal with the kind of information in question; (b) has commercial value because it is secret; and (c) has been subject to reasonable steps under the circumstances, by the person lawfully in control of the information, to keep it a secret'. The TRIPS Agreement enjoins Member States to ensure effective remedies for trade secret misappropriation, including injunctive relief and damages. With the spread of trade secret legislation, strong remedies are being prescribed against trade secret misappropriations.

Many enterprises and industries are not aware that secret information is considered IP, and is often protected by legislation. Countries that have provided legislation include: Brazil, which in the 1996 revision of its IP law provides criminal sanctions against a person releasing or using without authorization, a trade secret to which such an individual has had access through employment contract or contract, with the concerned company or institution; Canada, which in its trade secret law has provided, inter alia, for breach of contract, breach of confidence, etc., as cause for action; France, which in its criminal code has provisions relating to theft of trade secrets, know-how and confidential business information; Germany and Italy, which provide strong legal protection for trade secrets, the latter treating trade secret theft as a crime; and Japan, whose national trade secrets law effective from June 1991 includes technical or business information that has commercial value and is administered as a trade secret. In Japan, it is considered infringement when a trade secret is obtained through theft, fraud or extortion, and where there is unauthorized disclosure and use of a trade secret for unfair competition. The United Kingdom also provides for effective protection of trade secrets, including search-and-seizure orders that could be issued to protect trade secrets and to preserve evidence. In countries which follow the common law tradition, trade secrets are protected even without legislation.

However, with technology changing rapidly, trade secret protection is, in some cases, being considered the most attractive, effective and readily available IPR.

## 1.4.6 Geographical Indications

Another distinctive sign in trade is covered by the expression 'geographical indications' which embraces both 'indications of source' and 'appellations of origin'. Geographical indications are defined as indications identifying goods as originating in the territory of a country, region or locality with a quality, reputation or characteristic attributable to its geographical origin. Thus, a geographical indication points to a specific place or region of production that determines qualities of the product. Geographical indications are understood by consumers to specify the origin and the quality of products. They help promote goods of a particular area.

The use of geographical indications is an important method of indicating the origin of goods and services. Geographical indications are source identifiers, indicators of quality, and are as valuable to producers from particular regions as are trademarks; they prevent unauthorized parties from using a protected geographical indication for products not from the particular region or from misleading the public as to the true origins of the product.

Geographical indications are protected in accordance with national laws. In recent years, a significant number of developing countries have provided for their protection. Protection of geographical indications has also been on the international agenda for quite some time. It is addressed to some extent in the Paris Convention (Article 10), and is dealt with more specifically by the Lisbon Agreement for the Protection of Appellations of Origin and their International Registration (1958, revised at Stockholm 1967 and amended in 1979; the latest regulations became effective on 1 April 2002). A broader and more concrete effort in this context was the inclusion in the TRIPS Agreement (Articles 22 and 23) of international minimum standards for protection of geographical indications.

According to Article 22.2(a) in respect of geographical indications, the TRIPS Agreement requires Member States to 'provide the legal means for interested parties to prevent the use of any means in the designation or presentation of a good that indicates or suggests that the good in question originates in a geographical area other than the true place of origin in a manner which misleads the public as to the geographical origin of the good'. It is also incumbent on WTO Member States to prevent, according to Article 22.2(b) of the TRIPS

Agreement, any use which constitutes an act of unfair competition within the meaning of Article 10*bis* of the Paris Convention. It should be noted that an obligation to protect geographical indications exists only with regard to such indications that are protected in their country of origin (cf. TRIPS Agreement Article 24.9).

Geographical indications and trademarks should be distinguished from each other. Whereas geographical indication identifies a geographical area to which a quality, reputation or other characteristics of a product is attributable (e.g., champagne or Darjeeling tea; both refer to places of origin of a product), a trademark identifies an enterprise which offers a product in the market (e.g., Toyota or Coca-Cola). As for the linkage between trademarks and geographical indications, Article 22.3 of the TRIPS Agreement provides that a Member State shall 'refuse or invalidate the registration of a trademark which contains or consists of a geographical indication with respect to goods not originating in the territory indicated, if use of the indication in the trademark for such goods in that Member State is of such a nature as to mislead the public as to the true place of origin'. Both geographical indications and trademarks can be used to promote the competitiveness of businesses and growth of national economies.

### 1.4.7 Layout Designs of Integrated Circuits

Layout designs of integrated circuits constitute a relatively new type of IP protection given to advances in semiconductor technology. The owner of such a protection has the right to prohibit all others for a period of at least ten years, from the reproduction, importation, sale or distribution for commercial purposes of a protected layout design or integrated circuit. The ten-year protection term requires, in this case, only novelty in expression. While the creation of a new layout design of an integrated circuit may involve sizeable investment, its copying may cost just a fraction of such investment. Here again, strict and effective enforcement is necessary.

It may be germane here to quote an example from French law. It lays down, inter alia, that the topography of a semiconductor product that is the result of its creator's own intellectual effort, be the subject of a deposit that confers the protection under their law, at the National Institute of Industrial Property. According to Decree No. 89-816 of 2 November 1989 concerning the Protection of Topographies of Semiconductor Products, a deposit shall relate to one topography only, comprising a declaration of deposit containing sufficient information to identify the depositor, the topography and the date and place of its first exploitation. This Decree also lays down that as soon as the deposit is found to be in order, it shall be registered. Registration shall be notified to the applicant and announced in the Official Industrial Property Gazette (BOPI). According to Article L622-6, the prohibition set forth shall take effect on the day of deposit or on the date of first commercial exploitation if the latter is earlier. It shall vest in the registered owner until the end of the tenth following calendar year. However, any registration relating to a topography that has not been commercially exploited within a period of fifteen years from the date on which it was fixed or encoded for the first time shall cease to have effect. During the two months prior to the expiration of the term of protection, the owner of the deposit may request either the return of the documents or their retention for an additional, renewable period of ten years. The request for retention shall be acceptable only if it is accompanied by payment of the prescribed fee. In the absence of any request for return or retention, the documents relating to a deposit may be destroyed.

Reproduction, under the aforesaid French law, by any third party, of the protected topography is prohibited, as is the commercial exploitation or importation of such a reproduction or of any semiconductor product incorporating it. This prohibition does not apply to reproduction for evaluation, analysis or teaching purposes, nor is it binding on the bona fide acquirer of a semiconductor product, although such acquirer shall be liable for appropriate indemnification if he or she intends to engage in commercial exploitation of the product so acquired.

To take one other example, in China, the Regulations on the Protection of Layout Design of Integrated Circuits, adopted at the 36th Executive Meeting of the State Council on 28 March 2001, were promulgated by Decree No. 300 of the State Council, and became effective on 1 October 2001. These were formulated in order to protect the exclusive right of layout design of integrated circuit, encourage innovation of integrated circuit technology and promote development of science and technology.

### 1.4.8 Database Protection

IP protection of databases is going to be an important issue for science, researchers and innovators. Databases are collections or compilations of records that are organized for easy access and retrieval. Many of the databases are also 'unoriginal' in the sense that they do not meet the originality criterion as recognized in the Berne Convention and the WIPO Copyright Treaty. As a result, such databases are not protected by copyright. Although databases can be in any of a variety of formats, the growth of databases in electronic formats, both as standalone products on media such as CD-ROMs and as online products and services, has increased the need for their legal protection.

Advances in information and communication technologies will mean protection of digital databases of factual information. The Internet will disseminate the data rapidly. However, emerging technologies will prevent such dissemination. Once again the interest of the database creators and those who want access to it for scientific, education and library communities will have to be considered seriously.

There is protection for databases under the laws of both developed and developing countries. For original databases copyright protection is available, whereas for non-original databases some form of special protection exists. Many European Union (EU) countries have sui generis database protection laws pursuant to Directive 96/9/EC of the European Council. Mexico's Federal Copyright Law also provides for the protection of non-original databases. Several multilateral agreements also cover the protection of databases. Article 10(2) of the TRIPS Agreement which deals with the protection of databases states that: 'compilations of data or other material, whether in machine readable or other form, which by reason of the selection or arrangement of their contents constitute intellectual creations shall be protected as such. Such protection, which shall not extend to the data or material itself, shall be without prejudice to any copyright subsisting in the data or material itself'. Article 5 of the WIPO's Copyright Treaty of 1996 also has a similar provision.

The protection of databases gives rise to a number of complex economic issues. According to an economic analysis by Prof. Yale M. Braunstein[7] of the School of Information Management and Systems, University of California, in most countries, databases qualify for IP protection through copyright and trademark legislation. They may also be protected de facto through a contract system between the database supplier and the user. The protection for databases under copyright law is limited. In a 1991 case, the US Supreme Court denied protection to a telephone directory on the grounds that the collection of names, addresses and telephone numbers was not an original creative work.

In Europe, sui generis protection for a database is conferred irrespective of 'selection or arrangement' criteria, based instead on 'substantial investment' criteria.

Incidentally, provisions of the European Union's Database Directive include:

(a) the copyright criterion of originality, requiring a database to be its author's own intellectual creation, with a requirement that no other criteria may be applied to determine a database's eligibility for copyright protection;
(b) the copyright criterion of originality requiring a database to be its author's own intellectual creation, with a requirement that no other criteria may be applied to determine a database's eligibility for copyright protection;
(c) the concept of the sui generis right, with its own restricted acts of extraction and re-utilization, protecting a maker's investment and distinct from copyright protecting the author's creativity;
(d) lawful user rights applying to copyright and the sui generis right, but differently expressed for each; and
(e) application of the principle of Community exhaustion of the copyright distribution right in a copy of a copyright database by the first sale in the Community of that copy with the consent of the copyright holder.

The most significant contribution of the European Commission's proposal for the directive on the legal protection of databases was the introduction of a sui generis right to protect collections which, although expensive to compile and commercially valuable, lacked any element of human intellectual creativity. Such collections were thought to be inappropriate for protection by copyright under the Database Directive[8] as adopted. The maker of a database who can show that there has been qualitatively and quantitatively substantial

---

[7] 'Economic impact of database protection in developing countries and countries in transition'; study prepared by Yale M. Braunstein, WIPO's document No. SCCR/7/2 4 Apr. 2002: <www.wipo.int/documents/en/meetings/2002/sccr/pdf/sccr7_2.pdf>.

[8] EU Directive 96/9/EC on the Legal Protection of Databases: <http://eur-lex.europa.eu/LexUriServ/LexUriServ.do?uri=CELEX:31996L0009:EN:HTML>.

investments in either obtaining, verifying or presenting database contents is to have a sui generis right to prevent extraction and/or re-utilization of the whole or of a substantial part, evaluated qualitatively and/or quantitatively, of the contents of that database.[9] The sui generis rights requirement of substantial investment is a counterpart to the copyright requirement of intellectual creativity.[10]

Under the sui generis regime, the EU has adopted legislation to provide sui generis protection in respect of databases. The idea here is to prevent unauthorized use of data compilations, even if non-original.

### 1.4.9 Protection of Plant Varieties and Plant Breeders' Rights

IP protection has been conferred around the world in relation to plant materials in a number of ways. Historically, IPRs were applied primarily to mechanical inventions or artistic creations. The application of IPRs to living things is of recent origin. Vegetatively propagated plants were first made patentable in the United States in the 1930s. Protection of plant varieties in the form of Plant Breeders' Rights (PBRs) became widespread in the second half of the twentieth century. The US model of plant patents is distinct from normal (utility) patents. One can allow normal patents on plants or parts thereof, such as cells. One can patent plant varieties as is the practice in the US and in a few other countries. One can allow patents on deoxyribonucleic acid (DNA) sequences. What actual form of legislation a given nation uses for its plant protection depends upon its own state of development and the strategies that the nation uses to protect its national interests.

The TRIPS Agreement provides in its Article 27.3(b) that its Member States 'shall provide for protection of new plant varieties either by patents or by an effective sui generis system or by any combination thereof'. Plant variety protection is ultimately linked to, and is a form of, industrial property rights. Protection of plant varieties has certain features in common with patents for industrial inventions. Both forms of protection grant to their holders a form of exclusive right thereby providing an incentive to pursue innovative activity.

One of the key issues in this context is related to the ways and means of recognizing the contribution of farmers to the conservation and development of plant genetic resources. Giving recognition to farmers for their contributions to conservation and innovation, as well as ensuring increased spending on agricultural R&D, are essential ingredients for meeting the food requirements of the growing world population – expected to be in the region of eight billion by the year 2020. The challenges in this area can also be met only through new technologies and not through technologies of half a century ago. New technologies are needed to tackle new problems and must be protected through IPRs. Indeed, issues of generation, valuation, protection and exploitation of IP are becoming critically

---

[9]   Art. 7(1): EU Directive 96/9/EC on the Legal Protection of Databases.

[10]  Art. 3(1): EU Directive 96/9/EC on the Legal Protection of Databases.

important all around the world. Exponential growth of scientific knowledge increases demand for new forms of IP protection as well as access to IP-related information.

Protection of PBRs is granted to breeders of new, distinct, uniform and stable varieties of plants. Beginning from the date granted, PBRs offer protection for at least fifteen years. Many countries, both developed and developing, have exceptions for farmers to save and replant the seeds and to use such seeds for future breeding.

In many countries, the system of protection of new varieties of plants is dealt with by the Ministry of Agriculture, and in recent years it has acquired importance, since policy-makers are becoming increasingly aware of its value in the development of agriculture as well as protection of food, fibre, and renewable raw materials. This awareness is fostered by the trend towards privatization of the plant variety and seed sector.

New varieties of plants giving a higher harvested yield or providing resistance to plant pests, diseases, etc., are an essential factor in increasing productivity and product quality. It is important to identify a system that is suitable to the particular agricultural or socio-economic circumstances of a given country.

Breeding new varieties of plants requires investment in terms of skill, labour, material resources and funds, and may take many years. A new variety, once released, may in many cases be readily reproduced by others so as to deprive its breeder of the opportunity to profit adequately from his investment. Granting a breeder of a new variety the exclusive right to exploit his variety both encourages him to invest in plant breeding and contributes to the development of agriculture, horticulture and forestry.

The relevant international treaty in this field is the International Convention for the Protection of New Varieties of Plants (UPOV), which was signed in Paris on 2 December 1961, and subsequently amended in 1972, 1978 and 1991. It had fifty-two states as members as of 15 April 2003. Some additional countries are in the process of drafting laws conforming with the UPOV Convention. Although Article 27.3(b) of the TRIPS Agreement allows a fair degree of freedom to states in designing their plant variety protection system either by patents or by an effective sui generis system or by any combination thereof, the UPOV Convention has become the standard accepted by most states.

To be eligible for protection, a plant variety must fulfil certain basic conditions. It must be clearly distinguishable from any other variety whose existence, at the time of application, is a matter of common knowledge; it must be sufficiently uniform, subject to the variation that may be expected from particular features of its reproduction by seeds or vegetative propagation; it must be stable in its relevant characteristics, that is, remain unchanged after repeated reproduction or propagation or, in the case of a particular cycle of reproduction or propagation, at the end of each such cycle; and it must be new in the sense that it must not have been commercialized prior to certain dates established by reference to the date of application. It must also be given a variety denomination, that is, a name whose use will be mandatory in commercial transactions with the variety even after the termination of protection.

The effect of protection is that the authorization of the right-holder will be required for certain acts of exploitation of the variety for the production for purposes of commercial marketing, the offering for sale and the marketing of the protected variety and certain other varieties. The 1991 Act of the UPOV Convention provides, in particular, that the authorization of the right-holder would also be required in respect of harvested material (for instance, rice for consumption), but only if the right-holder has not had reasonable opportunity to exercise his right in relation to the corresponding seeds or propagating material.

This right rarely implies that the breeder enjoys a monopoly, for it is in the nature of agricultural production that varieties must be used by many farmers. The right could, therefore, be considered as one to assist in establishing partnerships. In the case of specialized crops, such as ornamental plants (roses, for example), the breeder will endeavour to organize production and trade in such a way that both himself and his partners will benefit from the exploitation of the variety. In the case of most food crops, suppliers could provide quality seeds to farmers.

The right granted to the breeder is subject to important limitations. Most countries provide an exception to the breeder's right under which farmers may freely produce seed for use on his own farm ('farmers' privilege'). Like most other IPRs, the breeder's right does not extend to private activities for non-commercial purposes. The exclusive right includes only production for commercial marketing; it does not extend to production of propagating material that is not for commercial marketing. Hence, production of seeds, for example, by a farmer for subsequent sowing on his own farm, falls outside the breeder's protection.[11]

### 1.4.10 Copyright

Copyright protection does not need the formality of registration of literary and artistic works. Copyright law, unlike that for protection of inventions through patents, protects the form of expression of ideas, not the ideas themselves. The copyright system, which protects an original work of an author that is fixed in a tangible form of expression, is concerned with the publication and communication of the creative output of authors. Copyright law protects creativity in the choice of words, musical notes, colours and shapes and relates to literary and artistic creations, for example, in the form of novels, poems, paintings, music and cinematographic works.

Copyright covers every original work of authorship, irrespective of its literary or artistic value or merit. In most European languages other than English, copyright is known as *le droit d'auteur* or author's rights. Copyright legislation protects against unauthorized use of the expression of certain ideas and in most countries it is declaratory. It is designed to promote intellectual creativity by providing to authors and creators of literary and artistic works, the exclusive rights in the works, thus encouraging them to create. Since for a new work to be created, the projected return needs to be higher than the expected costs, strong copyright protection, effectively implemented, is necessary for encouraging investments, in what has been aptly called 'the trading system of works of the mind'. Particularly, the

---

[11] Shahid Alikhan, *Socio-Economic Benefits of Intellectual Property Protection in Developing Countries* (WIPO, Mar. 2000), 18 to 21, <www.wipo.int/ebookshop?lang=eng&cmd=display_pub&cat_id=1165& cart_id=810414-80336318>.

investment necessary for the creation of works (in the case of filmmaking, book printing or architectural works for instance) or their exploitation (book publishing or record manufacturing, for example) will be more easily forthcoming if effective protection exists. In fact, often such protection is indispensable for obtaining these investments.

Copyright owners have the right to prevent all others from making copies of their works; the right to control the act of reproduction of their works; and the right to authorize rental of copies of certain categories of their works, for instance, musical works, audiovisual works and computer programs. Right of rental is important since rental of certain works is becoming a method of commercial exploitation. Duplication, display, translation and adaptation of a work protected by copyright also need authorization of the owner of such rights. As far as rights of copyright owners who choose cyberspace as a medium of expression are concerned, copyright infringement in cyberspace would possibly have to be treated like copyright violations in other areas.

These normal rights of copyright owners are also described as economic rights. They are distinct from moral rights of authors or artists, which are personal to the author or artist of copyright material and cannot be assigned or transferred, as is the case with economic rights. In a large number of other countries the rights of the author are based on his personal, intellectual, natural or 'moral' right that accrues for being the creator of the work, including the right to publish the work, to be acknowledged as its writer and creator and most importantly to have its integrity preserved. The work is seen as an expression of the author's mind, and being the extension of a specific personality, it is the natural property of the author. Moral rights are protected independently of the author's economic rights. Thus, even after sale of his or her economic rights, the author has the moral right to claim authorship of his or her work, to be recognized as the creator of the work, and to object to its distortion, mutilation or any other derogatory action in respect of his or her work which could be prejudicial to the author's or artist's honour or reputation. Thus, moral rights are a right of integrity, that is, the right not to have a work subject to derogatory treatment, and a right of attribution, that is, a right to be acknowledged as the author whenever and wherever the work is made public, and to be publicly recognized as the creator of the concerned work.

In the field of copyright, creative intellectual activity is encouraged by attributing to the authors, as creators of literary and artistic works, exclusive rights in their works. These rights also provide a legal basis for contractual arrangements/agreements between the author and the producer or distributor of the expression of the author's ideas, whether it be in the form of a book, a play, music performed in a theatre or other public place or as an audio or visual recording or programme broadcast by radio or television. The duration of protection of copyright works is much longer than that in the case of industrial property; normally, it is author's or creator's lifetime plus at least fifty years. It is limited to the boundaries of the country concerned. For nationals of the 150 countries (as of 15 April 2003) that are members of the Berne Convention for Protection of Literary and Artistic Works, protection is automatically granted in the rest of the 149 Member States. The main limitation on copyright, however, arises from the fair use doctrine that enjoins conditions under which copying for non-commercial uses is permitted.

24

The role of copyright in development at the national level is to encourage creativeness; promote tertiary industry (books, entertainment, records, films, etc.); promote the activities of the media (radio, television, cinema, press); while at the international level, it is to facilitate cultural exchanges; achieve integration in international relations (membership of multilateral treaties); and increase the role of countries within the international community.

It should be noted that while protection of IP is becoming increasingly acceptable in both the developed and the developing countries, some states in Asia and Africa have still not adhered to any international copyright convention. However, some of these states have domestic copyright laws. This could be due to lack of information, professional expertise, absence of motivation or non-existence of a proper mechanism for negotiation and valorization of copyright deals. Such non-adherence could result in financial losses to governments and to copyright owners.

As mentioned earlier, copyright, which deals with literary and artistic works, is a statutory right that does not require protection through registration and accrues in respect of the literary and artistic work without such formality. This is not the case where industrial property is concerned. Yet often, for their effective management in the marketplace, works protected under copyright require to be registered, not with the government, but generally with a society of authors, composers, musicians and the like. Such societies collectively manage the copyright on behalf of the authors, for a fee. Efficient and effective management of copyright, as for other IPRs, is essential for business enterprises, as it impacts on their performance and their competitiveness.

Thus, collective administrations or societies of authors and composers can help creators of literary and artistic works through collection and distribution of royalties due to them. These are normally in the private sector. However, the industrial property administrations in charge of receiving and registering applications after time-consuming procedures of examination, are either a part of the relevant government ministry or linked to it as an autonomous statutory body with an independent or semi-independent status.

## 1.5 NEW CHALLENGES

Since the first reported grant of IPRs in the year 1421 in Italy, the IP system has evolved substantially in scope, content and coverage. Not only have the means of its protection, management, exploitation and disclosure become more and more technology-savvy, but the commercial stakes in authorized dissemination have substantially increased. Likewise, IP as a system and as a polity has made deep inroads into the total system of governance of a country be it in trade and commerce, education and research and amongst the bureaucracy and judiciary, to name just a few.

While the almost volcanic eruption of sophisticated new technologies provides new opportunities, they are also posing new challenges. The opportunities lie in the enormous possibilities for the creation, distribution and use of works, and in turn these considerations pose challenges of multinational shades and hues requiring the adaptation of the system of protection of both copyright and rights neighbouring on copyright or related rights. Some of these potential challenges are enumerated below.

## 1.5.1 Emerging Technologies as IP Dissemination Sources

Reprography, tape recording and computer storage have made the reproduction of literary and artistic works easy, comparatively inexpensive, and within reach of such a large number of users that control of reproduction by the copyright owner is often impossible. The technology that enables cable television and satellite broadcasts knows no national boundaries, often making effective legal control of the content distributed by such technologies difficult.

With the development of printing and subsequent new technological means for dissemination of works of the mind, the possibilities of production of multiple identical copies of literary and artistic works at relatively low or insignificant costs have increased tremendously. While these developments have increased the demand for such works, they has also increased the need to protect the author, his assignees and publisher against unauthorized reproduction. In effect, the higher the potential market for a work, the greater the need for effective protection by legal and/or technological measures.

The impact of these rapid changes has led to certain new developments. Some experts feel that these developments have thrown the copyright system into crisis given the flood of new digital technologies and expected further waves of technological progress. The other view is that while copyright is in a difficult period of transition, it is certainly not in a crisis, at least not in the sense that it is in a state of decadence or is becoming obsolete.

Such dilemmas raised by technological progress are not new phenomena. When national copyright laws were promulgated during the eighteenth and the nineteenth centuries, legislators took into account certain traditional ways of using literary and artistic works. 'It was Queen Anne who brought about the fundamental turn in the year 1710 when she gave the right to authorise the printing of works to the authors themselves . . . the civil law system has more than one root. The most decisive one goes back in history to the time of the French Revolution, when authors' rights in their literary and artistic works were recognized.'[12] Later, in the second half of the nineteenth century, at the behest of the International Literary and Artistic Association, the Swiss Federation convened diplomatic conferences in Berne in 1884, 1885 and 1886. It was at the last of these conferences that the Berne Convention for the Protection of Literary and Artistic Works was adopted. The Convention fixed a minimum level of protection which each Member State must grant to nationals of other Member States.

Even around the time when the Berne Convention – the oldest multilateral treaty in the field of international copyright – was adopted in 1886, new types of changes had begun to occur, leading, slowly at first, but at a rapidly accelerating pace later, to the present qualitatively new situation.

While one cannot fully anticipate where the frontiers, if any, of these developments may be, it is clear that already innumerable numbers of protected works could be fed into

---

[12] Dr Mihaly Ficsor, Director of the Centre for Information Technology and Intellectual Property in Budapest, Hungary, and former Assistant Director General of WIPO, Feb. 2003.

computer memories with easy and direct access to them through satellites, cables and telephone lines, making it simple to reproduce, distribute, view, store and/or use them in private homes and offices with the aid of sophisticated terminals.

In view of the new possibilities of using protected works, a major problem raised by these technological developments for international copyright is piracy: illegal reproduction and distribution of protected works and other flagrant infringements of copyright. Redefining fair-use exceptions is, however, one way of redefining what is permissible and what is otherwise illegal and considered copyright infringement or piracy.

### 1.5.2 Creating Linkages between IP Stakeholders

To derive optimal benefit from the IP system, every country should proactively encourage the development of links between R&D institutions, business enterprises and universities. At the same time, industry and business should increasingly strengthen their contacts with researchers in universities and R&D institutions for various consultancy requirements. Likewise, R&D institutions and university researchers should equally strengthen their links with enterprises to evolve research programmes and activities tailored to the needs of such enterprises. This would help to shift the responsibility of generating new technologies from government to private officials, industrialists, entrepreneurs and academics, as well as to universities and other institutions of higher learning and research. As yet, no country can claim that its populations are aware of or understand the IP system's role in promoting the success of an enterprise, business, R&D institution or of the country itself in the twenty-first century.

Therefore, a greater awareness of the economic value of IP needs to be built for the private sector as well as for national development and growth. More attention should be paid regarding how the IP system can be utilized to promote national inventiveness and creativity. Such awareness could be effectively ensured through the media, the press, the radio and TV networks.

The small- and medium-sized enterprises (SME) sector is yet to be fully informed of the economic value of IPRs. Much worse, many inventors, innovators and creators of intellectual works are not aware of the basic parameters of IP laws or how to commercialize their inventions.

Most importantly, at the national level there should be a political will to adopt or adapt an IP system that will guard national interests and simultaneously remain compatible with international agreements. Towards this end, knowledge promotion, education and training, integration of education and industrial policy, with the necessary infrastructure development, as well as promotion of social justice, are factors to be considered for effective implementation. In this process, the IP system is itself a factor to be reckoned with in the process of technology transfer, technology development, industrial and economic progress, export trade, identification of new markets and their retention, and in the promotion of inventive, innovative and creative activities.

IPR protection is not meant merely for indulging in legal quibbles or law school debates; rather, the issue threatens significant economic fallout. IPRs are key components of the infrastructure required for economic growth. Suitably designed and adapted to national needs, they can be harnessed to promote socio-economic development, develop national indigenous technological capacity, generate export opportunities through enhancement of competitiveness and help attract foreign investment, particularly through joint ventures. Technology-based companies are facing and will continue to face exciting times that would constantly change the practices in many industries. In this evolving scenario, IPR protection is becoming a priority for managements that are willing to confront the realities of competition.

While most countries have gained experience in administering a legal system which protects IP, it is necessary to enhance basic awareness, upgrade legislation, strengthen infrastructural capabilities and fill in the many gaps that still remain in these areas.

### 1.5.3 Interfacing Legal, Business, and Management Systems

Constantly updating legislation, modernizing infrastructures and administrations and making them increasingly market-oriented and user-friendly, together with collecting and computerizing patent documentation, making it available to industry, establishing and/or modernizing the collective administration of copyright are all essential prerequisites to strong IP protection. Such protection, with adequate, modernized and well-enforced IP legislation, will undoubtedly improve the confidence of technology licensors and may assist in the ease of transfer of technology. Thus, it would help in attracting foreign direct investment (FDI) under conditions stipulated in Chapter 3. Attracting such resources in some high-tech areas (e.g., drugs and pharmaceuticals) becomes more difficult if IPR protection is not strong or is ineffective.

Good management of national enterprises and R&D institutions should encourage young technocrats to innovate, even if it takes time to promote inventiveness in the production of new, better and cheaper technologies. This is equally true for well-managed collective administration of societies for authors' rights. Efficient functioning of such societies enables low-cost collection and distribution of copyright royalties to creators of works. This encourages authors to write and provides the education system with better textbooks, written by nationally renowned writers and experts, which may be more relevant to national requirements.

Those countries which have effectively used the IP system to expand their manufacturing and services activities have been able to improve their export performance, and their national standard of living has steadily and measurably improved. With the internationalization of trade, technology and investment, the fear of erosion of economic sovereignty and of invasion of economic space is real and omnipresent. To overcome this fear and to face the reality of increasing competitive pressures from the increasingly skilled, low-cost, technical manpower in a sizeable number of countries, enterprises and national economies concerned will have to constantly improve their technological capacity by creating a technologically skilled workface, working in a dynamic, flexible enabling environment that provides the requisite stimulus for generation and utilization of new knowledge and for the creative expression of ideas. A key ingredient in providing such an environment is a well functioning IP system.

Businesses and enterprises should be encouraged to promote an inventive and creative spirit among their employees. Moreover, a conscious effort to do so is essential to help inventors to commercialize their inventions. In the process of economic reforms and growth, the adoption and use of an effective IP system that promotes inventive and creative activity is a sine qua non and in the larger national interests. Promotion of such inventive activity should be done in a systematic manner at every stage of the innovation process, starting from the stage of conception of a new idea for solving a technical problem through invention development, testing and, ultimately, commercialization of products and services based on such inventions. Technological progress is an important means of attaining economic growth and social prosperity and the IP system is an important resource in helping to accelerate innovation promotion and technology development as well as a significant factor in growth. Economic growth, with the utilization of the IP system, is becoming global, and not confined only to industrialized countries.

For reaping the real socio-economic value of the IP system, national industry associations and their local branches, where these exist, should pay more attention to the use of this system in the growth of SMEs, which also should be encouraged to follow improved management practices. While the big industries usually have a fairly high level of knowledge and expertise concerning the latest inventions in their field of technology (also concerning trademarks and industrial designs), it is the SMEs which need to be increasingly apprised and helped to integrate such information. They often adapt sooner to technical changes. SMEs are fairly significant employers and are units of technological innovation. These micro-enterprises are the sole sustenance of some 300 million people worldwide. They should, as a deliberate policy, be assisted by simplifying regulations and procedures for them and by facilitating access to credits, markets and training. The opportunities for SMEs to make more informed decisions and encourage innovation management could also prime the national technological base.

There is often a lack of clear appreciation of the important economic and technological impact that IPR protection can have on enterprise management and competitiveness. Such effective protection helps increase the efficiency with which inventive activity can be generated and used by encouraging the creative initiative of employees and by investment in R&D and marketing. Enterprises should, in the present competitive world, develop a deliberate policy of encouraging employees to invent, securing protection for their inventions and checking on and avoiding infringing the rights owned by others.

At the national industrial property or patent office level, patent applications should be processed expeditiously so that inventors are encouraged to register their inventions nationally. An ineffective or weak physical infrastructure will have a regressive effect, both qualitatively and quantitatively, on invention promotion. Most national patent offices need enhanced resources for accelerating their computerization. This would not only improve their basic services but also strengthen the patent information services. Better services will enable the industrial property office to charge higher fees, which might set the stage for such an office to become a financially autonomous institution, as is already the case in many countries.

In order to promote economic growth through technology development with the aid of the IP system, awareness-building programmes on IPRs and their protection should be regularly held at the national and sub-national levels. This will help to develop a progressive awareness in business, R&D institutions, and in university circles and help to change the 'mindset' among the general public at large. Such programmes should target not only industry technocrats, intellectuals, universities and the public at large, but also the police, customs and the judiciary, which play an important part in enforcement. Development of specialization amongst judges in the field of IP is also needed.

As a country advances scientifically and technically, an IP 'culture' needs to be assiduously and deliberately promoted. This would encourage market-oriented innovative and inventive activity, scientific and technological creativity, modernization of IP infrastructure and administration and human resource development required for these purposes.

Likewise, teaching of intellectual property should become an essential part of the law faculties in universities, in institutions of higher learning and in institutes of engineering, management and scientific research.

The socio-economic benefits of IP protection stem from the qualitative competitiveness of products and services produced and delivered through the use of the IP system. Thus, effective IP protection stimulates creativity and innovation by providing rewards, thereby resulting in a continuous stream of new and better processes, products and services. The management and commercialization of IP can result in benefits including increased revenue, increased operational efficiency,improvements in existing IP assets and opportunities for local industrial and enterprise development.

The qualitative competitiveness that the system generates helps to create jobs in the industries and businesses concerned, with a higher quality labour force through training associated with the transfer of technologies. In respect to the cultural industries, the IP system rewards the creative talent of authors and performers through collection and distribution of royalties due to them, as well as by helping them to reach local and foreign distribution outlets for their works.

IPRs and their protection are increasingly becoming a key part of the national economic agenda in a number of countries. They are fast becoming an integral part of the national economic policy, science and technology policy and education policy.

It is necessary to repeat and to emphasize that socio-economic growth depends increasingly on international competitiveness of the economy, of industry and of business. Such competitiveness is driven by knowledge-based technological progress which, in turn, is encouraged, promoted and substantially helped through an appropriate IP system. Effective use of the IP system by governments and by the private sector, as well as the strict enforcement of IPRs by the judiciary and the enforcement agencies, are essential ingredients of sustainable socio-economic development in a knowledge-driven, market-oriented environment.

# CHAPTER TWO

# GLOBALIZATION AND INTELLECTUAL PROPERTY

- *Nature of Globalization and Role of the World Trade Organization (WTO)*
- *Challenges to Intellectual Property (IP) Protection and Role of the World Intellectual Property Organization (WIPO)*

## 2.1 POWER OF GLOBALIZATION

In view of the realization that impediments due to non-liberalization in world trade could adversely affect global economic development, over the last quarter of the previous century, economic openness has been increasing, leading to qualitative changes in international economic integration, resulting in higher levels of trade across borders. This integration within the global economy is a process that has already gained momentum with the explosion of knowledge, science and technology.

Indeed, economic globalization has come to stay. Global inter-dependency of business enterprises continues to grow. Many feel that globalization per se is not a problem, but that national instruments, which can manage and control any unfavourable impact of globalization while enhancing its benefits, are necessary.

Constantly improving travel and communication systems have greatly facilitated business transactions, the exchange of ideas and views and social and economic interaction between individuals and institutions. The range and scope of economic activity amongst inhabitants of different countries is increasing. With advances in information and communication technology and easier and cheaper communications, the spread of the benefits of creativity and innovation has also been facilitated. Intra-industry trade and outsourcing has likewise significantly increased, as has foreign investment and flow of financial capital.

Globalization is, for many, neither a dirty word nor is it new. Innovative and dynamic societies throughout history have been, to a lesser or greater extent, cosmopolitan. Since the 1980s, governments in a number of developing countries have been following open-market policies for promoting their trade and for engaging more actively with the world economy, which has yielded positive results in respect to their economic growth:

Globalisation means many things to many people . . . it has opponents, often highly vocal, and supporters, sometimes unattractively brash. Little wonder, then, that popular coverage of globalisation focuses on its costs, real and imagined. . . . Yet there is a wealth of economic evidence demonstrating that globalisation brings great benefits . . . it offers the opportunity for a higher rate of sustainable growth – growth that translates into longer, healthier lives and improved living standards . . . the true benefits strongly outweigh the costs.[1]

With globalization, economic growth appears to have accelerated and widened. Per capita incomes have uniformly grown through the post-World War II period not only in the developed but also in the developing countries. Between 1990 and 2005, developing countries witnessed an average annual growth rate in their gross domestic product (GDP) of 4.33%, whereas in developed countries it was 2.37% for the same period.[2] The developing countries could have done better but for the fact that their populations during the same period grew at a much faster rate. Again, whereas GDP per capita rose by 2.4% in 1990 in developing countries, it rose by 0.3% in developed countries. Also, in the last decade, a large number of developing countries have economically outperformed most industrialized countries.

This is evident from the fact that between 1994 and 2003, exports from the developing countries witnessed a higher average annual growth rate of 11% as compared to developed countries, which had an average annual growth rate of 5% for the same period. Likewise, the exports from low-income countries witnessed an annual growth rate of 9% for the corresponding period – amounting to 209 billion United States dollars (USD) in 2003.

However, to its critics, globalization 'is a force for oppression, exploitation and injustice . . . these may be extreme positions', but at the same time 'it is important to understand why the sceptics are wrong, why economic integration is a force for the good; and why globalisation, far from being the greatest cause of poverty, is its only feasible cure . . . some of the sceptics are opposed not just to globalisation or even to the market economy, but to the very idea of economic growth. The anti-globalists themselves, somewhat self-contradictorily, use the information-spreading aspect of globalisation to great effect. Organising a worldwide protest movement would be much harder without the World Wide Web, but the web itself is merely one dimension of globalisation'.[3]

In this context, Prof. Amartya Sen, of Trinity College, Cambridge University, and Nobel Prize Winner said in his Alfred Deakin Lecture at Melbourne (May 2001), that 'the protestors often describe themselves as "anti-globalization" but are they really? They can hardly be, in general, anti-globalization, as these protests are in fact the most globalized events in the contemporary world'. In the same address he also remarked that 'we live in a world of unprecedented prosperity – incomparably richer than ever before. The massive command over resources, knowledge and technology that we take for granted, would be hard for our ancestors to imagine . . . there is much evidence that the global economy has brought prosperity to many different areas', with 'the great advantages of contemporary technology, the well-established efficiency of international trade . . . and the social as well as economic merits of living in open rather than closed societies . . . Economic growth can be extremely

---

[1]    'Making Sense of Globalisation: A Guide to the Economic Issues,' published by the Centre for Economic Policy Research, London, Policy Paper No.8, Jul. 2002: <www.cepr.org/pubs/books/cepr/booklist.asp?cv-no=PP8>.

[2]    World Development Indicators, World Resources Institute: <http://earthtrends.wri.org>.

[3]    'Globalisation and Its Critics: A Survey of Globalisation', *The Economist*, 29 Sep., 2001.

helpful in removing poverty. This is because the poor can directly share in the increased wealth generated by economic growth and because increase in national prosperity can help in financing of public services (including healthcare and education)... the world needs more interaction, not less'.[4]

It is also important to mention here what Kofi Annan, then Secretary General of the United Nations, said in this context, that 'arguing against globalization is like arguing against the laws of gravity'.

## 2.2 LEVERAGING OF IP IN A GLOBAL ECONOMY

In the present global economic scenario, challenges and opportunities are generated by the fast eroding physical barriers to international transactions and the growing borderlessness of trade. In this situation, IP is acquiring an important role on the international stage.

Works of the mind, for instance inventions, trademarks, industrial designs, books, music and films, are used and enjoyed in all countries around the globe. International protection of IP 'acts as a spur to human creativity, pushing forward the boundaries of science and technology and enriching the world of literature and the arts. By providing a stable environment for the marketing of IP products, it also oils the wheels of international trade'.[5]

Intellectual Property Rights (IPRs) are assuming importance in international trade, investment, economic relations and economic growth. The thrust in every productive sector of the economy must be to invigorate domestic efficiency and qualitative management in a growingly open and competitive global economy, with greater opportunities for investments and exports.

Recognition of the creator and inventor, protection of their rights and the rights of those who invest in the making of their creations and/or commercialization of their creative products all contribute to sustainable economic growth. In the context of globalization of trading activity, companies are being attracted towards transborder strategic alliances, including joint ventures, co-production agreements, joint research, technology agreements and licensing arrangements.

The international trade in goods and services, protected by IPRs, is not confined to industrialized countries. It is an important factor in worldwide economic growth and in all knowledge and technology-based industries and businesses. IP signifies this advancing knowledge in the form of new ideas, new techniques, new processes and new products having economic value and commercial potential.

The world's major growth industries, for example, microelectronics, biotechnology and telecommunications, are already brainpower industries. It is their knowledge-based intangible assets which are providing industry and business with a competitive edge. The dominance of intangible knowledge assets will require major changes within management structures. Knowledge-based industries such as software development,

---

4    <www.abc.net.au/rn/deakin/stories/s296978.htm>.
5    World Intellectual Property Organization (WIPO) – An Overview – 2007: <www.wipo.int/export/sites/www/freepublications/en/general/1007/wipo_pub_1007.pdf>.

pharmaceuticals, biotechnology, engineering services, etc., operate in a highly competitive environment placing great demands on the speed of response in global market conditions. High operational efficiency and functional flexibility is crucial for such industries. National and transnational knowledge networks between the productive sector and the R&D sector will have to be consciously strengthened to leverage the opportunities provided by globalization.

In respect to issues of generation, protection and exploitation of IPRs, industries and businesses will also have to face up to the challenges in the knowledge market as they integrate with the global economy. IPRs and their effective protection will be crucial in a world of competition based on knowledge. Incorporating strong systems for the generation of IPRs, their documentation, valuation, protection and exploitation, will need a massive thrust.

Here there is, however, an issue that is causing concern. The governments in some of the rich industrialized countries are seen as protecting their own powerful corporations, who own a considerable amount of IP vis-à-vis the interests of the population in the poorer countries. This is considered as an attempt to assist the multinational corporations (MNCs) in obtaining a larger share in the benefits of globalization. While IPRs certainly need effective protection to ensure that inventors, innovators and creators are duly compensated, it equally needs to be ensured that the spread and diffusion of knowledge so created is facilitated and not inhibited. The ongoing negotiations at the intergovernmental level in respect to the international IPR regime should take into account the legitimate interests of both the innovators and the creators, and the needs of the users as well as the interests of the global society in general, so that a just balance is ensured.

In the policy paper referred to earlier in footnote 1, it is mentioned that:

> investment in knowledge is not like investment in ordinary capital goods. Many innovations require large investments of time, skill and other resources, often for a very uncertain return. Once made, however, they can be copied at low cost . . . so we face a trade-off: either reward innovation, with the risk that innovations once made will spread too slowly, or facilitate the spread of existing knowledge, with the risk that everyone will become imitator rather than innovator.

The patent system provides a compromise by granting a temporary monopoly as a reward for the creator of an invention for a fixed period of time, after which the innovation can be encouraged to spread. Thus, while it is justifiable to ensure that globalization per se does not undermine IP protection, 'when overall returns to innovation are rising it is legitimate to be concerned that the benefits of such returns should be widely shared . . . there is no fundamental disagreement that a compromise of some kind is needed'.[6]

Meanwhile, in the last decade and a half of the previous century, economic growth, food production and health had already become some of the primary drivers in the generation of new knowledge. Advances in knowledge have also brought up new issues. Advances in modern biotechnology have led to genetically engineered crops. An understanding of the

---

[6]  See fn. 1.

potential risks and rewards of such technology needs to be rationally addressed so as not to impede the progress that is achievable through the use of this new knowledge. Genetic engineering and the associated reproductive technologies on plants, animals and humans have also brought forth certain issues concerning greater regulation and involving social scientists and environmentalists. The processes of Globalisation, privatization and corporatization of research have brought in new dimensions. 'Globalisation increasingly subjects corporations to constraints of competition with each other, constraints that in some respects make the task of government easier'.[7] Again, 'globalisation tends to boost growth, and growth reduces poverty. The poor as well as the rich see their incomes rise as a result of increased economic growth'.[8]

Ever since cutting-edge advances in modern biotechnology, space technology, information technology and renewable energy technology and their deployment in national policies have become necessary, issues of IPRs and proprietary information have assumed greater importance. As a result, new models of the innovation chain and new paradigms of the science and knowledge society have begun to emerge. In this scenario, lack of information about the usefulness of IP protection has often led to a certain mindset amongst an important section of public opinion, largely based on misinformation. Empowerment of the society with knowledge concerning the potential socio-economic value of IP is crucial for completing the innovation chain.

It is thus necessary not only to enhance basic awareness but also to upgrade legislation, strengthen infrastructural capabilities and fill in the gaps that still remain in these areas. With fast emerging technologies, legislation is, with the time taken in the formalities of its modifications, usually a pace or two behind. Laws cannot be static and must be in step with the emerging technologies and national economic needs; hence the necessity of constantly upgrading and modernizing IP legislation.

The global system of IPRs will undergo considerable change in the current century. In the context of globalization, the national and international markets are becoming more and more integrated with the reduction in barriers to trade, technology and investment. Also, in the global economy of the current century, creation of knowledge and its protection are important for ensuring and promoting competitiveness and economic development. With the ongoing liberalization of the trade rules and regimes in a number of developing countries and countries in transition, simultaneous strengthening of their IPRs will ensure a more steady path to techno-economic growth.

## 2.3 INTERNATIONAL TRENDS IN GLOBALIZING R&D AND TECHNOLOGY

Industrial R&D collaboration in the developed world has been increasing exponentially. A strong and synergistic pairing of major players in countries such as the US and Japan, as well as in Europe, dominates the scene.

---

[7] Ibid.
[8] Ibid.

The R&D spending abroad by US companies is rising much faster than their domestic spending. IBM and Hewlett-Packard, for example, are estimated to do nearly 30% of their R&D outside the US. Reciprocally, the number of R&D facilities in the US set up by foreign companies has increased significantly. Around 250 R&D facilities in the United States are owned by more than one hundred foreign parent companies. These are mainly Japanese, German, British, French and South Korean parent companies.

Likewise, several US firms hold R&D facilities in Japan. Development of products for the Japanese markets is their main goal. Improvement of product quality and consumer acceptance are other goals – the main objective being, of course, to gain entry into the Japanese market. This obviously helps the US firms to improve their market access in Japan.

Let us now move on to Japan itself and see what the game plan is. The last few years have seen a remarkable change in the way the Japanese are approaching the issue of R&D globalization. They are starting with the fundamentals, namely by beginning to hire foreign scientists in Japan. Indeed, Japanese companies, known for their conservatism so far, have now begun to recruit foreign researchers based on their skills rather than their nationality; Fujitsu, Nippon Steel, Sony, Canon, etc., are good examples of this trend.

It is generally recognized that the Japanese globalization approach is to take over R&D-intensive corporations and even establishment of R&D centres abroad. The Japanese have, in fact, promoted a new concept of *'techno-globalism'*, which is being interpreted as the strong interaction between the internationalization of technology and the globalization of the economy. It actually implies widening cross-border interdependence between individual technology-based firms as well as economic sectors, especially through the restructuring of high and medium-tech industry. Incidentally, it is interesting to note that the intensity of such transnational cooperation and establishment of R&D facilities is the highest in high-tech areas, such as electronics, biotechnology and automotive industries. Several European companies have also set up such R&D centres at many locations worldwide or within the European Community.

In respect to globalization of technology, Archibugi and Jonathan[9] have identified three separate processes that are generally subsumed under the catchall expression 'globalisation of technology'. According to them, the term has three conditions, namely:

(a) international exploitation of national technological capabilities;
(b) international technology alliances; and
(c) globalization of innovation across countries.

Each of these three categories has its own manifestations and indicators, which can be measured in empirical terms. The approach adopted is generally as follows:

– global exploitation of technologies takes place through patents and licenses;
– global sourcing of R&D takes place through alliances and joint ventures with foreign companies or universities; and
– global production of R&D takes place through overseas subsidiaries.

---

[9] Daniele Archibugi & Michie Jonathan (eds), *Technology, Globalisation and Economic Performance* (Cambridge: Cambridge University Press, 1997): <www.cambridge.org/catalogue/catalogue.asp?isbn=9780521553926>.

In respect to international exploitation of national technological capabilities, the manifestation for domestic enterprises means the following:

– exports of high-tech products;
– relocation of production abroad;
– exports of technology through the medium of licensing agreements between foreign and domestic firms.

The indicators for measuring these are the following:

– international trade in high-tech products;
– quantum of foreign direct investment (FDI) inflows and outflows;
– number of licensing agreements.

Similarly, international technology alliances mean collaboration across borders among both public and business institutions to exchange and develop knowledge. Its manifestation is that the firms expand their non-equity agreements to share costs and risks of industrial R&D. Its indicator is the number and form of scientific and technical agreements.

Finally, and in this context, the generation of innovation across more than one country manifests in MNCs establishing their R&D units abroad, and patenting activities of MNCs attributable to research in foreign locations, etc.[10]

It is to be recognized that collaborative R&D is sweeping the developed world. We firmly believe that countries like India, for example, can become a part of this game plan in the coming decade, provided they understand the forces that are driving globalization of R&D and move speedily and aggressively.

## 2.4 DRIVING FORCES FOR GLOBALIZATION OF INDUSTRIAL R&D

The chain of steps from concept to commercialization necessarily crosses national boundaries today. Companies realize that to gain a competitive advantage they have to leverage their capabilities. The idea is to develop synergies and to make one and one equal to eleven and not just two! Many companies across the world today consider it unwise to attempt self-sufficiency in technology development, particularly in an era where the R&D costs are increasing rapidly. With trade barriers among countries disappearing fast, companies have to provide the best technology globally to their customers. The concept that technology could be acquired rather than re-invented is gaining momentum. As part of the global innovation strategy, several companies the world over are scouting for new ideas and patents, which the originator is unable to exploit for a variety of reasons. These companies believe that the surest way of becoming technically strong is through networking with premier organizations in those areas.

---

[10]   Ibid.

There is another interesting and subtle aspect to this issue. The globalization of R&D is closely linked to globalization of business and consequently to global competition of skills. The competitive advantage in high-technology business increasingly depends on underlying technical skills of the business rather than on particular products. As product life cycles become shorter, skill life cycles become longer. The product then is merely an intermediary between a company's skills and the market it serves. Rather than being the focus of corporate activity, products are actually transient mechanisms by which the market derives value from a company's skill-base and the company derives value from the market. The high-technology companies are therefore, asking as to what skills, capabilities and technologies should be built up, rather than asking a stereotyped question as to which markets they should enter and with which products.

In order to acquire a particular new skill and remain world class in all the core competencies of one's company, an extraordinary technology renewal effort is required. In such a situation, the demands on R&D increase, but the dichotomy is that the corporate investments in R&D decrease because of pressures on profit margins arising out of global competition.

One of the major driving forces is thus the increasing cost of research and resource demands, which even giant multinational companies cannot afford. The companies are concluding that they cannot justify in-house assembly of all the various skills and facilities needed to carry out developments, and the pace of change often denies them the time to do so. One dramatic consequence is that today competitive advantage lies in the power and effectiveness of the allied network, which a business team is able to assemble and manage in a short time, rather than in in-house capability. Furthermore, the skills necessary to compete in leading-edge technology over a broad front are rapidly becoming available globally – Brazil's smaller commercial aircraft and Portugal's design and production of moulds for plastics manufacture are good examples.

The focus is shifting to complementing internal efforts with an increased amount of external technology acquisition on a global basis. Therefore, external technology acquisition is assuming importance within leading corporations. R&D departments are increasingly being charged with the job of managing and restructuring the corporation's technology portfolio. Their success is being measured in terms of what they have brought to that portfolio. This new function is global in nature and not restricted to the four walls of a single research laboratory. In some of the companies, as high as 10% of the specialized R&D professionals are devoted to this activity.

Several factors are helping to accelerate the globalization of industrial R&D, but the most important factor that is helping the process of creation of 'seamless laboratories' around the world is the evolution of global information networks. Information is the most fluid commodity in the world, most easily and quickly moving from place to place. Consequently, those products, processes and services which are most fluid and hence able to take the earliest and fullest advantage of information technology, are becoming globalized rapidly. The internationalization of all professional services is essentially a consequence of this fluidity of information. Global information networks allow real-time management and operation of laboratories in any part of the world.

In this context, it is also relevant to consider, appreciate and strengthen the roles and impact of existing international intergovernmental institutions such as WIPO and World Trade Organization (WTO; the latter being the successor of the General Agreement on Tariffs and Trade (GATT)) in creating linkages between social, political, and economic dimensions of IP. As mentioned by Mart Leesti and Tom Pengelly:

> [I]nternational rule making and standard setting on a very broad range of intellectual property subjects takes place predominantly in WIPO and WTO. A large majority of developing countries are members or are becoming members of both organizations.... Availability of information technology and the Internet also enables easy access to a wealth of information on intellectual property policy subjects, as well as on the on-line databases and libraries of organizations like WIPO and WTO ... yet, 154 intellectual property offices around the world currently lack Internet connectivity.[11]

Let us now consider the erstwhile GATT and the Uruguay Round and its successor, the WTO, followed by the role of the WIPO.

## 2.5 URUGUAY ROUND AND THE BIRTH OF TRIPS

Globalization and the need for further trade liberalization as well as multilaterally agreed rules for the conduct of such trade led to the eighth and largest multilateral trade negotiations round, known as the Uruguay Round under the then GATT. With the successful conclusion of the Uruguay Round and the Multilateral Trade Negotiations on 15 April 1994, GATT was succeeded by an intergovernmental organization, namely the WTO. WTO, with its 'one member, one vote' rule, is an international institution that is a forum for negotiations between member governments. It publishes a vast amount of background material and is subject to intense media scrutiny. Its concentration is on continued trade liberalization. Member States could apply policies best suited for them in a non-discriminatory way, so that they do not constitute a barrier to trade.

The Uruguay Round, which started in September 1986, had extended over seven years. WTO's predecessor, GATT, was established in 1948, with twenty-three countries signing the first post-war multilateral agreement on trade liberalization, since protectionist beggar-thy-neighbour policies were considered to have caused, between the two World Wars, the recession in the 1920s and the depression in the 1930s. Unlike the earlier trade rounds, which concentrated on lowering customs tariffs on goods at the borders, the Uruguay Round was expanded in scope to address a broader range of issues.

After protracted negotiations, the mandate of the then GATT was expanded to encompass agriculture, textiles, investment, services and IPRs, with the primary purpose of

---

[11] Mart Leesti & Tom Pengelly, 'Capacity Building for Management of Intellectual Property Rights', by, published in UNDP's booklet *Cooperation South, 2002:* <http://tcdc.undp.org/CoopSouth/2002_dec/p40-65_capacity.pdf>.

establishing rules-based systems and reducing protectionism, which was not confined to any one group of countries, developed or developing.

The issue of inclusion of IPRs for the first time in trade negotiations was raised at the very outset of the Uruguay Round in 1986, despite objections from some major developing countries. Until then, IPRs had not descended in varieties of trade-related or non-trade-related. The controversy over the Agreement on Trade-Related Aspects of Intellectual Property Rights (TRIPS) heightened when, in December 1991, Arthur Dunkel, then Director-General of the GATT, submitted a complete draft accord to help negotiators concentrate on a draft final text. This led also to a debate between proponents and opponents of full patent protection for pharmaceutical products during the two years of negotiation thereafter. However, the Dunkel text on IP went into the Draft Final Act of the Uruguay Round virtually intact, after certain improvements were sought, obtained and included for developing countries such as, for instance, a ten-year transitional period for implementation of product patents for pharmaceuticals, that would give the pharmaceutical industry in certain developing countries an important transition period to adapt to the new regimes.

During the Uruguay Round negotiations between 1986 and 1993, the strategy of some of the developing countries was concentrated on containing the expansion of the TRIPS agenda. When the agreement was finally signed, they had obtained through the negotiations a number of improvements and flexibilities in the text, which seemed a good starting point. Most of the forward-looking thinkers in the developing world felt that they could concentrate on their ingenuity to use the flexibilities to their advantage, and that simply because the world's major trading partners were proposing something, it did not necessarily mean it was disadvantageous for developing countries.

The TRIPS Agreement, which entered into force on 1 January 1995, is administered by the WTO, and covers seven categories of IPRs. These are:

(a) Copyright and Related Rights
(b) Trademarks
(c) Geographical Indications
(d) Industrial Design
(e) Layout of Integrated Circuits
(f) Trade Secrets
(g) Patents (including micro-organisms and plant variety protection).

The Agreement also commits governments of Member States to enact and enforce IPR protection laws. The minimum standards that it sets in connection with enforcement in Part III of the Agreement elaborate on the general obligations, civil and administrative procedures and remedies, evidence, injunctions, damages and other remedies, provisional measures, special requirements related to border measures and criminal procedures.

The principal objective of the TRIPS Agreement was to strengthen and harmonize IPR standards among all signatory countries. Also, since it is a Paris Convention for Protection of Industrial Property plus, and a Berne Convention for the Protection of Literary and Artistic Works plus treaty, and since these two treaties administered by the WIPO have 164 and 150 countries respectively as members, it should help them in this process.

Incidentally, during most of the initial years since 1986, WIPO helped developing countries in comprehending the legal standards and norms for protection of IPRs. This was done through a series of meetings, held in Geneva with their representatives following the commencement of the Uruguay Round. An elaborate document was produced by WIPO in September 1988, entitled 'Existence, Scope and Form of Generally Internationally Accepted and Applied Standards/Norms for Protection of Intellectual Property'.[12]

Before the entry into force of the TRIPS Agreement in January 1995, countries had more flexibility in excluding certain sectors of the economy from patent protection in their national laws. Since a number of developing countries and least developed countries (LDCs) had weaker IPRs prior to the TRIPS Agreement, the Agreement places substantially greater burdens on these countries for reforming their IPR regimes. These burdens include the cost of developing institutional infrastructure to protect IPRs.

To ease the transition, however, the TRIPS Agreement established different compliance deadlines – January 1996 for developed countries and January 2000 for developing countries. LDCs, were given until 2006, which – at the Fourth Session of the WTO Ministerial Conference held in November 2001 at Doha (Qatar) – was further extended with respect to their obligation concerning patent protection for pharmaceutical products, until 1 January 2016.

The TRIPS Agreement, as it finally emerged, was expected to encourage the flow of technology. However, while deciding on its implementation, the developing countries will have to undertake adequate safeguards to protect their interests. The safeguard provisions under the Agreement allow for compulsory licensing and parallel importing. The TRIPS Agreement has important provisions for fair play in technology transfer, from which the developing world could and should benefit. Yet the actual benefit that has been derived by the developing countries so far has been minimal as has been mentioned in the report of the UK Commission on IPRs.[13]

Article 7 of the TRIPS Agreement states that 'the protection and enforcement of international property rights should contribute to the promotion of technological innovation and to the transfer and dissemination of technology, to the mutual advantage of producers and users of technological knowledge and in a manner conducive to social and economic welfare, and to a balance of rights and obligations'. Furthermore, Article 8.2 states that 'appropriate measures, provided they are consistent with the provisions of the Agreement, may be needed to prevent the abuse of IPRs by rights holders or the resort to practices which unreasonably restrain trade or adversely affect the international transfer of technology'.

During the last half of 1993, prior to the signing of the GATT's Uruguay Round Agreements and the TRIPS Agreement, it was clear that few in various countries believed that keeping out of the multilateral trade agreements and having to undertake bilateral trade negotiations with each of the other 116 negotiating countries then (now there are 146

---

12   <www.ipmall.info/hosted_resources/lipa/TRIPS.asp>.
13   Report of the UK Commission on Intellectual Property Rights (CIPR), London, Sep. 2002: <www.iprcommission.org/graphic/documents/final_report.htm>.

members of the WTO) would be realistic. Governments in a number of countries, including some of those which had spearheaded the move towards improvements in the draft agreement, and notwithstanding some reservations about TRIPS, had in the overall interests of their countries decided to accept the Draft Final Act of the Uruguay Round, since it was not possible to accept only parts of it and reject other parts.

## 2.6 TRIPS AS A LEVER OF GROWTH

Even in developing countries, many experts felt that the TRIPS Agreement could open new horizons for industry, including the pharmaceutical industry, and ensure success through competition. Too much was involved in the deal for most countries' economies to allow them to give in to objections to strengthening IPRs, especially as these were largely owned by certain limited interest groups. It was also clear, during the negotiation period, that in the post-GATT era the national industrial property and copyright legislations in a large number of countries would have to be revised. For instance, even during the later part of the negotiations, and even at the time of conclusion of the TRIPS Agreement, patent protection for certain subject matter was excluded in a large number of countries, for example, pharmaceutical product patents in forty-nine countries (both developed and developing); plant varieties in forty-four countries; food products in thirty-five countries; computer programs in thirty-two countries; and chemical products in twenty-two countries.

Pursuant to their TRIPS obligations, all members of the WTO are required to provide IPR protection as per an agreed set of minimum standards. Member States are expected to be committed to modernize and enforce copyright and industrial property legislations. With implementation still underway and industries still adjusting, not much empirical evidence is available on the effects of the legislative changes.

The technologically advanced world has always agreed that lack of effective IP protection is a disincentive for export of the latest technologies, while such protection, effectively enforced, is an encouragement for FDI in wide-ranging sectors of industry, including media and information technology. Many countries have been turning away from trade protectionism and towards liberalization which, together with adequate IP protection, are positive factors in promoting economic growth.

In one study it was suggested that cutting barriers to trade in agriculture, manufacturing and services by about one-third would boost the world economy by USD 613 billion.[14] In view of this possibility, the global multilateral processes and, through them, open trade, could also help the world's poorer countries and people, through expanded access to markets. According to estimates by the Tinbergen Institute of Rotterdam in the Netherlands, developing countries would gain USD 155 billion per year from further trade liberalization – over three times the USD 43 billion in average annual overseas development assistance. Thus, the risk for some of the developing countries is not through

---

14 Drusilla K. Brown, Alan V. Deardorff & Robert M Stern, 'Multilateral, Regional, and Bilateral Trade-Policy Options for the United States and Japan', Research Seminar in International Economics, University of Michigan, Working Papers No. 469: <http://ideas.repec.org/p/mie/wpaper/469.html>.

globalization, but through marginalization. Generally speaking, only more open economies have contributed to sustained economic growth and prosperity.

At the WTO's Fourth Ministerial Conference at Doha (November 2001), the Ministerial Declaration, while reaffirming its commitment to sustainable development, stressed that international trade played a major role in the promotion of economic development and the alleviation of poverty and that the multilateral trading system embodied in the GATT and its successor organization, the WTO, has contributed significantly to economic growth, development and employment throughout the last nearly fifty-five years. A need was, however, felt for serious consideration of mechanisms to compensate developing and LDC in the South for losses, in certain respects, from the strengthening of IPRs.

A separate 'Declaration on the TRIPS Agreement and Public Health' stressed the importance of implementation and interpretation of the TRIPS Agreement in a manner supportive of public health by promoting access to existing medicines as well as R&D into new medicines. Also, issues with respect to implementation of Article 23.4 of the TRIPS Agreement, concerning additional protection for geographical indications and issues relating to the extension of such protection of geographical indications to products other than those mentioned in the said article, would be addressed in the Council for TRIPS. It was also agreed that the TRIPS Council should examine the relationship between the TRIPS Agreement and the Convention on Biological Diversity (the full text of which Convention was opened for signature at the 1992 Rio 'Earth Summit'), the protection of traditional knowledge and folklore, and the Council shall take fully into account the development dimension.

The long-term effectiveness of the TRIPS Agreement depends on striking a balance between requiring strict adherence to the agreement and allowing flexibility, so that countries see it in their interests to comply.

The role of the WTO would be both to maintain the momentum launched at the earlier mentioned Ministerial Conference at Doha, and to build on its deliberations and on the Doha Development Agenda (DDA) especially in respect of development issues and integration of the interests of the smaller, vulnerable economies into the multilateral trading system. Also, it would involve taking positive steps to assist developing countries, including the least developed among them, in securing a share in the growth of world trade commensurate with the needs of their economic development. In this context, the Ministerial Declaration has spelt out that enhanced market access, balanced rules, and well-targeted, sustainably financed technical assistance and capacity-building programmes have important roles to play.

The WTO's Sixth Ministerial Conference held at Hong Kong, China in December 2005 reaffirmed the declarations and decisions adopted at Doha.

The developing countries also seem keen to obtain greater market access for their agricultural produce and value-added industrial goods as well as improved access for their service providers. And of course, the implementation of the Doha decision – which would enable many lower-income developing countries which face serious humanitarian consequences due to public health crises and which have negligible domestic drug

(21) Locarno Agreement Establishing an International Classification for Industrial Designs

(22) Nice Agreement Concerning the International Classification of Goods and Services for the Purposes of the Registration of Marks

(23) Strasbourg Agreement Concerning the International Patent Classification

(24) Vienna Agreement Establishing an International Classification of the Figurative Elements of Marks

With the technological revolution and IP having increasingly become a global issue, one of the challenges is to ensure that the IP system is developed internationally as a promoter of socio-economic growth while, at the same time, making acquisition of protection simpler and its enforcement more effective.

WIPO undertakes and continues to help in the establishment of norms, which obligate Member States to grant a certain level of protection to the creators and owners of IP. It is constantly endeavouring to develop new norms and standards in keeping with advances in technology and business practices as well as in response to specific concerns like traditional knowledge, folklore and biodiversity. It also provides practical assistance to developing countries in respect to the protection of IP, including advice on legislation when requested by Member States.

WIPO also promotes the teaching of IP law in universities. In 1981, the International Bureau of WIPO initiated the establishment of a non-governmental organization called ATRIP (International Association for the Advancement of Teaching and Research in Intellectual Property). It helps, inter alia, to establish model curricula and availability of teaching material in the law faculties and libraries of universities in developing countries.

Likewise, in respect to encouragement of inventions, WIPO has actively been promoting inventive work and activities in various countries and focusing on the potential for such inventiveness in developing countries. It was the International Bureau's support, in fact, that helped establish the International Federation of Inventors' Associations (IFIA). Also, in a number of its workshops and seminars, WIPO has been devoting necessary attention to the role of IP in the transfer of technology.

Further, in respect to patent information services, WIPO has offered various facilities that provide, free of charge, copies of patent documents to developing countries and furnish search reports upon request. There are around four million patents in force in the world, which constitute important catalysts for the newest innovative technologies. The patent office in a developing country could send a request to WIPO with a copy of the patent application, which it had received, seeking a report on the patentability of the concerned invention. These requests are attended to with the least possible delay. In addition, WIPO had been supplying, free of charge, copies of patent documents needed for various reasons such as background information in research projects or for negotiation of licensing contracts, etc. WIPO functions as an intermediary between the patent office in a developing country and the office (often in an industrialized country) that provides copies of the information needed.

In addition, WIPO helps to harmonize national IP legislation and procedures; provides services for international applications for industrial property; exchanges IP information; provides legal and technical assistance to countries; and assists in infrastructure development of IP offices and copyright administrations.

## 2.7.2 WIPO and the Challenges to IP

Insofar as challenges to IP protection and the role of the WIPO is concerned, one of the foremost of these, according to the Director-General of WIPO, as reported[15] in his New Year's message at the beginning of 2002, 'is the task of making the promise of intellectual property as a tool for economic development a reality. In this 21st century, intellectual property is a powerful driver of economic growth'. It helps in 'stimulating creativity and innovation, generating revenue, promoting investment, enhancing culture, preventing "brain drain" and nurturing overall economic health. Despite the importance of intellectual property to wealth creation and economic development, a gap continues to exist between developed and developing nations in terms of intellectual property asset ownership and use'.

Again, conscious of the fact that while the major business and industry organizations often use IP as an effective tool, small- and medium-sized enterprises (SMEs) do not often have the information necessary to do so, WIPO intends to continue its campaign to make IP utilization more accessible to all. The Member States of WIPO approved, in September 2000, a new programme designed to help the important sector of economic and business players comprising SMEs, and WIPO has been helping this considerable job-providing sector in most national economies and the global economy to understand the value of IP and to help them take increasing advantage of the IP system in order to improve their qualitative competitiveness and help create wealth.

Among the challenges WIPO will continue to address, according to the aforementioned message of its Director-General, will be 'how intellectual property works in practice, how it promotes investments and affects valuation, how inventions relate to research policies, how cultural industries can be supported by intellectual property policies, how trademarks relate to branding and licensing, how intellectual property assets are managed, how licensing operates to share knowledge and spread the value of intellectual property and how it can be protected'.

An important adjunct to WIPO's meeting its challenges in an increasingly globalized economy and market, and the consequent need for inculcating a forward-looking awareness, is the establishment of the WIPO Worldwide Academy (WWA),[16] with the purpose of serving as an educational institution for teaching, training and research in IP. It conducts professional training, policy training, as well as distance learning programmes, among others. The initial idea of a WIPO Academy intended to build awareness among

---

15 &lt;www.wipo.int/about-wipo/en/dgo/dgki_2002.html&gt;.
16 &lt;www.wipo.int/academy/en/index.html&gt;.

policy-makers mainly in developing countries, was implemented in 1993 with the first Academy course. About five years later it took the shape of an important WIPO institution and was named the WWA. It helps develop human resources with new training and teaching techniques, and uses modern public access media in disseminating knowledge of IP. Its activities include a Distance Learning Centre, launched in 1999, using Internet facilities.[17]

Also in 1998, WIPO set up a well-defined project – the WIPONET, a global IP network designed to provide a number of services which could further promote a global partnership in IP management and information sharing. It is a step by WIPO towards utilizing the potential which information technology offers in promoting the use and protection of IP. It is also designed to enhance international cooperation by facilitating the digital exchange of IP information amongst the various IP offices of its Member States.

Inadequate preparedness of many IP offices in many developing countries is a serious concern. The problem areas pertain to manual and paper-based operations; static manpower resources; rapid increase in the number of patent applications filed in recent years leading to inordinate delays in granting IPRs; non-uniformity in examination; inadequate quality of search facilities and tools; and lack of digital data and networks.

It is felt that it is necessary to ensure the sustainability and continued upgrading of WIPONET in the coming decades. It is equally necessary to expand awareness and understanding of the basic components of a modernized framework in the context of IPR services, namely re-engineering of work functions, automation and networking, shifting from paper-based operations to electronic record management, providing a legal framework for making electronic payment systems available, providing the ability to authenticate an originator and to maintain the confidentiality of data and records wherever needed. WIPO will be endeavouring to place IP-specific applications and information on WIPONET which will include support for international treaties dealing with protection of IPRs, for example the Patent Cooperation Treaty (PCT); and utilizing its sophisticated, robust and secure infrastructure to provide a conduit for areas such as Intellectual Property Digital Libraries (IPDLs).[18] Future developments will also include applications to further assist IP offices in enhancing their internal operations and data hosting facilities; leverage information technologies; and improve the retrieval of IP information through continued development of international classification of patents, trademarks and industrial designs as efficient search tools.

The delivery of these new services is expected to be demand driven, based on business requirements which cater to the needs of the IP community, especially those of the IP offices. WIPO is seeking the cooperation and assistance of these offices in identifying the need for new and/or enhanced services, which will facilitate the further

---

[17]  <www.wipo.int/export/sites/www/academy/en/about/pdf/pub466e.pdf>.
[18]  <www.wipo.int/ipdl/en/>.

development of WIPONET, and importantly promote global international cooperation in IP matters.

WIPONET will thus be making direct as well as indirect contributions in the efforts to modernize national IP offices. It will be a direct provider of systems and services. It will also be a facilitator for providing details on technologies and related standards and make a catalytic impact on the development of national information technology infrastructures. A word of caution here: Developing nations will have to take urgent steps to utilize these services effectively.

With the growing importance of electronic commerce, another growing IPR-related challenge being met by WIPO has been its assistance in establishing a method of settling commercial disputes through its Arbitration and Mediation Centre.[19] This Centre meets the need for a quick and inexpensive manner of settling commercial disputes as an alternative to time-consuming and costly court proceedings and assists individuals and companies around the world in respect to disputes concerning IP. The Centre has emerged as a leading dispute-settlement service provider in the context of challenges arising out of abusive registration and use of Internet domain names known as 'cybersquatting'.

Through international consultations, WIPO is also examining solutions to cybersquatting extending to international non-proprietary names for pharmaceutical substances, names of intergovernmental organizations, geographical indications and trade names, etc.

In addition to its assistance to developing countries, WIPO has been providing assistance to countries in transition from a centrally planned to a market economy system. With the demise of the Soviet Union in 1991, its successor states (most of which joined the Commonwealth of Independent States (CIS) (Commonwealth in Russian consists of two roots, 'common' and 'friendship')), the three Baltic States which declared their independence and successor states of former Yugoslavia, such as Slovenia and Croatia, also independent since 1991, have been provided with WIPO's cooperative assistance.

While in the globalized economy the challenges for WIPO, as its Director-General has stated, 'are exciting ones', the organization is, in addition to the directions enumerated above, taking positive steps for helping developing and capacity-constrained countries to modernize their IP infrastructures by constantly building awareness of the wealth-creating value of the system, so that they are able 'to shape, adapt to, and benefit from the changes and improvements'.

At the same time, considering the need for strengthening the IP system in the LDCs, the newly created LDC unit of WIPO has, in cooperation with other concerned divisions of the organization, been helping with activities concentrated on building and/or strengthening both the public and private sectors of these countries, including managerial skills, technical capacity, administrative and legal systems as well as physical and equipment infrastructure.

---

[19]  <www.wipo.int/amc/en/center/background.html>.

## 2.8 GLOBALIZATION AND WIPO/WTO

Since we are reflecting on the roles of WTO and WIPO in the context of globalization and IP, and the need for assistance to developing and, in particular, to LDCs as well as those in transition, it is germane here to mention that the new emphasis on the protection and enforcement of IPRs through the implementation of the TRIPS Agreement has added to the value of WIPO's work programme. This is particularly so since the TRIPS Agreement virtually complements and expands on some of the conventions and international treaties serviced by the WIPO and its predecessor organization for well over a hundred years.

An agreement[20] concluded in December 1995, and implemented between the WIPO and WTO on 1 January 1996, provided for cooperation in the implementation of the TRIPS Agreement including legal technical assistance. In July 1998, a joint initiative was launched for assisting developing countries and LDCs in meeting their obligations under the TRIPS Agreement by the year 2000 and 2006, respectively.

At the Fourth Session of the Ministerial Conference of WTO at Doha in November 2001, referred to earlier, the Ministerial Declaration stated, inter alia, that since 'international trade can play a major role in the promotion of economic development and alleviation of poverty', and since the 'majority of WTO members are developing countries', the Conference sought to place their needs as an important base of the Work Programme adopted in its Declaration. It also stressed the need to:

> make positive efforts designed to ensure that developing countries, and especially the least developed countries among them, secure a share in the growth of world trade commensurate with the needs of their economic development. In this context, enhanced market access, balanced rules, and well targeted, sustainably financed technical assistance and capacity-building programmes have important roles to play.

In the road map ahead for these two important organizations, it is germane here to refer to the new initiative launched by WIPO and WTO in June 2001 to help the LDCs to maximize the benefits of IP protection.[21] The WIPO Director-General termed the joint initiative as an expression of commitment to the LDCs, as providing them with an IP system was crucial in assisting them in view of the importance of IP as a tool for technological advancement, economic growth and wealth creation. The WTO Director-General felt that while implementation of their joint initiative obligations posed a challenge, it provided an opportunity for the LDCs to harness IP in order to accelerate their economic, social and cultural development and that this joint initiative, which offered varied forms of technical assistance, would help the LDCs promote their developmental goals.

To sum up, there is a growing awareness that IP protection is a crucial part of the new global trading system. International trade in goods and services protected by IPRs is increasing, and both developed and developing countries have recognized that it is in

---

[20]   <www.wipo.int/ip-development/en/legislative_assistance/>.
[21]   <www.wipo.int/ldcs/en>.

their interest to provide strong IPR protection so as to participate in the benefits of such trade.

IP issues in respect of certain industries, in the context of new technologies and growing international competition, are pinpointing the need to constantly review national and international regulatory systems. Traditional legal frameworks have had to undergo changes. The high costs of research and development, comparative ease of piracy-cum-counterfeiting and the global market pressures of the emerging technologies have increased the importance of national and international protection of IP. Faced with borderless markets, policy-makers are often confronted with the dilemma of absorbing new technologies nationally and encouraging their absorption internationally, without deviating from either their national IPR protection system or the international regimes regulating these rights. International harmonization of IP laws and regulations is thus becoming a constant priority in the face of globalization of trade and of new technologies.

# CHAPTER THREE

# NATIONAL ECONOMIC DEVELOPMENT STRATEGY AND INTELLECTUAL PROPERTY

- *Market Orientation*
- *Export Orientation*
- *Foreign Direct Investment: Joint Ventures*
- *Technology Transfer; Licensing; Technology Forecasting and Use of Patent Information in Forecasting Technology Trends*
- *Intellectual Property (IP) and Environmentally Sound Technologies*
- *Valuation of Intellectual Property*
- *International Treaties*

## 3.1 IPRs as Tools of Economic Strategy

The accelerated liberalization of economies in today's world has drawn universal attention to the importance of IP and its protection as well as its role in stimulating growth. Progressive liberalization of world economies is resulting in a greater movement of goods, services, labour and capital across borders. Multilateralism, promoted by institutions such as the World Trade Organization (WTO) and the World Intellectual Property Organization (WIPO), is aimed at strengthening and encouraging the use of IP as an integral part of the international trading system. The need to focus on a national economic development strategy which covers Intellectual Property Rights (IPRs) issues in a holistic framework is felt today even more than ever before.

Most countries have well-articulated economic policies that focus on market-oriented, export-led growth. Governments in most developed and developing countries are trying to improve the overall environment for investment by firms. Various types of regulatory and licensing controls had imposed numerous constraints, encouraged the proliferation of red tape and other impediments, which have increased the transaction costs and the risks of doing business in a non-transparent environment. Countries are gradually freeing themselves from such controls.

Governments worldwide are also beginning to appreciate the crucial role of knowledge in economic development. Knowledge enhances the value of human capital. Therefore, efforts are being made to focus on development of human capacity on the one hand and on the effective generation and exploitation of IP's tangible assets, which are products arising from harnessed human capital, on the other.

3.2 IPRS AS TOOLS OF BUSINESS STRATEGY: MARKET AND EXPORT ORIENTATION

IP law should ideally help promote human creativity and innovation without simultaneously restricting the dissemination of the fruits of such intellectual endeavours. A modern IP system has the potential to facilitate the use of IP assets in market transactions such as sale, licensing or franchising of these assets, facilitating mergers and acquisitions, joint ventures and other forms of strategic alliances from the R&D stage through production to marketing.

Franchising, for example, with its origins in France in the 1930s, has been developed and extended throughout the world. A franchising contract is basically a licensing arrangement concerning the use of the trademark or trade name of the IPR owner (franchiser) by another entity (franchisee) who agrees to follow the franchiser's directives covering the operation of the franchise system in respect, inter alia, of quality control and territorial restrictions. It also involves the supply of marketing know-how by the franchiser, who has developed a system for operating a certain business, to the franchisee, allowing the latter to use the system as prescribed by the franchiser in exchange for monetary compensation. Franchising is common, for instance in fast-food restaurants and in the hospitality industry as a whole. The franchising system thus allows the IPRs relating to trademarks, trade names, inventions, industrial designs, etc., along with the appropriate know-how to be used for the sale of goods and provision of services for users. The conclusion of a contract with franchising clauses needs to be considered during the course of technology transfer leading to marketing by manufacture or import, made available to a franchisee in respect to a product intended for sale to the public.

While creators gain from royalties or a lump-sum payment for the use of the products of their creation, over which they have a time-bound monopoly as extended under their national law, there is an increasing movement to extend harmonization of IP laws worldwide. With the growth of new technologies, the number, type and class of innovations that could be protected under the IP system is increasing. Procedures for registration, where such registration of rights is required, are becoming more and more standardized. The use of digital technology also facilitates this process considerably.

With the rise in knowledge-based innovation and production, competition today amongst businesses and industries is becoming more intensive. Also, with the declining time span for an idea to move into the marketplace and with the need for constant production of newly innovative products in highly competitive markets, enterprises are becoming more and more dependent on effective IP protection, to ensure that their sizeable investments in creating the IP assets are duly recovered and rewarded. The protection of IPRs is a priority for enterprises eager and willing to confront the realities of competition. Confidence in IP protection is a powerful stimulus for innovation. Strong IP protection is also an important factor in obtaining the transfer of the latest technologies as well as in attracting Foreign Direct Investment (FDI).

Attracting such resources in a world of hyper competition will become harder where domestic economic stability is not well entrenched and where integration with world markets for goods and capital is inadequate, and also where IPR protection is not strong or is ineffective.

National economic development strategies need to ensure not only effective management of the protection of IPRs of national creators and inventors, but also to help commercialize the results of such creativity and innovation. For most enterprises, a core concern is to remain ahead of their competitors. Often this involves making a small improvement in the quality of existing products, as compared with those of the competitor. It also entails, in the context of market orientation, the successful production, distribution and marketing, so as to maintain consistency in quality and timely availability of goods or services to customers in the marketplace. The process of commercialization involves development, testing and marketing of new processes, products and services in the marketplace for a commercial return. The protection of IP is viewed as an important part of the process of commercialization of such assets in the national as well as in the international marketplace.

Good management of the process of commercialization of IP assets requires assessment of its benefits, likely costs, value of competing products or technologies, estimated return, as well as extent of enhancement of reputation, etc. An IP asset that has a commercial value in its sale, or in licensing of certain rights in that asset to a third party, could be used to raise funds. Likewise, an IP asset could be considered operationally useful and valuable if it performs an important role in the operation of services provided by an enterprise, industry or business.

National enterprises need to be careful not to disclose their IP creations or inventions to a third party before their publication and commercialization, as to do so would certainly destroy the IP asset's commercial value. Premature disclosure or publication could also reduce the potential market value of IP assets by providing possible competitors with information about a possible market opportunity, thereby encouraging them to develop a competing asset.

Where a product or creation is considered to be competitive for export to external markets, the necessary export opportunity would need appropriate protection. This is best done through the advice of suitably qualified legal experts or patent attorneys.

3.3 FOREIGN DIRECT INVESTMENT: JOINT VENTURES

Strong and effective protection of IPRs and increased efficiency in the administration of IP are important incentives for attracting FDIs and technology transfer under certain circumstances. FDI often takes place through the setting up or acquisition of a subsidiary in a foreign country, over which the concerned investing enterprise has adequate management control.

With the removal of barriers and expansion of national economies into a number of countries, this strategy has caused a sizeable flow of funds and investments in the last two decades of the previous century. The World Development Report[1] of the World Bank, published in September 1998, however, indicated that FDI in developing countries was

---

[1] <www.worldbank.org/wdr/wdr98/contents.htm>.

concentrated in a few markets. It reported that in many developing countries, the total availability of private international capital and FDI could have been higher but for certain gaps in their respective IPR systems. The intimate link between such investment flows and the level of IP protection has been empirically established through numerous studies published in recent years.

Some of these studies show that stronger IPRs in developing countries would increase imports significantly from developed countries, as well as from other developing countries.[2] Strengthening IPRs is also effective in increasing imports of low-technology consumer items and is associated with the decline of indigenous industries based on imitation. These studies also imply that countries with little technological capacity may experience reduced imports because the patent laws have the effect of increasing import prices on average, and hence reduce import capacity. Other studies show the influence of stronger IPRs on foreign investment, licensing, and the transfer of technology.[3] Liberalization of national trade policies also provides the necessary incentive for FDI. Likewise with a country's improved technological capacity, both FDI and technology transfer through licensing are seen to increase.

According to a study published by the Centre for Economic Policy Research,[4] 'the factors that attract FDI include also, an educated, productive workforce and a predictable business environment, which are in the interests of the workers themselves'. Keith Maskus, has inferred that the multinational enterprises (MNEs) make multifaceted decisions about how they can serve foreign markets. MNEs may undertake horizontal FDI, in which the subsidiary produces products and services similar to those produced in the home country of the concerned MNE or vertical FDI, in which the subsidiary produces inputs or undertakes assembly from components. The more horizontal the investment, the greater the importance of strong IPRs. In this case, it is not surprising that countries moving up the FDI cycle find a growing interest in adopting stronger IPRs, an interest congruent with their own expanding abilities to produce new products and technologies.

Strong national IPRs help to attract FDI, technology transfer and licensing. China, for example, has emerged as a particularly large destination in this context. According to Sherwood,[5] strong IPRs play a much larger role in signalling to potential investors that a particular country recognizes and protects the rights of foreign firms to make strategic business decisions with few governmental impediments.

---

[2]    Keith E. Maskus & Mohan Penubarti, 'How Trade-Related are Intellectual Property Rights', *Journal of International Economics* 39 (1995): 227-248; and P. Smith, 'Are Weak Patent Rights a Barrier to U.S. Exports?,' *Journal of International Economic* 48 (1999): 151-177.

[3]    Keith E. Maskus, *Intellectual Property Rights in the Global Economy* (Washington D.C.: Institute for International Economics, 2000), 73-79: <http://bookstore.petersoninstitute.org/book-store/99.html>.

[4]    'Making Sense of Globalisation: A Guide to the Economic Issues,' published by the Centre for Economic Policy Research, *London, Policy Paper* No. 8, Jul. 2002: <www.cepr.org/pubs/books/cepr/booklist.asp?cv-no=PP8>.

[5]    Robert M. Sherwood, *Intellectual Property and Economic Development* (Boulder, CO: Westview Press, 1990).

FDI is also sensitive to variations in IPRs. The amounts of possible additional investment as a result of patent reforms could be large. Imports and FDI both embody technological advantages that can spill over into domestic economies, even under strong patent regimes. Thus, a dynamic benefit from rising activity flows could outweigh losses in the terms of trade for such countries. The likelihood of such an outcome depends on complementary factors, such as the ability to absorb and commercialize technologies, openness to trade and maintenance of competition.

The effect of stronger trademarks seems particularly important in increasing imports of relatively low-technology goods, e.g., some consumer goods. Firms with easily copied products and technologies such as pharmaceuticals, chemicals, food additives and software depend more on local IPR systems. A strong patent system and its enforcement are prerequisites for technology transfer and investment. Japan, for example, has effectively utilized the IP system, particularly in respect to patents, to develop its economy and competence in the aftermath of World War II, and has become a leading industrialized country. This has also helped Japan to promote FDI and technology transfer. Another example, the Republic of Korea, has overtaken a number of countries in respect to overseas patents granted by promoting a strong IP system. Similarly, Brazil and India, after modernizing their IP legislations, have observed significant growth in FDI and in the number of patent applications filed in their countries. The rate of patenting in some other developing countries has also increased in the last few years.

It may be inferred from this that investment and technology transfer are relatively sensitive to weak or ineffectively operated IPRs. FDI is also influenced by trade costs, market sizes and other locational advantages. Also, FDI in respect to complex but easily copied technologies is likely to increase as IPRs are strengthened because effective protection of patents, copyrights and trademarks ensures the necessary security. Again, since stronger IPRs would help reduce licensing costs, FDI could be displaced over time by efficient licensing. Experience shows that the possibility of transfer of the most advanced technologies increases with the strength of IPRs and their effective protection.

Stronger IPRs in developing economies could thus promote long-term growth, as they would attract additional FDI and licensing as well as joint ventures and will spur further follow-up innovation and technology spillovers. This outcome is far more likely, however, if the implementation of stronger IPRs is accompanied by complementary policies that promote dynamic competition.

### 3.4 PROMOTING TECHNOLOGY TRANSFER THROUGH LICENSING

Facilitating the access of third-world countries, as well as countries in transition, to required technologies constitutes one of the key elements in accelerating the pace of their economic and social development. Such access is generally through licensing contracts or technology transfer agreements which not only allow exploitation of the legal rights protected in respect of patents, trademarks, industrial designs, etc., but also provide the necessary expertise and technical assistance in the exploitation of those rights.

The objective of concluding a licensing contract is the transfer by the licensor and acquisition by the licensee of a given technology. Further, it expands the right to exploit that technology in the making of, or in the use or sale of, a given product or in the application of a given process through which a product can be obtained. Licensing is probably the most common method of technology transfer and concerns granting of a right or license to use the technology in return for agreed payments, usually a royalty linked to sales volume or value. Licensing is also important in foreign business relations. It provides the main means of using IPRs of foreign companies by local national enterprises. It is a legitimate way of promoting the transfer of technology, because it is received from the proper source; normally with the full assistance of the licensor. Such transfer of technology is not only a legitimate activity, but also helps to create employment and increase the geographic area of sales. However, any possible dangers due to lack of awareness or experience in respect to negotiating licensing contracts should be guarded against. Here again, suitable legal advice could be obtained from licensing specialists.

The prospective technology seekers in some developing countries face serious difficulties in their commercial dealings with technology holders in the developed countries. These arise from a variety of reasons. Some arise from the imperfections of the market for technology. Some could be attributed to the relative lack of experience and skill of enterprises and institutions in the concerned developing countries in concluding adequate legal arrangements for the acquisition of technology. Some also arise due to government practices, both legislative and administrative, in industrialized as well as in developing countries.

Strong IP protection, adequate legislation and enforcement of IPRs are perceived as playing a significant role in indicating to potential investors that the country concerned will protect its rights in making business decisions, with the least possible government impediments. Transfer of technology, in principle, will be facilitated, since the foreign investors and licensors will be assured that their technology will not be exposed or revealed to competitors.

The agreed basis for a technology transfer transaction is like that in any other business transaction. Each party assesses the costs involved compared to the benefits expected and, on that basis, reaches a price which the transferor is prepared to accept and the transferee is prepared to pay. A business and financial assessment needs to be done by considering diverse factors. For instance, one must consider whether the acquisition of technology will carry with it some added benefits such as higher market profile and whether the price being asked carries hidden costs. For example, is the licensor also responsible for the maintenance and enforcement of the IPRs concerned?

An optimal licensing agreement should provide fairly adequately for the objectives of the parties to the agreement. Licensing choices, such as those regarding ownership, may be made at different points in the development life cycle of the IP asset concerned, affording it some flexibility. However, since normally the licenses are between parties in different countries, the currency of payment and the amount of license fees need to be specified at the then applicable exchange rates.

If the technology being sought is not specific, but covers a whole production complex, a turnkey arrangement is often contracted. The contractor, if he may be called so, takes the responsibility for establishing the operating plant, training the staff and supervising its initial operation. The contractor may then hand over to his client, or the entity which is the recipient of the technology, the entire plant that has the capacity of operating in accordance with certain agreed performance standards. The contractor party to the turnkey project normally undertakes to supply to the client the design details of the concerned industrial plant, as well as the necessary detailed technical information relating to its operation. The contractor is responsible for the design, construction and commissioning of the plant concerned, but often does not help develop local technological capacity. In a licensing arrangement, on the other hand, development of indigenous technological capacity is much less constrained. It is often, as a via media, that joint ventures are preferred.

A joint venture involves an association of persons for a joint undertaking in which the parties contribute in different ways, such as through provision of working capital and money, patent rights, technology and marketing skills. The parties should identify precisely what each one's inputs will be and how the joint venture arrangement will be managed, including raising the required capital, marketing plans, resolving of disputes, etc. Expert advice may be needed concerning international legal aspects. A joint venture could be a contractual association, a trust, a company such as a limited liability company or other form of ownership.

## 3.5 TECHNOLOGY FORECASTING BASED ON PATENT INFORMATION

In the context of technology licensing, technology transfer and joint venture undertakings, it is necessary to mention that technology forecasting is an important activity. Through the use of national patent information services for assessing technology trends, forecasting and technology road-mapping can be considerably assisted. It is an activity which seeks to map the evolution of technology in the areas of interest to a particular country or enterprise in its quest to appropriate benefits from science-intensive technological opportunities in the medium- to long-term perspective of international competitiveness.

One method of forecasting for the likely evolution of a particular technology area is based on a systems analysis and study of patenting activity covering that area. Technology forecasting usually helps focus on specific technologies that may have a potential of affecting a particular industrial sector and thus provides a systematic analysis of the possible consequences of certain emerging technologies. It could also highlight certain technological elements of product design as well as possible future technological developments.

Anticipating and understanding technological change is an important challenge for policy-makers in government as well as industry and business sectors. Scientists in R&D institutions as well as engineers, managers and technocrats in important national enterprises should be made aware, through technology forecasting, as to when, where and how the future technological advances are likely to take place. This could help the concerned institutions and enterprises in aligning their research or corporate business agendas appropriately.

Insofar as the small- and medium-sized enterprises are concerned, as their survival in the increasingly competitive world would certainly depend on constant innovation, it is necessary to help them with the latest developments of easily understood sources of technology forecasting, since they too need to be technologically informed. For both the private and public sectors of industry and business, tough economic competition is the primary driver of technological innovation and hence the key motivator for conducting technology forecasting.

## 3.6 Promoting Environmentally Sound Technologies

Environment, ecology, economics, equity and ethics need to be balanced by all nations. A national economic development strategy can collectively utilize the IP system for ensuring, to the extent possible, that the environment is free from pollution. For access to environmentally friendly technologies, countries could use the information available through patent documents. These provide the most up-to-date technological information in the world; in fact, there is no superior source of information, since 95% of all the relevant technical information is found in these detailed documents. Technological information can be obtained from many sources, but none provides the coverage of technological information as do the patent documents. From these documents it is possible to get the necessary technical details regarding a variety of inventions. If an invention is under patent protection, the information could provide particulars regarding the identity of the owner, who could then be contacted for authorization to use the invention concerned, if needed.

National development strategies should help encourage access to environmentally sound technologies on terms that are favourable to both the transferor and the transferee. At the same time, it needs to be publicized that not all such inventions are protected, because in many cases the protection might have expired. Such inventions which are not protected and are, therefore, in the public domain could be freely used. Again, since fewer of these patent applications are registered in many of the developing countries, environment friendly inventions could be freely used in those countries where they are not protected. However, in respect to the ever-improving and latest of technologies, which may still be needed for environmental protection but which may at any given point in time be covered by patent protection, necessary, special funding should be provided to enable the transfer and use of such technologies, especially among small- and medium-sized enterprises. It should also be possible, where such new technologies are needed but are still protected under IP and patent rights, to include their transfer as a possible accompanying part of large capital projects. In the context of national economic development strategies designed for promoting competitiveness in this twenty-first century, it would also be necessary to reduce barriers and provide incentives for the transfer of privately owned, environmentally sound technologies.

Agenda 21 as formulated at the United Nations Conference on Environment and Development (UNCED) in Rio de Janeiro in 1992 (now coordinated by the United Nations

Commission on Sustainable Development and implemented through national and local authorities) recommends,[6] in the case of privately owned technology, the purchase of patents and licenses on commercial terms for their transfer to developing countries on non-commercial terms as part of the programme of cooperation for development, taking into account the need to protect IPRs. Agenda 21 also recommends promoting long-term collaborative arrangements between enterprises of developed and developing countries for the development of environmentally sound technology, for promoting cooperation in, and related to, such technology transfer, as well as for building a trained human resource pool and infrastructure. The technical assistance in the field of environmentally sound technologies should be tailored to the actual needs of the development process in developing countries. Agenda 21 also recommends 'promoting joint ventures between the suppliers and recipients of technology. Together with direct foreign investment, these ventures constitute important channels for transferring environmentally sound technology, and sound environmental management practices, which could be transferred and maintained. Sustainable economic growth requires necessarily environmentally sound economic growth'.

Also:

> tapping this pool of knowledge and recombining it with local innovations to generate alternative technologies should be pursued .... Enhanced access to environmentally sound technologies should be promoted, facilitated and financed as appropriate, while providing fair incentives to innovators that promote research and development of new environmentally sound technologies. Governments and international organisations should promote effective modalities for the access and transfer in particular to developing countries of environmentally sound technologies through formulation of policies and programmes for effective transfer of such technologies that are in the public domain, and creation of favourable conditions to encourage the private and public sectors in developing countries, to innovate, market and use environmentally sound technologies.

The Agreement on Trade-Related Aspects of Intellectual Property Rights (TRIPS) has important provisions for fair play in technology transfer from which the developing world should benefit. Article 7 of the TRIPS Agreement states that 'the protection and enforcement of IPRs should contribute to the promotion of technological innovation and to the transfer and dissemination of technology, to the mutual advantage of producers and users of technological knowledge and in a manner conducive to social and economic welfare, and to a balance of rights and obligations'. Furthermore, Article 8.2 states that 'appropriate measures, provided they are consistent with the provisions of the Agreement, may be needed to prevent the abuse of IPRs by right holders or the resort to practices which unreasonably restrain trade or adversely affect the international transfer of technology'.

There are concrete examples to show that technology transfers to the third world have not taken place when they were needed most. The 1990 Montreal Protocol on Substances

---

[6]    <www.un.org/esa/sustdev/documents/agenda21/index.htm>.

that Deplete the Ozone Layer ran into conflicts over commitments to ensure fair and favourable access for developing countries to chlorofluorocarbon (CFC) substitutes protected by IPRs. The 1992 Convention on Biological Diversity aims to ensure fair and equitable use of genetic resources, partly through technological cooperation, and calls for its technological provisions to receive greater attention. The TRIPS Agreement calls for technology transfer to the least developed countries, yet that provision has not been translated into action to the extent expected.

The transfer and dissemination needs of the developing countries have to be seen from the point of view of the capacity of those in need of accessing the technologies, particularly where the cost of technology may be prohibitive due to economies of scale and other reasons. In such cases, in order to implement the related provisions of the TRIPS Agreement, commercially viable mechanisms will have to be found.

The formulation of a national economic strategy for promoting and protecting IP is increasingly becoming a crucial point of consideration in the context of technology acquisition through licensing, transfers, turnkey arrangements and joint ventures. Patent information is being used in technology forecasting. Patent information could be valuable in locating technologies for environmental improvement. Since a sizeable number of them are in the public domain, they could be utilized without the need for payment of compensation. This is important, since acquiring technologies as well as implementing ever emerging new innovations become expensive, often resulting in constraining development in the short or medium term.

## 3.7 VALUATION OF IP

IP enhances the value of the underlying technological or business assets. It may be the only asset of value in a start-up firm. Thus it is very important to place a value on IP at several stages in enterprise development, particularly in the valuation of IP in the privatization context. A report issued by Pricewaterhouse Coopers in 1999 found that the global IP licensing market had soared over the previous ten years to reach more than USD 100 billion.[7] It has further been shown that valuations of IP assets, such as trademarks, have grown to become an important component of a firm's capitalization. According to Interbrand, in 2001, the worldwide trademarks of Coca-Cola, Disney, and Ford were 61%, 54% and 66%, respectively, of the capitalization of those companies, and were worth USD 69 billion, 32.5 billion and 30 billion, respectively. It is interesting that only a decade or so previously, very few companies entertained such a concept of trademark valuation.

Valuation of IP[8] helps in assessing the commercial parameters for supporting and sustaining the IP investment, in raising its necessary financing and in the course of acquisitions

---

[7]  Kamil Idris, *Intellectual Property: A Powerful Tool For Economic Growth* (Geneva: WIPO, Feb. 2003), 61: <www.wipo.int/about-wipo/en/dgo/wipo_pub_888/index_wipo_pub_888.html>.

[8]  Gordon W. Smith & Russel L. Parr, *Valuation of Intellectual Property and Intangible Assets,* 3rd edn (New York: John Wiley and Sons, 2000), 175, 215: <www.amazon.com/Valuation-Intellectual-Property-Intangible-Assets/dp/0471362816>.

and mergers. It also assists in corporate accounting considerations, particularly in transfer pricing, joint venture negotiations, etc. The value of IP assets depends on, inter alia, its competitiveness, quality and function. Valuation models used for determining the value of IP assets must take into consideration both business parameters as well as legal issues, since the effect of legal considerations on business projections are key to deriving a quantitative value for IP assets.

A wide range of valuation methods are being used, and knowledge of at least the future costs of creating IPRs is needed as part of almost all of these methods.[9]

Conventionally, the valuation techniques and methodologies could be based on a cost approach, a market approach or an income approach.[10]

While the cost-based approach helps in evaluating assets of the business undertaking, valuation of multiple related assets and replacement costs, the market approach is based on the type of IP, relative market share protected, comparable royalty rates, profitability of the protected product, type of legal protection and exclusivity in regard to licensing terms.

Again, the cost-based approach provides an indication of the value of aggregating all the costs necessary to recreate the property under consideration. This method, however, does not allow for consideration of future benefits that may accrue from the concerned IP.

The market-based approach is used mainly to value the asset by studying the prices of comparable assets in an active market. This approach is quite beneficial when the elements of a like transaction in respect to similar property, disclosure of pricing information and reasonable knowledge of all relevant facts are available to the transacting parties.

The income-based – also known as the economic-based – approach depends on the legal life of the asset, its useful life based on technological advances, market changes, marketing support, assessment of the value of the revenue stream of future discounted cash flows and on similar other facts and data. IP valued using this approach considers profits, growth potential and investment risk. For evaluating early-stage technology, the income approach in the form of discounted cash-flow analysis is quite useful but it must reflect factors like time and money required to transform that particular technology into a commercially viable product or service.

While discussing the issue of pricing intellectual property at early-stage technologies, Razgaitis[11] introduces and explains six methods for valuation and pricing that are somehow linked to the market's expectation of value:

Method I: The Use of Industry Standards Method considers the range of published royalties (and other forms of payment) from technology licenses within an industry

---

9   Richard Razgaitis, '*Valuation and Pricing of Technology-Based Intellectual Property* (New Jersey: John Wiley & Sons, 2003).

10   S. Khoury (1998), 'Valuing Intellectual Properties', in *Profiting from Intellectual Capital: Extracting Value from Innovation*, ed. P.H. Sullivan (New York: John Wiley & Sons, 1998).

11   R. Razgaitis, 'Pricing the Intellectual Property of Early-Stage Technologies: A Primer of Basic Valuation Tools and Considerations', in *Intellectual Property Management in Health and Agricultural Innovation: A Handbook of Best Practices*, eds A. Krattiger et al. (UK: MIHR, and US: PIPRA), 2007: <www.ipHandbook.org>.

category and uses that information to guide valuation of a technology currently under consideration.

Method II: The Rating/Ranking Method considers several existing license agreements for similar technologies. It then compares and ranks a technology currently under consideration against the existing license agreements in terms of stage of development, scope of IP protection, market size, profit margins and other such factors.

Method III: The Rules of Thumb, such as the 25% Rule Method, which apportions anticipated profits from the commercial use of the technology between the seller and buyer.

Method IV: The Use of Discounted Cash-Flow Analysis with Risk-Adjusted Hurdle Rates Method seeks to split expected returns but adjusts basic profit-and-loss accounting terms to take into account the timing of investments and returns and the risks borne by both parties. The method involves different structures of payments that are possible, as they affect both timing and risk.

Method V: The Advanced Tools Method applies statistical methods, such as Monte Carlo simulations, to discounted cash-flow models to test the influence of various value assumptions and license terms on the possible outcomes of a deal.

Method VI: The Auctions Method allows parties to bid on the technology based upon their own independent efforts at valuing the technology, thus comparing their respective valuations, identifying the highest valuation and striking a price based on that highest valuation.

In the case of technology transfer transactions, there is no set formula for the valuation of technology per se. The transferee must consider the value of the benefits flowing in his particular situation and compare it with the true costs of acquisition as compared to alternative opportunities. There are other aspects which the transferee should consider. These include, inter alia, whether the technology being transferred is about to be supplanted by new developments; whether the technology is appropriate for the infrastructure that is available; questions of exclusivity, i.e., whether the arrangement will provide the transferee with exclusive access to the transferor's technology or whether others will be licensed to use the technology concerned; and whether the transferor will be competing in the market or whether the transferee will have exclusive access to that market. Incidentally, the recognition of IP as a component of enterprise strategy also encourages the assessment of its value.

## 3.8 INTERNATIONAL TREATIES

For enhancing their competitive strategies in respect to export orientation of products of creativity and innovativeness protected by IPRs, it is necessary that countries both developed and developing, as well as those in transition, participate in and adhere to the international multilateral treaties governing the protection of IP.

The main treaties are: the Paris Convention for the Protection of Industrial Property concluded in 1883; the Berne Convention for the Protection of Literary and Artistic Works concluded in 1886 (both administered by the WIPO); the TRIPS Agreement concluded on 15 April 1994, entered into force on 1 January 1995 and administered by the WTO; the Lisbon Agreement for the Protection of Appellations of Origin and their International Registration concluded in 1958; and the International Convention for the Protection of New Varieties of Plants (UPOV Convention) of 1961, as revised at Geneva in 1972, 1978 and 1991.

In addition, to enable and facilitate national creators and innovators to have multi-country registration of their patents and trademarks, adherence to the subsidiary treaties to the Paris Convention – namely the Patent Cooperation Treaty (PCT) which was adopted in 1970 and entered into force in 1978, and the Madrid Agreement Concerning the International Registration of Marks (the Madrid Union) signed in 1891 and entered into force in 1892; as well as the Hague Agreement Concerning the International Deposit of Industrial Designs, adopted in 1925 within the framework of the Paris Convention – is strongly recommended.

All member countries of the Paris Convention (there were 173 Member States as of June 2008) can adhere to the subsidiary treaties. While adherence to these subsidiary treaties does not require any membership fees or financial contribution, it offers considerable advantages.

In respect to the PCT, with only a single international application at the patent office of the applicant's country and designation of any or all of the states that are party to the PCT (as of 21 February 2008, there were 138 such states), it is possible to seek patents for an invention in the respective countries, thus saving, inter alia, several registration and/or translation charges. The number of international applications under the system has gone up from around 20,000 in 1990 to more than 156,000 in 2007 and is continuing to grow rapidly.

An analysis of the major PCT applicants in 2007 from developing countries shows that the Republic of Korea, China and India occupy the top three positions. Although the advanced nations dominate the PCT filing list, the rate of growth of filing from the developing world has been impressive.[12] For instance, the Council of Scientific & Industrial Research (CSIR) – India's largest publicly funded R&D organization – has been the consistent leader in filing patents in foreign countries since 2002. CSIR is dedicated to undertaking industrial research. It shows the increasing awareness of such institutions towards IPR protection. The transformation of CSIR into a leading organization in the emerging knowledge economy began in 1996, when it actively promoted an 'IP Management Policy'. The organization today is laying emphasis on web-based marketing of technology licensing of patents and other forms of IPRs to Indian and foreign firms.[13]

Likewise, adherence to the Madrid Agreement and its Protocol enables owners of trademarks to obtain protection in countries party to the Agreement or the Protocol (as of 31 December 2007, there were eighty-one states party to the Madrid Agreement) at much less expense. A country that is a party to the treaty also receives from WIPO a share in certain

---

[12] <www.wipo.int/pressroom/en/articles/2008/article_0006.html>.
[13] <www.patestate.com/liceser.htm>.

fees collected by that organization and profits of the Madrid Union. Importantly, it helps in attracting foreign investors, since it will be easy and inexpensive for foreign trademark owners to thus have their marks protected.

A system almost similar to the Madrid Agreement is provided for in respect to international registration of industrial designs, in the Hague Agreement concerning the International Deposit of Industrial Designs, adopted in 1925. This is a WIPO-administered treaty, in the framework of the Paris Convention. As of 18 June 2008, the Treaty had fifty-one Member States. According to this Agreement, an applicant can file a single international deposit either with WIPO or with the national office of a country, i.e., any party to the said treaty. The design would then be protected in all of the Member States unless specifically refused. The international procedure under this treaty also lessens the work of offices of states that are party to the said treaty and also helps them obtain revenues from it.

The WIPO Copyright Treaty (WCT) and the WIPO Performances and Phonograms Treaty (WPPT) were adopted at the end of 1996 to provide solutions to certain problems arising out of economic, social, cultural and technological developments, particularly in the information and communication fields. As of June 2008, WCT and the WPPT had sixty-five and sixty-four Member States, respectively. Adherence to these treaties, also referred to as the Internet Treaties, would foster creation and use of literary, artistic and musical works as well as the production and use of performances and phonograms. It will eventually assist national economic development strategies in respect to their export orientation.

IP protection is an important determinant of economic growth. It also helps enterprises to recover the costs of their innovation expenses. The IP systems must be so developed that they bring in socio-economic well-being. It bears repetition to emphasize that for this purpose it is necessary for countries to accept the challenge of constantly upgrading their national IP systems, both legislative and infrastructural, to increase the opportunity for transfer of top-grade technology and also for developing competitiveness in the national and international market. New methodologies need to be constantly devised and updated to help users obtain, maintain, exploit and enforce IPRs.

CHAPTER FOUR


# PROTECTION OF CULTURAL HERITAGE, BIODIVERSITY, TRADITIONAL KNOWLEDGE AND PRACTICES, FOLKLORE AND SUSTAINABLE SOCIO-ECONOMIC DEVELOPMENT

*– Incentives and Rewards for Protection of Intellectual Property (IP)*
*– Interface with the IP System*


## 4.1 THE NATURE OF TRADITIONAL KNOWLEDGE

The role of traditional knowledge (TK) with its spiritual, cultural and economic values is being increasingly recognized today. Such knowledge has been used for centuries by indigenous and local communities under local laws, customs and traditions. Such knowledge encompasses the totality of all knowledge and practices, whether explicit or implicit, used in diverse facets of life. This knowledge, which is the result of a community's cooperative effort, is built on the foundation of past experiences and observations. The products based on TK are important sources of income, food and healthcare for large parts of the population in developing countries in particular and, in turn, for their sustainable socio-economic development.

TK evolves over a period of time by contributions of members of a particular society. TK is generated by societies in 'laboratories of life' and is continuously tested, evaluated and used over a period of time. What makes TK special is the way it is acquired and used. The social process of learning and sharing knowledge, which is unique to each culture, lies at the very heart of its traditionality.

TK is dynamic, as it evolves in response to the changing context. Both its form and content changes in response to a dynamic process of verification, adaptation and creation. TK includes a broad range of subject matter, such as agricultural, ecological, medicinal and biodiversity-related knowledge; expressions of folklore in the form of music, dance, song, handicrafts, designs, stories and artwork; elements of languages, such as names, geographical indications, and symbols; and movable cultural properties.[1]

Western societies, in general, had neither recognized the value of TK nor the obligations associated with its use. These societies also looked at TK as information in the 'public domain', which was freely available for use by anybody. The idea of the acknowledgement

---

[1]  'Protection of Traditional Knowledge Global Intellectual Property Issue'. WIPO/ ISESCO Conference on Intellectual Property, Baku, 21-23 May 2001. Number: WIPO-ISESCO/IP/BAK/01/INF/4 <www.wipo.int/ meetings/en/details.jsp?meeting_id=4307>.

of and benefit sharing with the creators of TK was not discussed or debated. It is only recently that such debates have evolved. The value of blending TK with modern scientific knowledge to create innovative solutions in areas ranging from agriculture to health is being increasingly discussed now.[2,3]

This chapter analyzes the incentives and rewards for protection of Intellectual Property (IP) and the interface of TK with the IP system.

### 4.1.1 Folklore

Folklore comprises characteristic elements of the traditional artistic heritage developed by a community. Folklore, in general, includes folk tales, folk poetry and riddles; folk songs and instrumental music; folk dances, plays and artistic forms of rituals; and drawings, paintings, carvings, sculptures, textiles, carpets, costumes, basket weaving, needle-work, pottery, mosaic, woodwork, metal ware, jewellery, musical instruments and architectural forms.

### 4.1.2 Cultural Heritage

Cultural heritage includes folklore, ethnographic materials, such as products of pharmacopoeia, traditional medicine (TM), etc. Historic monuments and groups of buildings and sites also form a part of cultural heritage.

Monuments comprise various architectural works, works of monumental sculpture and painting, structures of an archaeological nature, inscriptions, cave dwellings, etc. Groups of separate or connected buildings which, because of their architecture, their homogeneity or their place in the landscape are of outstanding universal value from the point of view of history, art or science are also a part of cultural heritage.

The sites comprise works of a human or the combined works of nature and human, and areas including archaeological sites, which are of outstanding universal value from the historical, aesthetic, ethological or anthropological point of view.[4]

The heritage of indigenous people represents all moveable property and includes all kinds of literary and artistic works such as music, dance, songs, ceremonies, symbols and designs, narratives and poetry; all kinds of scientific, agricultural, technical and ecological knowledge, medicines and rational use of flora and fauna; immovable cultural property such as sacred sites, sites of historical significance and documentation of indigenous people's heritage on film, photographs, videotape or audiotape.

---

[2] R.A. Mashelkar, 10th Zuckerman Lecture on *'Nation Building through Science & Technology: A Developing World Perspective'*, (London: Royal Society, 11 Jun. 2003. <www.biodevelopments.org/innovation/ist1hires.pdf>.

[3] R.A. Mashelkar, 'Ayurveda for the Future', *Evidence-based Complimentary and Alternative Medicine (ECAM)* 5, (2008): 129-131.

[4] <http://whc.unesco.org/en/conventiontext>.

## 4.1.3 Biodiversity

Biodiversity includes the variability amongst living organisms, covering all sources including, inter alia, terrestrial, marine and other aquatic ecosystems. In developing countries, which are 'capital poor' and 'resource rich'; plant genetic resources and other forms of biodiversity contribute significantly to this richness. The access to those resources and associated TK can substantially benefit formal scientific research centres as well as enterprises.

## 4.1.4 Traditional Medicines

The World Health Organization (WHO) defines traditional medicine (TM) as the sum total of all the knowledge and practices, whether explicable or not, used in diagnosis, prevention and elimination of physical, mental or social imbalance and relying exclusively on practical experience and observations handed down from generation to generation, whether verbally or in writing. Healthcare providers worldwide incorporate many of these into their mainstream activities.

TM plays a crucial role in healthcare and serves the health needs of the vast majority of people in developing countries. Access to modern healthcare services and medicine may be limited in some developing countries. TM becomes the only affordable treatment available to poorer segments of people, especially those in remote communities.

TM is largely based on medicinal plants, indigenous to those countries where the system has been in vogue for several centuries. The effort is on accessing them either directly or through the use of modern tools of breeding and cultivation, including tissue culture, cell culture and transgenic technology. IP issues linked to such endeavours are beginning to be debated more widely now.

In Asia, there are codified systems of TM as well as non-codified medicinal knowledge; the latter includes folk, tribal or indigenous medicine. In India, for example, folk traditions are passed on orally from generation to generation. Folk medicine has emerged from several centuries-old traditional beliefs, norms and practices. These are passed on through oral traditions. They constitute people's healthcare culture, home remedies or folk remedies. Knowledge of TM may be possessed by individuals. In some cases, for instance, healers use rituals as part of their traditional healing methods. This often allows them to create knowledge monopolies. The codified knowledge has more sophisticated foundations, expressed in thousands of manuscripts covering all branches of medicine. Examples are Ayurveda, Siddha, Unani and the Tibetan tradition.

Plants used for medicinal purposes may also often have a symbolic value for the community. Medicinal plants, and to a lesser but important extent, animal products, form the 'materia medica' of these traditions. Other tradition-based creations, such as expressions of folklore, have at the same time taken on new economic and cultural significance.

The protection of TM under Intellectual Property Rights (IPRs) raises two types of issues. First, to what extent it is feasible to protect it under the existing IPR system. Certain aspects of TM may be covered by patents or other IPRs. There have also been many proposals to develop sui generis systems of protection. Such proposals are based on the logic that if inventors and innovators in the 'formal' system of innovation receive compensation through IPRs, holders of TK should be similarly treated.

World Intellectual Property Organization (WIPO) has also been sensitive to these concerns. At a conference held in India in October 1998, under the aegis of WIPO, an agenda for the future of IPRs in the field of TMs was prepared, which prioritized activities in this area. These included the development of standards for the availability, scope and use of IPRs in TM in Asian countries, systematic documentation of TM for protection purposes, regional and inter-regional information exchange and compilation of the requisite databases, etc.

## 4.2 TK PROTECTION AND PROMOTION: STRATEGIES

The protection of TK can be considered from two perspectives. Protection may be granted to 'exclude' the unauthorized use by third parties of the protected TK. Protection, on the other hand, may also mean the 'preservation' of TK from uses that may erode it or negatively affect the life or culture of the communities that have developed and used it. Protection of TK is a necessary, but not sufficient, requirement for its preservation and further development. In fact, the Global Knowledge Conference in 1997 emphasized the need to learn, preserve and exchange TK.[5]

Some of the objectives of TK protection are:

- Preserving and conserving TK;
- Increasing awareness of the value of TK among TK holders and others;
- Enabling communities to continue using TK in the context of their traditional lifestyles;
- Preventing the unauthorized use of TK;
- Encouraging TK-based innovations;
- Commercializing certain types of TK;
- Sharing equitably the benefits arising from the commercial use of TK;
- Controlling and monitoring access to TK for varying purposes including research, commercial applications or use by other traditional communities;
- Encouraging the conservation and sustainable use of biodiversity;
- Promoting social justice and equity;
- Recognizing traditional customary laws and practices;
- Providing guarantees for the participation of local and indigenous communities in the policy and decision-making processes related to TK; and
- Recognizing the important role of women as holders of TK and to ensure their participation in decision and policy-making processes.

---

[5]  <www.worldbank.org/afr/ik>.

Mashelkar[6] has discussed the issues concerned with 'economics of TK'. He emphasizes the concerns of the developing world about appropriating the elements of the collective knowledge of societies into proprietary knowledge for the commercial benefit of a few. Developing countries, therefore, need assistance to build national capacities in terms of raising awareness on the importance and potential of TK for development. These knowledge systems need to be protected through national policies and international understanding linked to IPRs, while providing for their development and proper use as community knowledge and community innovation.

Local communities or individuals do not have the knowledge or the means to safeguard their property. This is because we operate in a system which has its origin in very different cultural values and attitudes. The communities have a storehouse of knowledge about their flora and fauna – their habits, their habitats, their seasonal behaviour and the like. As a matter of natural justice, we need to give them a greater say in the study, extraction and commercialization of their biodiversity. We need a balanced policy that does not impede the advancement of knowledge, while at the same time provides for valid and sustainable use and adequate IP protection with just benefit sharing.

The issues of the economics of community knowledge are truly complex. Many indigenous cultures appear to develop and transmit knowledge from generation to generation within a system. However, individuals in local or indigenous communities can distinguish themselves as informal creators or innovators, separate from the community. Furthermore, some indigenous or traditional societies recognize various types of IPRs over knowledge which may be held by individuals, families, lineages or communities. It follows that discussion of IPRs and TK should draw more on the diversity and creativity of indigenous approaches to IPR issues.

Correa[7] has articulated the options of applying the existing modes of IPR protection to different components of TK that are currently considered practicable:

– Some elements of TM may be protected under patent laws. However, since most of the TK is not contemporary and has been used for long periods, the novelty and/or inventive step requirements of patent protection may be difficult to meet.
– It would be easier to comply with a more flexible novelty requirement such as that for plant varieties in International Convention for the Protection of New Varieties of Plants (UPOV) for plant varieties that had been previously commercialized or disposed of for purposes of exploitation.
– Some valuable TK may be kept secret, such as in cases of applications of plants for therapeutic purposes.
– Holders of TK may be protected against disclosure under unfair competition rules.

---

[6]   R.A. Mashelkar, 16th Dr. CD Deshmukh Memorial Lecture on '*Economics of Knowledge*', 1999: <www.nif.org.in/Economics_of_Knowledge>.

[7]   Carlos M. Correa, '*Traditional Knowledge and Intellectual Property*' (Geneva, Switzerland: Quaker United Nations Office, Nov. 2001): <www.qiap.ca/documents/TKcol3.pdf>.

- Geographical indication may, in some cases, be a suitable mechanism to enhance the value of agriculture products, handicrafts and other TK derived products.
- Copyright can be used to protect the artistic manifestations of TK holders (especially artists who belong to indigenous and native communities) against unauthorized reproduction and exploitation.
- Development of a sui generis regime of IPRs, which is specifically adapted to the nature and characteristics of TK, is also possible. Although this approach has received considerable attention, little progress has been made in terms of actually implementing this kind of protection.

As an interesting sui generis system, Possey & Duttfield[8] and Possey[9] have proposed the concept of Traditional Resource Rights (TRR).

TRR defines many 'bundles of rights' for protection, compensation and conservation. The change in terminology from IPR to TRR is meant to build on the concept of IPR protection and compensation, while recognizing that traditional resources – both tangible and intangible – are also covered under a significant number of international agreements that can be used to form the basis for a sui generis system.

A TRR-type sui generis system is expected to synergize and harmonize the human rights commitments of the governments with biodiversity conservation, sustainable development and global trade agreements. Governments are expected to help in the development of instruments such as Material Transfer Agreements, Information Transfer Agreements, contracts and convenants.

## 4.3 IPRs & TK

The Convention on Biological Diversity (CBD) has addressed the issues linked to TK in a holistic manner. The CBD's large and diverse constituency open to non-governmental organizations (NGOs) has provided an intergovernmental forum where these issues have been debated with a certain measure of coherence.

Two extreme views have so far surfaced in the debates in the CBD and other fora. The first view seeks the extension of IP protection to cover TK. The second pertains to treating such knowledge as a public good. The proponents of the first view argue that extending IP protection to TK will in fact promote technological innovation, as it would facilitate the dissemination and development of that knowledge in the modern economic context. An example of how the IP system can be utilized to commercialize a traditional cultural property system or prevent its misuse is the way in which Aboriginal and Torres Strait Islander artists in Australia have obtained[10] a national certification trademark, which is

---

[8] Darrel A. Possey & Graham Duttfield, '*Beyond Intellectual Property*', (Ottawa: International Development Research Centre (IDRC) 1996).

[9] Darrel A. Possey, '*Traditional Resource Rights*' (The International Union for the Conservation of Nature (IUCN), Gland, 1996).

[10] Marianna Annas, 'The Label of Authenticity: A Certification Trade Mark for Goods and Services of Indigenous Origin' *Aboriginal Law Bulletin* 3, Mar. 1997: <www.austlii.edu.au/au/journals/AboriginalLB/1997/20.html>.

intended to promote the marketing of their art and cultural products and deter the sale of products falsely claimed to be of aboriginal origin. Recognition of IPRs in TK would serve as an incentive for indigenous communities to conserve their environment.

The industrialized countries must ensure that indigenous and local people receive a fair and equitable share of benefits arising from the use of their TK and the commercialization of their genetic resources. Local innovators, entrepreneurs and holders of TK must partner to enable the exploitation of TK.

The Honeybee Network in India, for example, works to protect the IPRs of grassroots-level innovators.[11] This network helps to document and disseminate their innovations and has compiled a database of more than 10,000 entries. This activity is based on the fundamental belief that when peoples' knowledge is collected and recorded, they should not become poorer for sharing their knowledge and insights. Further, if any income is generated by developing peoples' knowledge, they must be rewarded with a fair share of this income.

Another example is in the People's Democratic Republic of Laos, where the government established the Traditional Medicines Resource Center (TMRC).[12] This organization is working with the local healers to document details of all TMs with a view to create a practice of benefit sharing. The TMRC is also collaborating with the International Cooperative Biodiversity Group (ICBG) in efforts to create new medicinal products. Any monetary benefits as well as new knowledge emerging from the collaboration will be shared with all the involved communities.

Some opponents of the extension of IP protection to TK argue that sharing financial benefits will destroy the social basis for generating and managing such knowledge. They argue that TK, having been a community property passed on from one generation to the next, would be privatized under IP law protection and this may deny access to such knowledge.[13]

The grant of IPR can help convert traditional knowledge into a marketable commodity. Mere preservation of such knowledge in its cultural context alone cannot serve a wider public good. The other view is that ethnobotanical knowledge is integrative and holistic. It is most meaningful in the place where the plants exist. Therefore, it has to be viewed in the appropriate ecological and cultural contexts. It should be managed and used by local residents.

The other view is that IPR protection provides value to the specified properties of plants that may be detached from their natural and cultural context, since these may be replicated through artificial selection in a laboratory or greenhouse. This enables the creation for a wider possible public good, rather than leaving the benefits solely to a confined locale.

TK has been increasingly used for providing the 'technical lead' in biodiversity prospecting. A number of pharmaceutical companies rely on TK of indigenous and local

---

[11]  <www.sristi.org/cms/en/our_network>.

[12]  Mary Riley, 'The Traditional Medicine Research Center (TMRC)': <www.strategicnetwork.org/index. php?loc=kb&view=v&id=4959&mode=v&pagenum=1&lang>.

[13]  J. Mugabe, 'Intellectual Property Protection and Traditional Knowledge: An Exploration in International Policy Discourse'. Paper prepared for WIPO, (Geneva: December, 1998).

people in their screening activities for identifying the biologically active constituents, which may have potential commercial market. Indigenous and local people should be able to share, in a fair and equitable manner, the benefits arising from the appropriation of their knowledge and its subsequent use in drug development. Though the need to protect TK and to secure a fair and equitable sharing derived from the use of biodiversity and associated TK has been recognized, there is no agreement on the most appropriate and effective models to achieve this.

## 4.4 Loss of TK

There is a growing concern about the increasing loss of plant and animal species as well as destruction of habitats, as well as the loss of knowledge concerning these. Destruction of ecosystems takes place with the expansion of agricultural lands and deforestation that accompanies the harvesting of timber and other forest products. This is all a physical loss.

On the other hand, the loss of knowledge takes place due to over-emphasis on oral traditions, lack of documentation and appropriation of TK with no rewards for the holders of that knowledge. Extinction of some of the groups possessing this knowledge is also a contributory factor. Apparently, about eighty-five Brazilian Indian groups became extinct in the first half of the twentieth century.

Loss of TK also could be due to the advent of new technologies. In India, for example, the Bhotiya tribe inhabit higher altitudes in Garhwal Himalayas. They traditionally dyed their wool using herbal dyes, which were fast and cheap. But with the development of road networks into the formerly inaccessible areas, synthetic dyes from the markets of Punjab became easily available to the Bhotiya community, at much cheaper rates. Thus the availability of synthetic dyes brought the traditional wool dyeing technique to the verge of extinction.

## 4.5 Biopiracy of TK

The grant of patents on non-original innovations (particularly those linked to TMs), which are based on what is already a part of the TK in the developing world, has been causing great concern in these countries. Protection of TK is a sensitive issue. Grants of wrong patents, firstly, created tension amongst those who possessed this knowledge. Secondly, the challenges to such patents and their subsequent revocation have brought out the real reasons for granting such wrong patents. They further led to new initiatives, such as the creation of Traditional Knowledge Digital Libraries (TKDLs), and caused changes in the International Patent Classification (IPC) systems. In the following, we will describe some of these cases.

### 4.5.1 Challenge to Patents Based on TK

#### 4.5.1.1 Turmeric (Curcuma long)

Turmeric rhizomes are used as a spice for flavouring in Indian cooking. Turmeric is an effective ingredient in medicines, cosmetics, etc. Traditionally it has been used to heal wounds. There was an attempt to patent TK of the wound-healing properties of turmeric in the US. which was later revoked by the US Patent and Trademark Office (USPTO).

This is a landmark case. Therefore, full details as reported by Mashelkar,[14] who led this revocation from India, are captured below:

> Two US-based Indians, Suman K. Das and Hari Har P. Cohly were granted US patent 5,401,504 on 28 March 1995 for the use of turmeric in healing wounds. The patent was assigned to University of Mississippi Medical Center, US. This patent claimed that the administration of an effective amount of turmeric through local and oral routes to enhance the wound-healing process was a novel finding. The CSIR, however, could locate thirty-two references (some of them more than one hundred years old and in Sanskrit, Urdu and Hindi) which showed that this practice was well known in India prior to the filing of this patent. The formal request for re-examination of the patent was filed by CSIR at USPTO on 28 October 1996.

The first office action in the re-examination was issued by USPTO on 28 March 1997, which rejected all six of the claims based on the references submitted by Council of Scientific & Industrial Research (CSIR) as being 'anticipated by the submitted references' and therefore considered invalid under 35 U.S.C. 102 and 103.

After receiving the first action, the University of Mississippi Medical Center, to whom the turmeric patent was assigned, decided not to pursue the case and transferred the rights to the inventors, who decided to file a response. The inventors argued that the powder and paste had different physical properties, i.e., bio-availability and absorbability. Therefore, they argued, one with ordinary skills in the art would not expect, with any reasonable degree of certainty, that a powder material would be useful in the same application as a paste of the same material. The inventors further mentioned that oral administration was available only with honey and honey itself was considered to have wound-healing properties.

In the second office action, the examiner rejected all the claims once again and made his action final. He made it clear that the paste and the powder forms were equivalent for healing wounds in view of the cited art.

Subsequent to the second rejection, the inventors had an interview with the examiner and deleted claims 5-6 and also restricted the invention to a 'non-healing surgical wound' as supported by the two case histories mentioned in the patent, stating that there was no disclosure or suggestion of using turmeric in surgically inflicted non-healing wounds. They requested that the examiner allow the amended claims.

On 20 November 1997, the examiner rejected all the claims once again as being anticipated and obvious.

The re-examination certificate was issued on this case on 21 April 1998, bringing the proceedings to a close.

---

14   R.A. Mashelkar, 'Intellectual Property Rights and the Third World', *Current Science* 81 (2001) 955: <www.ias.ac.in/currsci/oct252001/955.pdf>.

The following points are interesting to note:

– The turmeric case was a landmark case in that this was the first time that a patent based on the TK of a developing country was challenged successfully and USPTO revoked the patent. This eventually opened up the path to the creation of TKDL, Traditional Knowledge Resource Classification and finally inclusion of TK in the International Patent Classification System.
– Amidst the loud protest against 'biopiracy' and 'theft' of India's biodiversity and TK by foreign nationals, it is interesting to note here that the patents were filed by Indians (Das and Cohly), the re-examination in USPTO was done by an Indian (Kumar) and the re-examination was sought by an Indian institution (CSIR).

### 4.5.1.2 Neem (Azadirachta indica)[15,16]

Neem extracts can be used against hundreds of pests and fungal diseases that attack food crops; against skin diseases; and even against meningitis. In 1994, the European Patent Office (EPO) granted a patent (EPO Patent No. 0436257) to the US corporation W.R. Grace Co. and the US Department of Agriculture for a method of controlling fungi on plants through hydrophobically extracted neem oil.

In 1995, a group of international NGOs and representatives of Indian farmers filed a legal petition against the patent. They submitted evidence that the fungicidal effect of extracts of neem seeds had been known and used for centuries in Indian agriculture to protect crops and thus was a prior art and unpatentable.

In 1999, the EPO determined that according to the evidence all features of the present claim had been disclosed to the public prior to the patent application and thus the patent was not considered to involve an inventive step. The patent granted on neem was revoked by the EPO in May 2000.

### 4.5.1.3 Basmati[17]

Rice Tec. Inc. had applied for registration of a mark 'Texmati' with the UK Trademark Registry. It was successfully opposed by the Agricultural and Processed Food Exports Authority (APEDA), India. One of the documents relied upon by Rice Tec as evidence in support was US Patent 5,663,484 granted by the US Patent Office on 2 September 1997, and that is how this patent became an issue for contest.

This US utility patent claimed a rice plant having characteristics similar to the traditional Indian Basmati rice lines, and with the geographical delimitation covering North, Central or South America, or the Caribbean Islands. The patent had twenty claims covering not

[15] S. Biber Klemn & T. Cottier, '*Rights to Plant Genetic Resources and Traditional Knowledge: Basic Issues and Perspectives*', (Oxfordshire, UK: CABI Publishing, 2006), 136.
[16] Ulrike Hellerer & K.S. Jarayaman, '*Greens persuade Europe to revoke patent on neem tree . . .*': <www.nature.com/nature/journal/v405/n6784/full/405266a0.html>.
[17] R.A. Mashelkar, 'Intellectual Property Rights and the Third World', *Current Science* 81 (2001): 955: <www.ias.ac.in/currsci/oct252001/955.pdf>.

only the novel rice plant but also various rice lines; resulting plants and grains, seed deposit claims, method for selecting a rice plant for breeding and propagation. Its claims 15-17 were for a rice grain having characteristics similar to those of Indian Basmati rice. The said claims 15-17 would have come in the way of Indian exports to the US, if legally enforced.

Evidence from *Bulletin* of the Indian Agricultural Research Institute (IARI), New Delhi was used against claims 15-17. The evidence was supported by the germplasm collection of the Directorate of Rice Research, Hyderabad, since 1978. The various grain characteristics were evaluated by Central Food Technological Research Institute (CFTRI) scientists and accordingly claims 15-17 were opposed on the basis of the declarations submitted by CFTRI scientists on grain characteristics.

Eventually, a request for re-examination of this patent was filed on 28 April 2000. Soon after filing the re-examination request, Rice Tec chose to withdraw claims 15-17 along with claim 4.

Above are examples of cases that were successfully contested. On the other hand, there are cases which remain unresolved, or in which the concerned patent offices have not agreed with the claims of the challenges and have not revoked the patents, or the inventors have abandoned their claimed patents. Some examples of these cases are given below.

### 4.5.1.4 Kava (Piper mythesticum)[18]

Kava is an important cash crop in the Pacific, where it is highly valued as the source of the ceremonial beverage of the same name. More than one hundred varieties of kava are grown in the Pacific, especially in Fiji and Vanuatu, where it was first domesticated thousands of years ago. In North America and Europe, kava is now promoted for a variety of uses. The French company L'Oréal has patented the use of kava to reduce hair loss and stimulate hair growth.

### 4.5.1.5 Ayahuasca (Banisteriopsis caapi)[19]

For generations, shamans of indigenous tribes throughout the Amazon basin have processed the bark of B. *caapi* to produce a ceremonial drink known as 'ayahuasca'. The shamans use ayahuasca (which means 'wine of the soul') in religious and healing ceremonies to diagnose and treat illness, meet with spirits and divine the future.

An American national, Loren Miller, obtained a US Plant Patent (No. 5,751 issued in 1986), granting him rights over an alleged variety of B. *caapi* which he had collected from a domestic garden in the Amazon and had called 'Da Vine', and was analyzing it for

---

[18] 'Traditional knowledge of Biodiversity in Asia-Pacific: Problems of Piracy & Protection', 2002. <www. grain.org/briefings/?id=97> and 'Fijian Perspectives on TRIPS 27.3(b)', 1999: <www.grain.org/bio-ipr/ ?id=106>.

[19] Leanne M. Fecteau, 'The Ayahuasca Patent Revocation: Raising Questions About Current U.S. Patent Policy': <www.bc.edu/bc_org/avp/law/lwsch/journals/bctwj/21_1/03_TXT.htm>.

potential medicinal properties. The patent claimed that Da Vine represented a new and distinct variety of B. *caapi*, primarily because of the flower colour.

The Coordinating Body of Indigenous Organisations of the Amazon Basin (COICA), which represents more than four hundred indigenous tribes in the Amazon region, along with others, protested against the wrong patent that was given on a plant species called B. *caapi*. It protested that ayahuasca had been known to be native to the Amazon rainforest, and cultivated for generations for its traditional medicinal uses, so Loren Miller could not have discovered it and should not have been granted such rights, which in effect, appropriated indigenous TK. On re-examination, USPTO revoked this patent on 3 November 1999. However, the inventor (Loren Miller) was able to convince the USPTO on 17 April, 2001, and the original claims were re-confirmed and the patent rights restored to the innovator.

### 4.5.1.6 Quinoa (Chenopodium quinoa)[20]

Quinoa is a staple food crop for millions in the Andes, especially Quechua and Aymara people who have bred a multitude of quinoa varieties. One traditional quinoa variety, Apelawa, is the subject of US patent No. 5,304,718 held by two professors from Colorado State University who claim the variety's male sterile cytoplasm is key to developing hybrid quinoa. On 1 May 1998, the 'quinoa' patent was abandoned by the inventors.

### 4.5.1.7 Phyllanthus Amarus[21]

The plant *Phyllanthus amarus* is used for Ayurvedic treatment for jaundice. A US patent has been granted for its use against hepatitis B. The plant *Piper nigrum* is used for Ayurvedic treatment for vitiligo (a skin pigmentation disorder). A patent has been granted in the UK for the application of a molecule from *Piper nigrum* for use in the treatment of vitiligo.

### 4.5.2 Successful Cases of Benefit Sharing

In contrast to the above two categories, where patents were either revoked or not revoked but the holders of knowledge were uninvolved in any financial transactions, there are cases where the originators of knowledge either received or were promised some benefit. Such an interesting case is discussed below.

### 4.5.2.1 Hoodia (Hoodia gordonii)

Hoodia has been used for centuries by the San tribes, who live around Kalahari Desert in Southern Africa, to suppress appetite during hunting trips. In 1963, CSIR included Hoodia

---

20  <www.etcgroup.org/upload/publication/pdf_file/411>.
21  Gerard Bodeker, 'Indigenous Medical Knowledge: the Law and Politics of Protection', 2000: <www.oiprc.ox.ac.uk/EJWP0300.pdf>.

Gordonii, a Kalahari desert cactus, in a research project on edible plants based on ethno-botany of the San.

In 1995, the South African CSIR patented Hoodia's appetite-suppressing element (P57) and its consequent potential to cure obesity. In 1997, P57 was licensed to British Biotech Company, Phytopharm. In 1998, Pfizer acquired the rights to develop and market P57 as a potential slimming drug and cure for obesity (a market then estimated to be worth more than 6 billion British pounds (GBP)) from Phytopharm for USD 32 million.

The San people, upon learning about the exploitation of their TK, launched legal action against CSIR and the pharmaceutical industry in June 2001. They claimed that this was a clear case of biopiracy and that CSIR had failed to comply with the rules of the CBD, which require the prior informed consent of all stakeholders, including the original discoverers and users.

There were negotiations for a benefit-sharing agreement, despite complications as to who should be compensated, that is, the persons who originally shared the information, their descendants, the tribe or the entire country. The San are nomads spread across four countries.

On 24 March 2003, a landmark agreement was signed, features of which are of generic significance to all such agreements. As reported by Petro Terblanche,[22] the benefit-sharing agreement signed with the San states that 'both parties commit themselves to the conservation of biodiversity by, inter alia, applying legal "best practices" with the collection of any plant species for observation, and by ensuring that no negative environmental impacts flow from the proposed bioprospecting collaboration'. The agreement also acknowledges the importance of TK, stating that 'San people are custodians of an ancient body of traditional knowledge . . . related inter alia to human uses of the Hoodia plant . . . '.

It adds: 'The CSIR acknowledges the existence and the importance of the traditional knowledge of the San people, and the fact that such body of knowledge, existing for millennia, predated scientific knowledge developed by Western civilisation over the past century.' The benefit-sharing agreement will also benefit the San financially: the CSIR will pay the San 8% of all milestone payments it receives from Phytopharm as well as 6% of all royalties that CSIR receives once the drug is commercially available. Existing CSIR study bursaries and scholarships have also been made available to the San and talks will be held to agree to future bioprospecting for the benefit of both parties.

Potential earnings will be put into a San Hoodia Benefit Sharing Trust, whose trustees will consist of one CSIR nominee; three San representatives from the Khomani, Xun and Khwe communities; one representative from the Working Group of Indigenous Minorities in Southern Africa (WIMSA); one South African professional; and a non-voting observer from the South African Department of Science and Technology.

Beneficiaries will include the San from the Khomani, Xun and Khwe communities of South Africa plus San communities elsewhere who are members of WIMSA and are identified by the trustees as eligible beneficiaries. The Agreement will remain in force

---

22  'Case Study: San/CSIR Hoodia Benefit Sharing', Symposium on Food Security and Biodiversity: Benefit sharing: <www.syngentafoundation.com/symposium_benefit_sharing_case_study_csir.htm>.

for the royalty period for as long as the CSIR receives financial benefits from the commercial sales of the products, with record-keeping provided by both the CSIR and the San Trust.

### 4.5.2.2 Need for Concerted Action

The developing world is concerned about the appropriation of elements of the collective knowledge of societies into proprietary knowledge for the commercial profit of a few enterprises. Some shared solutions are needed to protect these fragile knowledge systems through national policies and international understanding linked to IPRs, while providing for the development and proper use of the knowledge for the benefit of its holders. While focusing on safeguarding community knowledge, simultaneous efforts should be made to enhance community innovation, enterprise and investment.

In February 2002, a number of countries – China, Brazil, India, Indonesia, Costa Rica, Colombia, Ecuador, Kenya, Peru, Venezuela and South Africa, which are rich in bio-diversity – formed an alliance to fight biopiracy and press for rules protecting their people's rights to genetic resources found on their land.

### 4.6 USE OF TK FOR CREATING MARKETABLE PRODUCTS

Natural products are sources of new biochemical compounds for drug, chemical and agro-product development. These have been exploited by the biotechnology, pharmaceutical and human healthcare industries.

It has been estimated that the present world market of USD 60 billion for herbal products is expected to grow to more than USD 5 trillion by the year 2020. The biological diversity comprising the plants and animals from tropical countries is worth more than GBP 20 billion a year to major pharmaceutical companies. Unfortunately, very little money has gone back to the developing world.

Exploiting the treasure of biological diversity has led to the resurgence of interest in TK and medicine. This interest has been stimulated by the importance of TK as a lead in new product development.

Developing countries and their traditional communities have contributed considerably to the global pharmaceutical industry. Plant-derived prescription drugs in the US originate from forty species of which 50% are from the tropics. The twenty species generate about USD 4 billion for the US economy.

The commercial exploitation of these plants has been accompanied by appropriation of TK. To cite an example, in the 1970s the US National Cancer Institute (NCI) invested in large-scale collection of *Maytenus buchananii* from Simba Hills of Kenya. The lead for the collection came from the knowledge of the Digo communities – indigenous of the Simba Hills area – who use the plant to treat cancerous conditions.[23] The plant contains the

---

[23]   Krishna Dronamraju, '*Biological Wealth and Other Essays*', (New Jersey, USA: World Scientific, 2002), 7: <www.worldscibooks.com/lifesci/4864.html>.

biologically active constituent maytansine, which is considered a potential treatment for pancreatic cancer. The collected material was traded without the consent of the Digo community. Moreover, its knowledge of the plant and its medicinal properties was not rewarded.

Similarly, the NCI also collected another plant, *Homalanthus nutans*, from the Samoan rainforests, which contains an anti-HIV compound, prostratin. This collection was undertaken on the basis of TK.[24] NCI has also benefited from TK of local communities living around Korup Forest Reserve in Cameroon, from where it collected *Ancistrocladus korrupensis* to screen for an anti-HIV chemical, Michellamine B. The NCI and other drug research and development organizations have started investing considerable sums of money to prospect for plants containing useful chemicals and are also investigating the efficacy of TMs.

Some other examples provided by Naomi Roht-Arriaza for drug and cosmetic development based on TK include Eli Lilly's extraction of the rosy periwinkle plant,[25] and TK from Madagascar and commercialization of the resultant drug totalling USD 100 million with no returns to the local people. According to Possey,[26] less than 0.001% of profits from drugs developed from natural products and TK accrue to traditional people who provided technical leads for the research.

### 4.6.1 Cases of Benefit Sharing

One can cite some exceptions where a part of the benefit has accrued to the indigenous people. These include Shaman Pharmaceuticals and the Body Shop.[27] Shaman develops new therapeutics by working with indigenous peoples of tropical forests. The Body Shop is bioprospecting in the Kayapo area of Brazil; extensively drawing on TK of the Kayapo Indians. It has invested in ethnobotanical research for the development of new ingredients for its body-care products. The investment has proved to be a boon. In 1991, the Body Shop had at least three hundred products with annual sales of USD 90 million. By 1995, its annual sales stood at least at USD 200 million. The Body Shop also sponsors projects to assist local people to establish enterprises for processing crude products.

Another example of a benefit-sharing model for indigenous innovation relates to a medicine that is based on the active ingredient in the plant *Trichopus zeylanicus.*[28] Scientists at

---

24 <http://msig.ncifcrf.gov/abstract-0405.pdf>.

25 M.F. Brown, '*Who owns Native Culture?*' (Cambridge, USA: Harvard University Press, 2003), 136: <www.hup.harvard.edu/catalog/BROWOO.html>.

26 D. Posey, 'Intellectual Property Rights for Native Peoples: Challenges to Science, Business, and International Law', International Symposium on Property Rights, Biotechnology and Genetic Resources, (Nairobi, Kenya, 1991).

27 Jeremy MacClancy, '*Exotic No More: Anthropology on the Front Lines*', (Chicago, USA: University of Chicago Press, 2002), 310: <www.press.uchicago.edu/presssite/metadata.epl?mode=synopsis&book-key=33134>.

28 <www.williams.edu/go/native/jeevani.htm>.

Tropical Botanic Gardens and Research Institute (TBGRI), Thiruvananthapuram, Kerala, India, were on an expedition to areas inhabited by Kani tribals in 1987. Their interaction with the tribals led them to an observation of a plant that the tribals chewed to keep themselves energetic. They studied the properties of this plant by isolating and testing the active ingredients. They incorporated these ingredients into a product, which they christened 'Jeevani'. This product was shown to bolster the immune system. It was later found that it had immuno-modulation hepato-protection as well as aphrodisiac properties.

The development of this drug was possible only due to the indigenous knowledge of the Kani tribe residing in Western Ghat forests in India. TBGRI, which is the sole patent holder, struck an agreement with the tribal community to share a license fee and 2% of net profits. This was perhaps an early example of acknowledging the value of the indigenous knowledge held by a tribe, for which compensation in the form of cash benefits had gone directly to the source of the IP holders.

CSIR, Shaman, the Body Shop, and Jeevani have developed mechanisms of returning some of the benefits from the commercialization of medicinal plants and TK to the local people.

In the interest of the developing countries, it may be worthwhile to ensure that living organisms and their parts are not patented; that the rights of traditional farmers to use, exchange and save seeds be protected; and that the indigenous local farming community innovations are likewise protected.

## 4.7 PROTECTION OF TK THROUGH DOCUMENTATION

TK documentation data constitute an important form of non-patent literature with its specific characteristics making it a category of non-original databases. Some of those characteristics may necessitate specialized measures for TK data to be adequately integrated and recognized as relevant non-patent literature and as a non-original database.

If the development of such measures takes into account the needs and priorities of all stakeholders, they might:

– avoid the grant of patents for TK-based inventions which are not novel and non-obvious;
– avoid the costs of challenging such patents for TK holders and other interested third parties; and
– facilitate recognition of the technological value of TK by all users of non-patent literature, including IP offices, industry, researchers and the general public.

As mentioned earlier, the grant of patents on non-original innovations (linked to TMs), which are either based on what is already a part of the TK or a minor variation thereof, has been causing great concern to the developing world.

A recent study by an Indian expert group[29] examined 762 randomly selected US patents which were granted under A61K35/78 and other IPC classes, having a direct relationship

---

[29] R.A. Mashelkar, 'Intellectual Property Rights and the Third World', *Current Science* 81 (2001): 955: <www.ias.ac.in/currsci/oct252001/955.pdf>.

with medicinal plants in terms of their full text. Out of these 762 patents, 374 (49%) were found to be based on TK. A further study by a team of experts of the TKDL studied the USPTO, EPO and UKPTO patent databases in respect to medicinal plants (with respect to Unani system of medicine) in April 2003 and found more than 15,000 patent references compared with 4,896 references found in the year 2000, clearly demonstrating a three-fold increase. However, as per the study carried out in December 2005 at EPO, UKPTO and USPTO, the number of patents filed in these offices on medicinal plants have increased to 35,567. The possible number of patents granted by the Indian system of medicine each year is estimated at around 2,000. The fact that 2,000 patents are being granted each year for several medicinal plants implies that it is extremely urgent that the issue of patents on traditional systems of medicine be addressed.

Patent examiners in such patent offices that undertake substantive examination prior to grant of a patent face a difficulty. When considering the patentability of any claimed subject matter, they obviously use available resources for searching the appropriate non-patent literature sources. Patent literature, however, is usually wholly contained in several distinctive databases and can be more easily searched and retrieved than can be the non-patent literature prior art that will reside somewhere within many diverse sources. Therefore, there is a need to create more easily accessible non-patent literature databases that deal with TK.

With the help of developing countries, TK can be documented, captured electronically and placed in the appropriate classification within the IPC so that it can be more easily searched and retrieved. A TKDL would help to prevent the patenting of products based on TK.

Eventually, the creation of a TKDL in the developing world would serve a larger purpose in providing and enhancing its innovation capacity. It could integrate widely scattered and distributed references on the TK systems of the developing world in a retrievable form. It could act as a bridge between the traditional and the modern knowledge systems. Availability of this knowledge in retrievable form in many languages will give a major impetus to modern research in the developing world, which would add further value to this TK, an example being the development of an allopathic medicine based on a traditional plant based therapeutic. Sustained efforts to modernize the TK systems of the developing world will create higher awareness at national and international levels and will establish a scientific approach that will ensure higher acceptability of these systems for practitioners of modern systems and for the public at large.

A Task Force consisting of members from USPTO, JPO, EPO, China and India was constituted by WIPO in the 30th meeting of IPC Union (19-23 February 2001) to look into the possibility of integrating or interlinking Traditional Knowledge Resource Classification (TKRC) into IPC. In the 31st meeting of the IPC Union (25 February to 1 March 2002), the committee noted that the IPC, representing the worldwide system for classifying patent information, could also be successively applied for classifying non-patent documentation, such as TK documentation. However, only a few entries in the IPC were available for classifying this subject matter and substantial revision of the classification would be required in this regard, including the creation of a new subclass covering TK subject matter.

TKRC, devised by the Indian experts, is a classification system for the purpose of systematic arrangement, dissemination and retrieval of TK resources. It is expected to facilitate the digitization of TK and act as a meta library to provide language-independent storage and retrieval of digitized information. This is achieved by following the internationally well-accepted IPC structure which includes sections, classes, subclasses, groups and subgroups.

TKRC needs to be integrated into the IPC, which has been widely accepted by patent authorities globally for classification and retrieval of information. Once TKRC is integrated into IPC, it will offer a uniformly acceptable solution, which will serve as an instrument for the orderly arrangement of documents relating to traditional medicinal plants and other TK resources. It will serve as a basis for selective dissemination of information on traditional resources to all users of non-patent information.

For documenting TK, TKRC needs to be globally accepted. TKRC relates to more than 2,000 medicinal plants, information on processes for the preparation of drugs and its uses, details of plants used, therapeutic compound formulations, compositions and doses and diseases in which they are used, as well as a list of documents wherein such information is available and has already been completed by Indian experts. This classification will need to be enhanced at a global level.

India took an initiative to create a TKDL on the codified TK on Indian systems of medicine, which are Ayurveda, Unani, Siddha and Yoga. The medicinal formulations present in 148 books are being transcribed into five international languages – English, French, German, Spanish and Japanese – in patent application format.

The information present in fifty-nine Ayurvedic texts has been transcribed. So far, 81,500 Ayurvedic formulations have been transcribed. Images of plant, animal and mineral resources used in the formulations have also been incorporated into the database. Over 1,07,000 formulations from Unani texts and 12,000 formulations from Siddha have been transcribed. In 2008, activities on TKDL were expanded to Yoga, in which 1,500 postures have been identified and 500 postures have been transcribed. Under the TKDL project so far a total of 2,01,500 formulations similar to turmeric usage for wound healing or neem for antifungal properties have been transcribed and the database is present in 28 million A4 sized pages.[30]

Once the NTKDLs have been created, they may be included in the official list of International Search Authorities (ISA) relating to non-patent literature.[31] Presently, there are 135 non-patent technical journals in the lists of ISA. It will also be useful for IP offices to review patents granted on non-original inventions which are part of the TK systems. Revocation of such patents by IP offices will go a long way in addressing the emotional concerns of the developing world on the issue of IPRs based on indigenous

---

[30]   V.K. Gupta, Council of Scientific & Industrial Research, India, 2008 (private communication).
[31]   *'The Protection of Traditional Knowledge: Revised Objectives and Principles'*, WIPO document: WIPO/ GRTKF/IC/9/5: <www.wipo.int/edocs/mdocs/tk/en/wipo_grtkf_ic_9/wipo_grtkf_ic_9_5.pdf>.

knowledge. On 29 June 2006, the government of India approved providing access to the TKDL database to International Patent Offices under a non-disclosure agreement for the purpose of search and examination by patent examiners.

The IPC Union has decided to include about two hundred sub groups on medicinal plants in contrast to one subgroup, A61K 35/17, available at present. In the 32nd IPC Union meeting held by WIPO in Geneva in February 2003, it was decided that the Task Force should continue its work on further development of classification tools for TK and to investigate possible patent classification aspects relating to components of biodiversity and folklore.[32] The Task Force must also consider how the future revised IPC could be linked to TKRC, which may be developed in various countries, and how best to organize access to TK documentation, which was in the public domain, including hyperlinking the IPC to TK databases. The Task Force has also recommended linking of TKRC developed by India with IPC. For linking IPC with TKRC, an IPC-TKRC concordance table was prepared and presented at the 35th IPC Union Meeting held in October 2004 at Geneva. The concordance has been developed for the subgroups under twenty-two main groups of IPC and the subgroups created for TKRC Ayurveda. Linking of IPC with TKRC has been approved in the 35th IPC Union meeting.

All of these ongoing developments are likely to have a significant impact on the system of search and examination that precedes the grant of patents based on TK. These developments may significantly reduce the grant of wrong TK patents and in turn, will augur well for integrating TK into the knowledge base on industrial systems.

---

[32]  <www.wipo.int/edocs/mdocs/classifications/en/ipc_ce_32/ipc_ce_32_3.doc>.

CHAPTER FIVE

# CULTURAL AND INFORMATION INDUSTRIES

*– The growing Importance of the Cultural and Information Industries*
*– Cultural Industries, Intellectual Property (IP) and National Identity*
*– New Systems of Delivery of Information Products*
*– Economic Contribution of the Cultural Industry*


5.1 THE IMPORTANCE OF CULTURAL INDUSTRIES

The economic value of IP for the cultural industries in countries, which are major creators of copyright material, has been well established. These industries contribute substantially to national economic wealth, and also rank in size with other major conventionally defined industries in many of such countries. These include both developed countries like the USA (with approximately 6.5% of the Gross Domestic Product (GDP) being contributed by such industries in 2005),[1] as also developing countries such as China (the corresponding figure being 6% of the GDP).[2] The importance to a number of national economies of the cultural or copyright-based industries, and of professions which are copyright-based and dependent on copyright protection for their commercial success and viability, is substantial.

Advances in technology have continuously changed the landscape of the cultural and information industries. The advent of videocassette recorder in the 1970s, digital revolution in the 1980s, Internet in the 1990s and Web 2.0 in late 2000s has made a huge difference. Further, it has invoked a challenge for the copyright laws to be constantly kept in step, especially with regard to the continuous changes on interpretations, adaptations, etc.

Copyright legislation protects, as well as encourages, creativity in literary, artistic and musical works. Copyright thus protects not only the author, but also safeguards the investments of those helping in bringing into a tangible form, the results of such creativity. The expression and exploitation of this creativity through records, films, broadcasts, performance in public, and publications, is an important activity. Copyright related activities have also recorded a sizeable growth in employment generation in a number of countries, in respect, inter alia, of authors, composers, musicians, photographers, commercial artists, computer analysts and programmers, librarians, as also of dancers, actors and other performing artists. Copyright-based industries, which pertain to industrial activity or

---

[1]   <www.iipa.com/pdf/IIPAEricSmithtestimonyOctober182007Testimony10172007.pdf>.
[2]   <http://english.peopledaily.com.cn/200505/25/eng20050525_186756.html>.

production using copyright materials, should be provided constant encouragement in order to enable them to maintain their share in the increasing world trade.

Meanwhile, new technologies are emerging at a rapid pace. Global information networks, the digital superhighways, electronic commerce, the national information infrastructure (NII), the global information infrastructure (GII), and the internet which was originally meant for researchers, and has now become a worldwide web connecting millions of users, are examples of the eruption of new technologies. The invention of computers and computer programs has led to introduction of digital technology.

The word 'digital' refers to the fact that computers work with digit-based binary systems. For a computer, there is, in terms of format, hardly any difference between a program and any type of data. It is all encoded in binary form. With technological evolution, images, texts, voices, sound, music, and even information necessary to reproduce a three-dimensional object such as a sculpture, can be stored in a digital form. For the computer, once these various elements have been digitized or put into digital format, they can be merged, transformed or mixed, to create new works. The 'global information infrastructure' covers telephone and telecommunications networks, cable and satellite communication agencies, broadcasting organizations, among others. This together with interactive digital networks, digital transmissions and delivery systems, are revolutionizing the concepts of copyright protection, and playing an important part in national competitiveness. Globalised information networks and the Internet economy are transforming life in respect of communication, trade, commerce, as well as of learning. The Internet, as a vehicle of global electronic commerce, is growing at an enormously rapid pace.

Creative intellectual activity in the fields covered by copyright needs constant encouragement. This can be provided by safeguarding the interests of authors and creators of literary and artistic works, by giving exclusive rights to them. Since copyright covers mass media communication, printed publications, radio and television broadcasting, films, and also extends, in a number of countries, to computer systems for storage of information, its value in an electronic age is considerable.

A country's creative and innovative capabilities and its cultural development have to be deliberately fostered and protected by adequate legislation. In this context, cyber legislation, rules and regulations are equally necessary for facilitating the growth of the information technology industries, and e-business ventures, in a networked and integrated world, and in a rapidly growing market for Internet services.

Strengthening of the IP system in the context of internationalization of trade, of Internet economics, of the multimedia age, and of information technology in the current century, is a constant necessity.

## 5.2 New Systems of Delivery of Information Products

With technological improvements, new methods have emerged through which products of creative activity can reach out to the public. With the utilization of new interactive technological systems, the traditional means through which literature, music or films are being made available to the public by business of selling books, video records, etc., are being overtaken. The interactive online systems are enabling access to databases, from which persons interested could have a book, a musical recording or a film transmitted to them over the wireless or cable. They could also read it on the screen, view it, or make copies thereof. Such online systems are also providing access to information from other countries.

The earlier accepted method of making these available through sale of physical copies is being replaced by transmittal of copies of works via receiving equipment. These in turn make it possible for receivers to produce their own physical copies instead of buying them at bookshops, music stores, and the like. The publishing, music and software industries, to name a few, are becoming increasingly vulnerable to often unauthorized delivery via the Internet.

For example, the emergence of the process of extracting digital content, such as audio or video from a CD or DVD to MP3 files on the hard drives of individual users, has increased substantially in recent times. Originally, the users used audio tracks from CDs to create a personal music compilation on their computers. However, with the proliferation of web-based file sharing or 'peer to peer' (P2P) application like Napster, which permitted users to share their personal audio and video collections online, there was a further proliferation of these practices. Once copyright-protected content is transferred to media controlled by users, it can be made freely available irrespective of its legally protected status.

The first file-sharing network, Napster, began operating in 1999 and immediately achieved widespread popularity among music users. By 2001 the company had been sued for copyright infringement by the Record Industry Association of America and was forced to shut down its operations. However, other P2P applications quickly emerged in Napster's wake. But like Napster other P2P programs already allowed people to pass smaller music files from one computer to another. But big files would clog the system. Then in 2004, another P2P software called BitTorrent was developed in Silicon Valley, USA. Essentially, the software breaks files into pieces and scatters them on users' hard drives. When someone requests a movie, the software gathers the pieces from the nearest computers on the network and assembles them only once they reach their destination. This allows a file to download much more quickly. Now audio, video and gaming industries are gradually warming up to the idea of using such tools.

Another disruptive model is that of YouTube. In February 2005, YouTube, a video sharing website was launched by two Silicon Valley engineers. YouTube, makes it easy for users to upload, view and share video clips. Initially YouTube started with user generated content, but soon thereafter, users started uploading short clips from movies and other copyrighted material. As a service provider of user generated content, YouTube has always maintained that the responsibility of uploading content lies entirely on the user. YouTube does not view videos before they are posted online, and it is left to copyright holders to issue a takedown notice under the terms of the Digital Millennium Copyright Act.

YouTube has been criticized frequently for failing to ensure that its online content adheres to the law of copyright. YouTube has been in the past sued for copyright infringement by media companies such as Viacom and the English Premier League. However, one cannot deny the popularity of YouTube among its users. According to a Nielsen Survey, as of July 2008, YouTube had 77 million viewers, which ranked it at number one video site in the world. YouTube video clips are also embedded in various websites across the Internet to provide video content in addition to plain text based information.[3]

As broadband connectivity becomes increasingly widespread, file sharing and distribution mechanisms such as BitTorrent and YouTube are creating new challenges for the copyright industry. To combat this, the copyright industries are adopting a variety of measures. These include stepped-up anti-piracy activities aimed at identifying and pursuing high-volume infringers, development of new business models for online content delivery using digital rights management (DRM) technologies, and allocating increased resources to awareness building programmes. At the international level, World Intellectual Property Organization (WIPO) is assisting in the campaign by actively promoting accessions to the 1996 WIPO Copyright Treaty and the WIPO Performances and Phonograms Treaty, both of which entered into force in mid-2002.

Again, the substantial growth of the software industry in a large number of countries around the world over the last decades, while highlighting the need of, and the demand for skilled information technology manpower, has been presenting the industry with a problem in respect of software piracy. With the availability of the modern copying equipment, and with pirates having equal access to the new technologies, book publishers, music publishers, record manufacturers, film producers as well as software producers, are faced with pirate competition on a very high scale. However, technology developments are rendering it also possible to have devices that permit automatic monitoring of the use to which this wealth of accessible material is being put to. Built-in information (watermarks) signals in the digitized version of books, music, films, and so on, could be read through electronic devices provided in the equipment made available to the public, and could render it possible to control the extent of utilization of works of a copyright owner.

National legislations should make it an offence to circumvent these technically in-built copy protection systems through any other technologically equipped system that could deactivate them, thereby making it possible to copy without compensation. Legislation and technology should thus be used to prevent copying without compensation or prior authorization, except for certain free uses of works as provided for in Articles 9(2) and 10 of the Berne Convention (Paris Act of 24 July 1971 as amended on 28 September 1979).

Insofar as computer software is concerned, as mentioned earlier, it is protected under copyright legislation in most countries. This enables software companies to prevent copying, which is important, as software products can generally be easily copied. However, copyright protects the 'literal expression' of computer programs, it does not protect the 'ideas' underlying the computer program, which often have considerable commercial value. There are divergent opinions around the globe on the protection for software related patents. Countries like US, Japan, Singapore and Australia have been granting software related patents and countries like India, Mexico, and U.K are generally against the grant of

---

[3]   <www.websiteoptimization.com/bw/0808/>.

such patents. Canada, Korea, and Taiwan are in the process of forming their policy towards this new category of patents.[4]

A legal framework for protection of software under national IP laws is, therefore, essential, so is its active and effective enforcement. As Robert Schware observes:

> software is a booming sector, and is growing faster than most industries. The market for computer software and services is global, intensively competitive, fast-changing and fast-growing ... The learning curves for domestic and international markets (in respect of developing countries) are different; the domestic software market being important base for skills, experience and establishing a track record that may later be applied to exports ... countries need to pay attention to domestic opportunities, since these have high returns in terms of gaining experience and innovation in software production, and provide training that allows a broadening of software exports.[5]

There is, however, a movement for open source software, an idea that matured in early 2000, but can be easily used for personal and business computing applications as well as for scientific R&D. The open source software is distributed with its source code in an accessible form. Indeed the basic idea behind open source software is simple. When programmers can read, redistribute, and modify the source code for a piece of software, it evolves through continued modification and adaptation. The real key here is that all participating programmers accept a license formula, which allows subsequent programmers to adapt and build on their works. This, of course, means that the open source movement is based on copyright. The business model, however, is different from that for the mainstream software sector.

As regards embedded software, the:

> market is growing rapidly as software is becoming an important source of functionality enhancement and differentiation in many traditionally non-computing industries ... An embedded software system is a combination of hardware ... microcode, drivers, an operating system, and an application that delivers functionality within traditional non-computing devices.[6]

The software sector is one of the fastest growing areas of the information technology market. To quote Prof. Carlos M. Correa of the University of Buenos Aires, Argentina, 'With world sales exceeding US$100 billion annually, the software sector is targeted by hardware suppliers and specialized software firms alike ... Software development is skill intensive. The availability of technical personnel is a key factor, albeit not sufficient, to ensure commercial success', especially as concerns developing countries. Again,

> despite the high degree of formalisation of knowledge involved in software development, considerable room is left for creativity and ingenuity ... Work on systems

---

4   <www.wipo.int/sme/en/documents/software_patents.htm>.
5   Robert Schware, 'Software Industry Entry Strategies for Developing Countries', in *World Development*, vol. 20, No.2, (Washington D.C: The World Bank, 1992), 143-164.
6   *The IT Industry in India : Strategic Review* 2003, published by the National Association of Software and Service Companies (NASSCOM), New Delhi, India, page 73.

software requires particular knowledge and skills . . . the production of packaged software poses higher quality and reliability requirements and entails substantially larger investments.

Also with the 'rapid pace of technological change and the short life cycle of products, force software companies to undertake research and development (R&D) and to invest in training for new technologies'. Further, while software firms in developing countries do take advantage of their cost factor, and though amongst these, 'India has gained considerable recognition as a technically reliable software producer; most firms in developing countries find it difficult to reach directly the potential end users'.[7]

An updated, modern copyright legislation and its enforcement is important. Such legislation helps in attracting and sustaining investments in the cultural industry and the information technology industry. The economic value of the cultural industry in the growth process of a number of countries, both developed and developing, is quite substantial. Its considerable contribution to national economies shows that it is likely to flourish even in the Internet and digital environment.

### 5.3 Economic Contribution of the Cultural Industry

The core of the cultural industry includes:

- book publishing;
- art printing and reprographic enterprises;
- journals, periodicals and newspaper industries;
- advertising;
- radio and television broadcasting;
- cable networks;
- sound recordings, musical and audiovisual works;
- the recording and music publishing industry;
- films, and television production companies;
- the motion picture industry

Also included are:

- the computer software industry including data processing.
- enterprises, businesses and/or institutions that produce or distribute cultural, educational or scientific material; and
- materials dealing with information technology or covering sophisticated technologies.

In addition to these are those other related non-core industries, whose activities are to some extent copyright dependent. These include industries and businesses that produce equipment needed for the use of copyrighted material, such as radios, portable digital music

---

[7]    Carlos Correa, 'Strategies for Software Exports from Developing Countries', published in *World Development*, vol. 24, No.1, 1996, 171-182.

players, television sets; computers, recording devices, as also the production of printers, copiers, binders, paper and printing machine manufacturers, all of which in addition to theatres, libraries, and so on, contribute to the output of the cultural industries.

The cultural and information industry, which has also become known as the copyright industry, is one of the fastest growing sectors of the economy in a number of countries, providing very sizeable employment and export possibilities. Its contribution to the gross national product (GNP) of a number of countries, including also developing countries, has been impressive. It is the economic value of the copyright industries and their growth potential that had prompted several studies, particularly in some of the countries which are major creators of copyright-based material.

Denis de Freitas, President of Honour of the British Copyright Council, thus commented on the role and importance of the copyright system:

> the copyright system as it now exists in virtually every civilised country is a vital part of modern society's infrastructure, serving the entire community ... It is the foundation on which the world's publishing industry rests, bringing the written or recorded word, carrying knowledge, ideas, understanding and entertainment to every literate person ... in the community ... The orderly acquisition and transfer of rights which take place within the copyright system are indispensable to the entire media – newspapers, journals, radio and television, and, of course, the whole world of entertainment theatres, concerts, films, record production, broadcasting. All depend upon a regular supply of literary, dramatic, musical and artistic works, the creation and dissemination of which is stimulated and regulated by the copyright system ... With the extension of the system to the protection of computer software, much of the industrial and commercial activity of a country involves the use of rights protected by copyright.
>
> Until recently no one had any real idea of what the economic dimensions of the copyright industries were; but in the last two decades, in several countries, independent research have been carried out which have produced some quite remarkable statistics.[8]

These arguments, made more than a decade ago, are even more valid today. For example, the United States, one of the fastest growing and most dynamic sectors of the U.S. economy is the copyright industry. In 2005 copyrighted industry in US generated substantial revenues from picture and video industry (USD 73.4 billion), sound recording industry (USD 18.7 billion), software publishing industry (USD 119.6 billion) and retail sales of video game software (USD 7.0 billion).[9]

There is a perception that compared to other sectors of an economy video games are very marginal in terms of their economic contribution. However, the fact is that Europe

---

[8]  'The Fight Against Piracy' by Denis de Freitas, Publication by the International Publishers' Copyright Council (IPCC), 1994.

[9]  Stephen E. Siwek, 'The True Cost of Copyright Industry Piracy to the U.S. Economy', IPI Policy Report-189.

generates USD 17.9 billion a year (using 2007 data).[10] United Kingdom USD 3.3 billion,[11] France (USD 3.12 billion)[12] along with Germany makes up the three largest video game countries in Europe. Nowadays video game industry plays a pivotal role in the international and regional economic arena. Video games are increasingly accessible via internet and mobile phones, which are expected to make up 33% of total revenues for video games in Europe by 2010. As of 2008, the European video gaming sector is already worth half as much as the entire European music market and exceeds the cinema box office.[13]

In South Korea, which is one of the emerging economies of the developed world, and which is rated as the eleventh largest trading nation, the cultural industry is well developed. As of 2008, South Korea's gaming industry is approximately USD 1 billion in market size.[14] Within the gaming industry, if one excludes the console-based gaming segment, which is largely controlled by Japan and USA, South Korea has a 15% market share of the worldwide gaming industry. According to market research firm – Pearl Research, South Korean gaming industry is expected to grow to more than USD 1.7 billion by 2009. South Korea already has a sophisticated IT infrastructure with 80% of households connected to the Internet, which makes it easier for gamers to participate in the PC online games. More than 12 million Korean adults visit game portals every month.[15] Apart from gaming, South Korea has one of the highest adoption rates for online shopping. Approximately 67% of those in the age group of 20 to 30 years purchased online content in 2008. Of those who purchased digital content, 91% purchased music while 39% purchased community and avatar items from online services.

However, South Korea faces intense competition from the Chinese gaming companies.[16] China's lower development costs, relatively inexpensive rates for launching in North American markets and the ability to quickly reverse engineer games have become extremely vital competitive advantages for the country. To counter the Chinese competition, the Ministry of Culture, Sports & Tourism of South Korea is helping the gaming industry by organizing the best environment for game development, creating a global publisher and expert studio structure plan and fostering collaboration between big firms and smaller firms. Apart from this, the government of South Korea has committed a funding of USD 237 million to the gaming industry from 2008 to 2012. The funding will go towards sixty new gaming titles. Additionally, the government has vowed to expand exports of games to USD 3.38 billion per year.

Singapore is considered today as one of the world's stronger economies. Its competitiveness has been based on close cooperation between the State with a reputation for strict governance and business. Its active book publishing industry is protected by a sternly

---

10 &lt;www.forbes.com/home/2008/06/18/ubisoft-game-assassin-tech-innovationeu08-cx_mji_0618ubisoft.html&gt;.
11 &lt;www.gamedaily.com/articles/news/report-game-sales-blow-past-music-in-uk/?biz=&gt;.
12 &lt;www.newswiretoday.com/news/33025/&gt;.
13 &lt;http://europa.eu/rapid/pressReleasesAction.do?reference=IP/08/618&gt;.
14 &lt;http://blog.wired.com/games/2008/12/south-korean-go.html&gt;.
15 &lt;www.kdcstaffs.com/it/main_view.php?mode=view&nNum=5344&page=1&parts=Game&gt;.
16 &lt;http://gamingzealots.com/2008/12/04/south-korean-games-industry-threatened-by-the-chinese/comment-page-1/&gt;.

enforced copyright law, which has reduced piracy considerably. The total revenue from the information and communications industry was about USD 35.6 billion in 2007, providing an employment to more than 130,400 professionals.[17]

The cultural industry is also fairly well established in a number of developing countries. Let us see some concrete examples. China's film industry has produced, in the two decades up to the end of 2000, an average of 126 films annually, and imported and dubbed more than 800 foreign films; it has more than 30 film production companies and more than 2000 film distribution institutions, with an exceptionally large attendance in cinemas. Recently, in 2007, China's film production went up to 500 films. China is the world's largest TV market, with 378 million TV households and 152 million cable TV households by the end of 2007. As for digital cable TV, according to the data released by CMR-Union on 10 December 2008, China has 47.65 million digital cable TV subscribers up 97.39 percent year-on-year.[18]

China, already the world leader in cell phone use, has surpassed USA as the number one nation in Internet users.[19] As of December 2008, China is reported to have around 253 million Internet users. Online shopping turnover (Business-to-Consumer and Consumer-to-Consumer excluding online travel booking) reached USD $8.7 billion in 2007 with the level of online spending per consumer at about USD $147 in 2007.[20] China's software industry grew at a CAGR of more than 39% over the period from 2001 to 2007 to reach USD 74 billion and is further anticipated to grow at a CAGR of nearly 22% through 2012.[21] The Chinese gaming market of nearly USD 900 million is expected to be worth more than USD 6 billion by 2010.[22] The growing China game industry has more than 27 million gamers and it is predicted that there will be 60 million by 2010 consuming $1.8 billion of online games.

In India, within the copyright industry, the motion picture and music industry have been making significant economic contributions. A CII AT Kearney report[23] released in 2006, pegged the total market size of the Indian Film Industry at USD 1.8 billion in 2006. CII AT Kearney report had further estimated that the industry will reach a market size of USD 4.4 to 5.1 billion by year 2011. The report further states a wide-scale movie going audience with 3.7 billion movie tickets sold in 2006 alone. However, going forward, the emergence of home video market and challenges of piracy will significantly alter the growth trends in the film industry, especially the theatrical form of film exhibition. In 2006, home video rentals had a small share of 8% of the overall movie revenues in comparison to some of the developed markets where it contributes to more than 40%. However, this share is expected to grow to 14% by 2010. The key drivers that will enable this are the increasing penetration

17 <http://app.mica.gov.sg/Default.aspx?tabid=199>.
18 <www.interfax.cn/news/7379/>.
19 <www.cia.gov/library/publications/the-world-factbook/geos/ch.html>.
20 <www.slideshare.net/web2asia/successful-ecommerce-in-china>.
21 <http://en.wikipedia.org/wiki/Software_industry_in_China>.
22 <www.city-interactive.com/en/o-firmie-en/history.html>.
23 <www.ciionline.org/documents/executivesummarycii_ATkearneyup.pdf>.

of DVD players, which are getting more affordable by the day and the dropping prices of the original DVDs to combat the challenge of piracy. Similarly, the music industry in India has witnessed significant piracy. In India, pirated music is estimated to be one-third the size of the organized market. This is further aggravated by the drop in sales of physical formats due to the increased adoption of digital formats. This has resulted into the music industry shrinking in size from USD 250 million in 2000 to USD 155 million in 2006.Therefore, in view of the above, the future growth prospects in areas of the cultural industry, particularly in the film and music industries, India will have to step up systems to curtail piracy and at the same time embrace new digital technologies, which make the access to content more affordable and ubiquitous.

IT services industry in India,[24] is protected under its copyright law since 1984. This industry employs over 860,000 professionals as of 2007 and 2008. India is the most successful IT services provider among the developing countries. The revenues from IT services (excluding Business Process Outsourcing (BPO)) increased from USD 23.5 billion in 2007 to USD 31 billion in 2008. Out of this total of USD 31 billion, USD 23.1 billion came from exports and USD 7.9 billion came from the domestic market. While the US and the UK remain the largest export markets for India (accounting for about 61% and 18% respectively, in 2007), the industry footprint is steadily expanding.

The IT industry (BPO included) is on track to reach USD 60 billion in exports and USD 73-75 billion in overall software and services revenues by 2010. The competitive advantage of the Indian software industry was based on its cost-effectiveness, world-class quality, high reliability, rapid delivery, all of it powered by state-of-the-art technology know-how and domain knowledge.

Incidentally, in the context of the two developing countries mentioned above, viz., China and India, there has been a dialogue for possible cooperation in the software field, respectively between one hardware giant and another software giant, basically to put together their complementarities in order to further boost their international exports.

In Malaysia, the Intellectual Property Division of the Ministry of Domestic Trade and Consumer Affairs is in charge of IPRs.The Government at the highest levels is keen on using the IP system for furthering its economic development and global competitiveness assisted, with its private sector efficiency, and by an educated labour force, and with manufacturing growth at 12% per annum over almost two decades. According to a report released by the Malaysian Book Publishing Association in May 2008, its book publishing industry is estimated at USD 440 million per year.The future prospect for the Malaysian book industry remains bright. The general public's improved reading habit has caused the sales of general books, fiction and non-fiction for both adults and children, to increase steadily and significantly. Print runs for such general books have shown marked improvements, with the best-selling titles achieving print-runs of tens of thousands. The increasing population, higher GNP per capita, higher literacy rate and greater reading awareness have all contributed positively to the growth of the industry. The Malaysian government's emphasis on human capital development, better infrastructure and better governance

---

[24]   <www.nasscom.in/upload/5216/IT%20Industry%20Factsheet-Aug%202008.doc>.

have also provided a lot of impetus to drive the knowledge-economy forward. Buoyed by the economy, local publishers are beginning to venture into the regional and international markets.[25]

In spite of the cultural and information industry's significant contribution to both developed and developing countries, inexpensive and accessible reproduction technologies, however, make it easy for copyrighted materials to be pirated, which results in lost revenue. This translates into lost production of legitimate copyright products, which in turn means lost wages and lost purchases of upstream products and services.

In developed countries like the U.S., piracy has resulted in significant losses. In 2005 alone, piracy cost in motion pictures, sound recordings, business and entertainment software is estimated to be USD 25.6 billion in lost revenue. According to the October 2007 report of the Institute for Policy Innovation, the total costs to the U.S. economy due to copyright piracy are estimated to exceed USD 58 billion in lost output, 373,375 lost jobs, USD 16 billion in lost employee earnings and more than USD 2.6 billion in lost tax revenues.[26]

International Intellectual Property Alliance[27] (IIPA), was formed as a private sector coalition in 1984 to represent the U.S. copyright-based industries. IIPA claims that in China, hard goods piracy – motion pictures, records, books, videogames, and software – remains widespread. While most pirate products in the Chinese market are produced in China, imports of pirated products from other countries in Asia are also a problem. Internet piracy is an ever-growing phenomenon in China today, including peer to peer (P2P) piracy, unauthorized or pirate servers for entertainment software, and piracy in Internet cafés. Piracy levels for 2007 remained in the 85-95% range for most of the industries. The industries collectively estimated USD 3.5 billion in estimated trade losses due to piracy in China in 2007, not including loss data from the motion picture and entertainment software industry. The losses due to records and music piracy is at a 90% level having gone up from USD 206 million in 2006 to USD 451 million in 2007. Business software the losses in 2007 are at 80% having gone up from USD 2.17 billion in 2006 to USD 2.47 billion in 2007.[28]

In comparison, US trade losses due to India were estimated to be at USD 913 million by IIPA with USD 732 million coming from the business software industry alone. However, according to IIPA, these losses have gone down from 71% in 2006 to 69% in 2007. At the same time, the losses from records and music have gone down from USD 52.7 million in 2006 to USD 13.8 million in 2007.[29]

However, since 2004, a nationwide campaign for IPR protection has been carried out in China to end trademark, patent and copyright infringements – particularly in import and

---

[25] <http://mabopa.com.my/upload/attc/A%20Malaysian%20Report%20for%202008%20ABPA%20AGM.pdf>.
[26] Stephen E. Siwek, 'The True Cost of Copyright Industry Piracy to the U.S. Economy', Institute for Policy Innovation, IPI Policy Report No. 189 (2007).
[27] <www.iipa.com/aboutiipa.html>.
[28] <www.iipa.com/pdf/IIPAChinaTPSCwrittencomments092608.pdf>.
[29] <www.iipa.com/rbc/2008/2008SPEC301INDIA.pdf>.

export, wholesale markets, trade fairs, original-equipment manufacturer, printing and reproduction. In 2008, China outlined its new action plan on IPR protection, which deploys 280 detailed measures in 10 areas with focus on improving the IPR regime, and creating a legal market and cultural environment conducive to IPR protection. The specific measures involve timely revisions to IPR legislation, speeding up the revision of laws and regulations on punishment for IPR infringements, strengthening judicial protection and administrative law enforcement, defining the scope of IPRs to prevent its abuse, and launching extensive educational programs to promote moral standards, and condemning plagiarism, piracy and counterfeiting.

Through the IIPA, the U.S. continues to work with several local governments in enforcing stricter laws and reducing widespread copyright infringement. The IIPA states that countries such as Singapore, Taiwan and Brazil have been successful at reducing piracy levels to significant levels. For example, in Singapore, piracy levels are among the lowest in Asia at 5-10% for audio and video piracy and 39% for business software.[30]

## 5.4 COLLECTIVE MANAGEMENT OF COPYRIGHT

For the promotion of the cultural or copyright industries worldwide, it is imperative to ensure the protection of rights of the creators of copyrighted works, who contribute the very inputs needed for the sustenance and development of the said industries.

The rights of authors, composers and creators of literary, artistic, musical and dramatic works, as also the rights of beneficiaries of the so-called neighbouring or related rights, that is, of the performers, producers of phonograms and broadcasting organizations, and other such rights including those of publishers in the typographical arrangement of their books, are exclusive rights of the owners of such rights. They cannot, however, always be exercised by their owners. This is basically on account of the vast and ever increasing number of their users.

Their protection through collective management of rights becomes necessary because of the number, and other circumstances relating to their uses, which are not often practical to exercise on an individual basis. Similarly, the users cannot be expected to contact all the authors and performers of works they wish to use.

The collective administration of copyright and neighbouring rights is thus of considerable economic significance, and can help in the efficient exercise of authors' rights through a balanced system, which could not only serve the owners of rights, but also offers advantages to users, who could be enabled access to works in an organized manner and at reasonable rates.

As explained by an eminent international copyright specialist,[31] under a collective management system, the rights owners authorize the collective administration societies

---

[30]  <www.iipa.com/pdf/IIPAEricSmithtestimonyOctober182007Testimony10172007.pdf>.
[31]  WIPO's publication No. 855(E) of 2002 entitled 'Collective Management of Copyright and Related Rights' by Dr. Mihaly Ficsor.

to administer their rights, through monitoring the use of their concerned works, negotiating with prospective users, giving them licenses against appropriate fees, collecting such fees and distributing amongst owners of the rights. It is necessary, however, to ensure that there is an overall supervision concerning the rate and operation of tariffs vis-à-vis users that would enable the concerned government authorities to prevent any abuses. Also essential are appropriate legislative and administrative measures that would facilitate monitoring of the activities of collective management and administration. For efficient and effective administration of authors' rights by collective management societies, rights have to be adequately guaranteed by law.

Likewise, it is also necessary to ensure cooperation by the users. Enforcement measures and/or sanctions should be prescribed against users who may create obstacles that are considered unreasonable. Then again, the remuneration obtained by collective management societies after the deduction of the costs of administration, should be distributed among individual rights' owners, as much in proportion to the actual use of their works as possible. With the increasing application of digital technology, the advent of multimedia productions and the use of digital networks, i.e., the Internet, the exercise and management of creative works are facing new challenges.

New technological solutions, however, are being worked out to face these challenges equally with the use of digital technology. These include, inter alia, encryption technology, digital identification numbers, rights management information system, and anti-circumvention measures supplemented by contract law as well as through systems of database protection. New methods of licensing and monitoring use, as also of collecting and distributing remuneration are being, introduced. Strategic developments are likewise taking place to enable collective organizations to offer effective protection and management of rights to the owners of such rights, particularly in the electronic commerce environment. Technical machinery also embodying the latest digital technology is being developed in order to facilitate the formation of infrastructures for electronic management of collective administration of copyright.

In respect of such collective administrations and managements, it is preferable to have one single organization for the same category of rights in each country. Again, while as to whether the copyright collective administration should be a public or a private organization depends on the political, economic and legal traditions prevailing in the relevant country. Generally such organizations should be, and are in most countries, in the private sector. New and improved copyright legislation in different countries should include provisions for the establishment of such organizations.

These organizations functioning as Societies of authors or performing rights organizations exist in a number of countries. To take only a few examples, these are ASCAP in the United States of America, PRS in the United Kingdom, GEMA in Germany, SIAE in Italy, SGAE in Spain, SUISA in Switzerland, RAO in the Russian Federation, ARTISJUS in Hungary, ZAIKS in Poland, JUSAUTOR in Bulgaria; and in developing countries, again to take a few examples, these are ONDA in Algeria, SADAIC in Argentina, IPRS and the Authors' Guild in India, BMDA in Morocco, BSDA in Senegal.

As Dr. Mihaly Ficsor has remarked:

although it is in the field of musical 'performing rights' where the network of collective management organisations is the most complete, there are still several developing countries where no organisations exist or, even if they exist in principle, they do not function in practice. Both CISAC (the International Confederation of Societies of Authors and Composers) and WIPO have intensive 'institution building' programmes and 'incubator' projects in order to establish appropriate organisations in those countries and to improve the operation of the existing ones . . . In a few countries, collective management organisations do not have membership but act as representatives of composers and text-writers whose 'performing rights' they manage on the basis of statutory law.[32]

From some of the facts and figures recounted in this Chapter, it should be clear that the copyright-based cultural industries contribute quite substantially to socio-economic growth in both developed and developing countries as also in the countries in transition. Their encouragement through the establishment and enforcement of strong and effective IP system helps not only in sizeable contribution to the GNP of the countries concerned, but it also helps promote national identity internationally. Inter-regional and intra-regional flows of the production of the various cultural industries need to be deliberately encouraged through, inter alia, facilitation of licensing; negotiated royalty payments; bilateral sub-regional and intra-regional agreements on avoidance of double taxation of copyright royalties, etc. These should aim at easier mobility, identification and reduction of obstacles, facilitation of access under fair and reasonable terms, the adaptation of commercial practices in the flow of rights, strict enforcement of protection for copyright works, and tax incentives and remissions, which would certainly help further promotion of the cultural industries and their value-added contribution to the various national economies.

---

[32] Ibid., 41 and 42.

# CHAPTER SIX

# THE IMPORTANCE OF INTELLECTUAL PROPERTY FOR COMPETITIVENESS OF SMALL- AND MEDIUM-SIZED ENTERPRISES

*– Nature of Small- and Medium-Sized Enterprises (SMEs)*
*– Contribution of SMEs*
*– Creating IP Culture in SMEs*
*– Fostering Cooperation Amongst SMEs*

## 6.1 NATURE OF SMEs

SMEs are the backbone of most economies. They are the engines of sustainable employment generation and broad-based economic growth. There is no universal definition of SME. SMEs are independently owned businesses set up with the objective of making reasonable profits on the investment made. Generally, SMEs are defined on the basis of one or more quantitative parameters such as the number of persons employed, the annual turnover or the level of their investment. In some countries, the limits set in relation to the above criteria often vary depending on the nature of the SME's business or industrial activity and how the SME's particular purpose is defined by law, regulation or administrative instruction. Therefore, it must always be borne in mind that SMEs are an extremely diverse and heterogeneous group with a very wide range of needs and concerns. From the cottage handicraft-based industries to micro-technology and micro-electronics based industries, SMEs are as diverse as mankind is today. Their Intellectual Property (IP) needs and concerns are, therefore, dependent on the nature and scale of their operations and on their relationships with other entities and enterprises.

Generally, SMEs are small units, set up sometimes at the initiative of a few individuals and relying essentially on their entrepreneurial skills. These independent enterprises often cater to niche markets which may be localized. They are often suppliers of parts, components or sub-assemblies to larger enterprises. Normally they do not have a formal or strict hierarchical structure. Compared with larger enterprises, SMEs are more labour intensive and have relatively low-level technological assets. They often rely on low input levels in respect to raw materials, energy and labour. A small proportion of SMEs comprise high-tech enterprises, beginning their life in a technology incubator.

SMEs are the focus of most governments worldwide.[1] SMEs implement fresh thinking and ideas for developing as well as launching improved and new products and services

---

[1]  The New SME Definition User Guide and Model Declaration, European Commission, 2005: <http://ec.europa.eu/enterprise/enterprise_policy/sme_definition/sme_user_guide.pdf>.

which could sometimes be ahead of the competition in a dynamic and ever-changing marketplace. Of the new products and services that come to the marketplace from SMEs, some do spectacularly well, others just manage, and still others do poorly. SMEs grow through various phases with a range of possibilities, from one end of the spectrum – spectacular success—to the other end – failure.

SMEs often provide the breeding ground for entrepreneurs and for the interrelated flow of trade. They could help promote innovative new technologies, managerial growth and competitiveness as well as absorption of technological innovations and exploitation of indigenous research findings due to their comparatively lean organizational structures. Again, due to their inherent flexibility, they could be encouraged to promote industrial diversification in response to market changes. SMEs are also responsible for rural and social development. As such, practically all governments worldwide have placed SMEs high on their list of priorities and generally provide numerous SME support services covering a broad spectrum of inputs and activities so as to enable SMEs to realize their full potential.

## 6.2 CONTRIBUTIONS OF SMEs

SMEs the world over comprise a widely divergent spectrum of establishments, engaged in economic activities ranging from micro and rural enterprises to modern industrial units using sophisticated technologies. The figures in Table 2 below are indicative of the contributions of SMEs across diverse economies.[2]

Table 2. Contribution of SMEs across Diverse Economies

| Country | Share |
|---------|-------|
| **Organization for Economic Cooperation and Development (OECD)** | |
| Canada | 99.7% of all establishments |
| | 60% of employment |
| France | 99% of all establishments |
| | 53% of output of industrial, commercial and service sectors |
| | 65% of employment |
| | 26% of manufacturing exports |
| Germany | 95% of all establishments |
| | 57% of corporate value-added output |
| | 70% of employment |

*(continued)*

---

[2] SIDBI Report on SSI Sector 2000 (<www.sidbi.in/>); also *Handbook on Foreign Direct Investment by Small & Medium Sized Enterprises, Lessons from Asia,* UNCTAD, Geneva, 1998; Trade and Development Board, Commission on Enterprise, Business Facilitation and Development, UNCTAD, Geneva; SMEs Export Contribution – UN Country-wise Statistics.

Table 2. Contribution of SMEs across Diverse Economies (*continued*)

| Country | Share |
|---|---|
| Italy | 99% of all establishments<br>71% of employment<br>53% of exports |
| United Kingdom | 99% of all establishments<br>Under 40% of manufacturing output<br>44-66% of employment |
| United States | 99.7% of all establishments<br>40% of total economic activity output<br>50% of employment<br>31% of exports |
| *Asia and Pacific* | |
| China | 99% of all establishments<br>60% of gross industrial output<br>73% of employment<br>40% to 60% of exports |
| India | 95% of all industrial establishments<br>40% of industrial output<br>80% of industrial sector employment<br>35% of exports |
| Japan | 99% of all establishments<br>52% of output<br>72% of employment<br>15% of exports |
| Malaysia | 92% of all establishments<br>15% of output<br>18% of employment<br>15% of exports |
| Republic of Korea | 90% of all establishments<br>47% of gross output<br>71% of employment<br>40% of exports |
| Singapore | 97% of all establishments<br>41% of output<br>58% of employment<br>16% of exports |
| Taiwan | 97% of all establishments<br>81% of output |

*(continued)*

Table 2. Contribution of SMEs across Diverse Economies (*continued*)

| *Country* | *Share* |
| --- | --- |
| | 79% of employment<br>48% of exports |
| *Western Asia* | |
| Egypt | 90% establishments<br>9% of manufacturing output<br>11% of employment |
| Jordan | 93% of all establishments<br>41% of employment |
| *Africa* | |
| Ghana | 91% of total enterprises<br>16% of employment<br>6% of the gross domestic product (GDP) |
| Nigeria | 97% of total enterprises<br>50% of industrial output<br>50% of employment |
| *Latin America and the Caribbean* | |
| Argentina | 35% of output<br>45% of employment |
| Brazil | 92% of all establishments<br>61% of output<br>67% of employment |
| Mexico | 90% of all establishments<br>31% of output<br>45% of employment |
| Trinidad & Tobago | 96% of all establishments<br>40% of output<br>58% of employment |
| Uruguay | 71% of all establishments<br>23% of output<br>57% of employment |

For most SMEs, numerous challenges bedevil their day-to-day operations and the implementation of their business strategies. In this era of globalization and the internationalization of markets, many SMEs have new opportunities, but at the same time, most of them also face a new environment that has brought new challenges, both at the policy level and at the operational level, as they face new investors, new customers and new competitors. In this highly competitive environment, the real strength of a successful SME lies in its ability to access and effectively use new or original knowledge to remain ahead of the competition. As such, to survive and grow, SMEs concerned with quality production must continuously benchmark their performance vis-à-vis their real and potential competitors. Therefore, they put a huge emphasis on continuously scanning the external environment for discerning new benchmarks, be it in financial performance or quality and/or delivery of the product/service. Quality per se is no longer a competitive edge, as quality is expected almost routinely of a good SME on a consistent basis. Continuous improvement in a hyper-competitive environment seems to be the only way for an SME to evolve and grow. Continuous improvement in delivery performance implies a need for greater flexibility coupled with total reliability.

### 6.3 Hurdles Faced by SMEs

SMEs may face several hurdles. Some of these may be due to external obstacles. These may include limited access to financing, or sometimes, a lack of qualified human resources. High levels of regulations and red tape, bureaucracy, taxation and rigidities of the labour market can deny SMEs access to internal markets. Lack of a well-coordinated approach across all government departments with areas directly affecting SMEs can hurt them. Special types of public-private partnerships are important. Lack of well-designed, efficient information, networking, partnership or benchmarking services can also affect SMEs.

Additionally, there are internal obstacles in the SMEs. These could be cultural, with resistance to structural change, lack of understanding of IP protection, lack of qualified human resources as well as low levels of trust in public services and programmes for SMEs. What is most important is access to innovation, particularly in the area of technology.

International partnering, networking and clustering within localities are some of the best ways to build and sustain the kind of competitiveness that SMEs need to survive and grow in a globalizing economy.

### 6.4 Creating IP Culture in SMEs

In this changed scenario, governments face numerous challenges to create a conducive environment for SMEs to operate with confidence. The continued good health of the SME sector in national economies is vital and cannot be overstressed, as SMEs account for a very large percentage of employment in the industrial sector: generally from 40% to 60% of industrial production and from 15% to 50% of direct exports of most countries worldwide. Governments that have followed a holistic approach to the needs and concerns of national SMEs have fared comparatively better than others. Due to the increasing role of knowledge and technology in improving competitiveness, more and more governments are encouraging and facilitating SMEs to make effective use of the IP system to improve their competitiveness in the domestic and global marketplace. The IP system provides the mechanism to prevent those who do not have the rights to protected new or original knowledge and technology from using them without prior authorization of its owner(s), thereby preventing 'free-riding'. More importantly, the IP system provides the basis for greater security in developing trustworthy business and customer relationships of all kinds, including the provision of documentary evidence needed for the resolution of disputes in a fair and transparent manner, based on the rule of law.

Adequate protection of an SME's IP is a crucial step in turning ideas into business assets with real market value. It also helps in the enterprise's business development and competitive strategy: from product development to product design, from service delivery to marketing and from raising financial resources to exporting or expanding the business abroad through licensing or franchising. It helps in acquisition and exploitation of technological innovations by preventing competitors from imitating any product. It further helps them to obtain access to new markets, enhance access to finance and acquisition of venture capital, enhance the enterprise's market value, avoid wasteful investment in R&D and marketing, and create corporate identity.

Additionally, the urgency of providing IP-related support to SMEs to remain viable comes into sharper focus when it is noted that in highly competitive markets, as product lifecycles are continuing to shorten, the importance of promoting innovative and creative activities and technological development amongst SMEs is the key to generating new or original knowledge.

Intellectual Property Rights (IPRs) can play a major role in the following areas for increasing the competitiveness of SMEs:[3]

- acquisition and exploitation of technological innovations;
- preventing competitors from copying or closely imitating a company's products;
- obtaining access to new markets;
- acquiring venture capital and enhancing access to financing;
- enhancing the market value of the company;
- avoiding wasteful investment in R&D and marketing; and
- creating a corporate identity.

The needs and concerns of SMEs are different in different countries. For example, SMEs in many countries vary from rural-based small units to independent enterprises producing goods for specific markets. They also comprise specialized companies producing specific specialized end products. Most of the smaller enterprises rely on low-cost raw materials and also on comparatively lower-cost labour. Those in the rural areas are labour-intensive units using comparatively low-level technologies. High-tech start-up companies employ very highly educated and skilled professionals and technicians in emerging sectors of the economy such as software, biotechnology and advanced materials, and are often linked to publicly funded R&D institutions, science parks and business incubators.

It is clear that given the heterogeneous nature of the SME sector, the development of policy measures and implementation of practical interventions will have to be customized according to the needs and concerns of specific SMEs. In most countries, a relatively

---

[3]    <www.wipo.int/about-ip/en/studies/publications/ip_smes.htm>.

smaller percentage of the total SMEs is actually export-oriented and/or high-tech, while the vast majority of SMEs is barely able to compete in the marketplace. The performance of SMEs, especially of those in the high-growth, high-tech and/or high-export categories, can be further improved through proper and effective use of the IP system. However, most studies undertaken, be they in developed or in developing countries, show that SMEs in general are not well-informed about the potential benefits of using IP assets in their business strategy.

It is, therefore, crucial for policy-makers worldwide to adopt and implement customized measures to help the SMEs play a dynamic role in promoting and sustaining economic growth.

## 6.5 POLICY INTERVENTIONS BY GOVERNMENTS

Governments should, as a deliberate policy, assist SMEs by simplifying regulations and procedures for them by facilitating their access to credit, new technologies, markets and training.

The main challenges for policy-makers are as follows:

- that international SMEs remain competitive;
- that at-risk SMEs should be assisted to adapt, and wherever possible, to become inter-nationally competitive;
- that they resist pressures from insulated SMEs for protection and, where appropriate, assist these SMEs to adjust to increased international competitiveness.

For reaping the real economic benefits of IP, industry associations should also pay attention to the use of the IP system by SMEs. While the big industries usually have fairly high levels of knowledge and expertise concerning the protection of inventions through trade secrets or patents as well as the role of trademarks and industrial designs, it is the SMEs that need to be apprised and helped in this regard.

Governments in a number of countries, both developed and developing, as well as those in transition, have been assisting SMEs in their respective countries in making effective use of the IP system. This will develop their competitiveness both in national and international trade.

To take just a few examples from across the globe, in Nigeria, the National Office for Technology Acquisition and Promotion[4] (NOTAP), an agency under the Federal Ministry of Science and Technology, has undertaken some initiatives aimed at assisting national SMEs to use IP through the Patent Information and Documentation Centre (PIDC), established in NOTAP with the assistance of World Intellectual Property Organization (WIPO). As in many other countries, SMEs in Nigeria constitute the majority of enterprises and are considered to be the engine of growth. NOTAP has been promoting an awareness-building program whereby technological information in patent documents is used to sensitize

---

[4]    <www.notap.gov.ng/>.

entrepreneurs and enterprises on the usefulness of such information as a catalyst for wealth creation and as an innovative instrument for supporting SME development and growth.

NOTAP is also disseminating technical information in patent documents among researchers, inventors, innovators and students with a view to improving the quality of R&D, and to encourage greater inventive and innovative activities. NOTAP assists inventors and researchers in SMEs, inter alia, in patenting their inventions and innovations through assistance in drafting of patent applications; assisting SMEs to avoid unauthorized use of protected IPRs which could make them liable for infringement action; and helping SMEs to upgrade their products and processes through the use of new technology and the identification of possible licensors. Apart from these services, NOTAP also provides technology advisory and extension services to SMEs, through research institution-industry linkage programmes.

In the Republic of Korea, the Korean Intellectual Property Office[5] (KIPO) and the Korean Patent Attorneys Association (KPAA) have, through a business cooperation agreement entered into in December 2000, initiated a programme that provides SMEs with free patent management services, from pre-filing to registration. Currently, several patent agents throughout the country are providing free consultation services to SMEs. KIPO also provided additional fee reductions for SMEs from January 2001 until 2005 as per the government's Fee Regulation approved on 23 December 2000, in order to encourage IP creation and acquisition activities. Since September 1999, KIPO has carried out SMEs IPR Acquisition Campaign, in cooperation with the Korean Chamber of Commerce. The purpose is to raise IPR awareness and to encourage IPR acquisition among small- and medium-sized enterprises (SMEs).

Similarly, in Singapore, measures to facilitate the use of the IP system by SMEs include the provision by the Patent Application Fund[6] (PAF) of financial assistance for covering part of the costs of patent applications, including drafting, legal and filing costs. Its aim is to encourage SMEs in Singapore to apply formally for the protection of IPRs. The PAF was established in 1992 by the Singapore National Science and Technology Board (NSTB) and is administered by the IP Office. The fund supports 50% of the legal, official and other related fees incurred in the process of applying for a patent, up to a maximum of 30,000 Singapore dollars (SGD) for each invention. The PAF is believed to have contributed significantly to the increase in patenting activity by financially assisting companies and independent inventors to seek patent protection for their inventions.

In India, the small-scale industry sector's output contributes almost 40% of the gross industrial value-added and 45% of the total overall exports (direct as well as indirect exports) and is the second largest employer of human resources after agriculture, employing around 20 million persons. The development of the small-scale sector has therefore been assigned an important role in India's national plans. The Small Industries Development Organisation (SIDO) is the national SME development agency and works as part of

---

[5]  <www.kipo.go.kr/kpo2/ek/?catmenu=KIPOENG>.

[6]  <www.edb.gov.sg/edb/sg/en_uk/index/our_services/for_individuals/patent_appication.html>.

the Ministry of Small Scale Industries of the Government of India.[7] Set up in 1954, SIDO provides services to small industries through entrepreneurship development and through testing centres, R&D, consultancy, etc. Its strength lies in its reach of almost one hundred offices and more than 2,500 mostly technical staff. It networks with SME intermediaries and state governments. A series of sensitization workshops was organized in different parts of the country, each of which included a lecture on patents and one on e-commerce to alert the industry on the shape of things to come. These workshops have yielded encouraging results. Apart from spreading awareness, they have helped to highlight instances of SME success stories in the exploitation of the IP system.

In its annual convention in 2002, a detailed presentation on IPRs was scheduled in order to sensitize top decision-makers. SIDO is now working with WIPO on customizing guidelines on trademarks and industrial designs from an Indian perspective. On the anvil are training workshops, so that in each of its offices SIDO is able to position at least one officer who is IP savvy.[8]

While most institutional support services and some incentives are provided by the central government, others are offered by state governments in varying degrees, to attract investments and to promote small industries with a view to enhancing industrial production and generating employment in their respective states.

Amongst Latin American countries, for example in Mexico, the Mexican Industrial Property Institute[9] (IMPI) established, in the year 2000, has regional offices to promote the use of IP by SMEs and researchers throughout the country. This decentralized mode of operations has helped to increase considerably the number of applications for patents, trademarks and industrial designs by Mexican enterprises, inventors and researchers.

Likewise in Peru, the National Institute for the Defence of Competition and Intellectual Property[10] (INDECOPI) has played an important part in the promotion of the use of distinctive signs (especially collective marks and appellations of origin) by groups of SMEs through training and also by publicizing the various mechanisms for the registration and promotion of IP.

In this connection the SME assistance service goes beyond guidance on the registration of distinctive signs; it also guides and assists in organizing the system and writing the rules of use for the distinctive signs. The inclusion of collective marks in corporate strategy has not only made it possible for smaller entrepreneurs to reduce their costs, but has also lent them greater competitiveness in the market. With this, the SMEs have been able to protect their goods at lesser cost, taking advantage of economies of scale and at the same time increasing client confidence.

---

[7]  <www.smallindustryindia.com/sido/sido.htm>.
[8]  <www.laghu-udyog.com/ssiindia//statistics/ssidata.htm>; <http:smallindustryindia.com/ssiindia/statistics/economic.htm>.

   Also 'Best Practices for Assisting SMEs to Use IP System, Ministry of Small Scale Industries, Government of India: <www.wipo.int/sme/en/best_practices/india.htm>.
[9]  <www.impi.gob.mx/>.
[10]  <www.indecopi.gob.pe/quienes-somos-ing.jsp>.

Similarly, the Cuban Industrial Property Office, through its Specialized Service for the Entrepreneurial Sector (or SESE, in its Spanish acronym), offers a series of information and advisory services on IP to SMEs. Within the framework of the SESE, the Department of Information of the Cuban Industrial Property Office acts as a link between the private sector and the technical areas of the IP Office. Services are customized to the needs of each enterprise and are accessible to all SMEs that express an interest in participating. The SESE includes assessment of the IP needs of the enterprise; state-of-the-art searches; training and advice on IP; and proposals and advice on the selection of trademarks and trade names, as well as trademark searches. The aims of the service are to promote technological innovation; refocus technology management on the basis of global trends; find out about threats, weaknesses, strengths and opportunities relating to the competitive context within which the enterprise operates; contribute to enhancing the corporate image of the enterprise; and redesign commercial and marketing strategies of the said firm.

Again, insofar as SMEs in the countries in transition are concerned, IP legislations have been modernized and WIPO has been assisting in institution building as well as in reaching out to a broad range of users of the IP system, in particular the SMEs. In this respect, WIPO seeks to work in partnership with institutions that are providing support to SMEs in order to include an IP component in their services. IP services to SMEs may range from the provision of information on state-of-the-art technologies to providing details on suppliers of technologies, based on the information available through patent documents.

One example of assistance to SMEs in developed countries is Austria's Innovation Agency, a public sector entity in charge of promoting the development of innovative companies and the commercialization of new technologies. Its main focus is on providing services to innovative enterprises and academic researchers to facilitate the establishment and development of technology start-up firms including SMEs. The Innovation Agency channels its services through five main programs, i.e., Technology Marketing Austria (Tecma); Seed Financing Scheme; Network for Market and Technology Information (Tecnet); the Business Angels Network; and the Impulse Programme Biotechnology.

Similarly, IP Australia has taken an active role in raising awareness and educating SMEs about the importance of the IP system. Its main activities in this area include reader-friendly publications; easy-to-use multi-media products; preparation of SME case studies; practical information on websites; and seminars for SMEs.

The Canadian Intellectual Property Office[11] (CIPO) fosters the use of the IP system and the exploitation of IP information and encourages invention, innovation and creativity in Canada. CIPO's outreach programme is targeted at Canadian SMEs, innovators and creators. It is intended to promote awareness of IP and encourage citizens and businesses to use, or make a more effective use of, the IP system to stimulate innovation and provide a competitive advantage in the marketplace.

In order to encourage the Danish SMEs to make use of the IP system, the Danish Patent and Trademark Office[12] (DKPTO) has embarked on a two-track approach. The first

---

[11] <www.cipo.ic.gc.ca/epic/site/cipointernet-internetopic.nsf/en/Home>.
[12] <http://int.dkpto.dk/>.

approach is to take domestic measures focused on supporting SMEs to overcome the challenges related to effective use of the IP system. The second approach is to initiate, through the government and within the framework of the European Commission and the European Patent Organisation, measures on the European level aimed at encouraging SMEs to use the IP system. The DKPTO has established a call centre with the objective of handling IP-related inquiries from SMEs. It provides library services and has launched a communication concept – profitgate – with the aim of disseminating strategic IP knowledge to SMEs.

In Finland, the Foundation for Finnish Inventions supports and promotes the development and exploitation of Finnish inventions. Legal advice and financial support for patenting inventions is an important part of the activities of the Foundation, which also provides advice and support for private inventors as well as researchers and SMEs in Finland. The activities of the Foundation include: promotion of inventive activities; evaluation of inventions; advisory services; financing of protection of inventions; financing of product development; and financing of marketing.

Likewise, in Germany the INSTI Project[13] was established in 1995 by the German Federal Ministry of Education and Research (BMBF), with the aim of creating an environment for inventors and innovations in Germany and to improve the transfer of R&D results into marketable products. INSTI provides assistance to SMEs, inventors and scientists on:

(a) patent information or training in using patent databases;
(b) information about the patent system;
(c) trademarks;
(d) the cost of patents;
(e) the possibilities of using legal protection for new products;
(f) practical aspects of innovations;
(g) launching new products nationally or internationally;
(h) establishing new business contacts;
(i) the exchange of experience; and
(j) financing, licensing or acquiring services of a renowned patent attorney.

The INSTI project has six special support programs of which the relevant ones for SMEs are the INSTI SME Patent Action, which offers financial support to SMEs that apply for the first time for a patent or utility model protection or have not filed for one in the five years prior to application; INSTI-Innovation Market, which enables SMEs to make use of their on-line database on new technologies, products and product ideas, and INSTI Innovation Training, to help increase innovative activity in Germany through enhancing the awareness of inventors and the business community in the field of innovation.

Similarly, in Ireland, support on IP to inventors and SMEs has been provided through the Intellectual Property Assistance Scheme since 1998. The main activities of the scheme are

---

[13]   <www.wipo.int/sme/en/best_practices/germany.htm>.

providing advice on the protection of inventions, funding patent applications and advising on the development and commercialization of inventions.

## 6.6 IP STRATEGY FOR SMEs

Before an SME can take advantage of IP assets, it has to acquire IP rights. A number of IP rights need to be granted or registered. Patent or trademark rights are not worth much unless they are adequately exploited. The IP strategy of an SME should at least consider the policies on acquisition, exploitation, monitoring and enforcement of IP.

IP audits are essential to ensure a better position for SMEs to capitalize on the potential benefits of their IP assets. IP audits provide complete information about the SME to its owner that is helpful in a number of ways.

To become competitive, SMEs must improve the quality of their products and services. To do so, they should be encouraged to use the latest technologies and follow improved management practices. In addition, SMEs should be enabled to use the IP system as a tool for their technological development and marketing strategy. SMEs need to be helped to strengthen themselves to face global competition, as their failure could cause widespread unemployment and aggravation of poverty, especially in developing countries. But even with the availability of the best idea or product and a stable network of support, an SME needs a solid, long-range plan in place before it can hope to succeed. Without such a plan, an entrepreneur or SME cannot meet unexpected contingencies and will almost certainly not have the necessary documentation needed to secure financing. So preparing a business strategy and plan is a key step. And integrating the IP strategy and plan into the business strategy and plan is something that must be emphasized at the outset.

The IP strategy of SMEs should take a holistic approach to the different types of IP assets. For SMEs, acquiring technology from the outside is perhaps more important than generating their own technology. Creating an IP culture in an SME is the first step, which begins by creating and implementing an action plan for protecting its business secrets that give it an edge over its competitors. It is important that the immense value of technical, business and legal information contained in patent documents be appreciated since access to and proper use of patent information has great potential benefits for an SME.

Given the vast number of SMEs and their heterogeneous character, there is a need to use multiple agencies and institutions to create such awareness. This requires various types of partnerships between public sector and private institutions that are working to improve the performance of the SMEs. Lack of adequate information or misinformation often results in SMEs developing perceptions of high costs involved in obtaining and enforcing IPRs, and that the system is time-consuming and complex, thereby discouraging its use. The basic message of IP must relate to the core concerns of SMEs; otherwise, it will not be perceived to be relevant. Hence, development of a policy framework for creating widespread awareness about the value of the IP system in enhancing the competitiveness of the SMEs has to be encouraged in the public sector, private sector and civil society.

For an SME to become and remain better than its present and potential competitors, use of new or original knowledge or/and creative expression of ideas is required. There is need for ensuring the use of better technological inputs promoting quality and developing for-ward-looking business plans and strategies. These steps will enable the sector to emerge as a vibrant constituent of growing national economies. By introducing the latest and newest technologies, SMEs could play a critical role in economic growth and help promote natural competitiveness through the use of the IP system in responding to consumer demands for better-quality products and services.

Technologies have become an important asset, especially for SMEs to strengthen not only their export competitiveness but also their domestic efficiency in the context of an increas-ingly open and competitive global economy. This will also provide SMEs with opportunities for attracting investment and enhancing exports. At the same time, SMEs must be able to communicate the message of consistent high quality production to their users in order to promote consumer loyalty.

In other words, an SME must be able to effectively market its products/ services. This invariably requires the creation of one or more trademarks in addition to a distinctive business name. Often, the trademark may pertain to an association of SMEs, that is, it may be a collective mark or the SMEs may benefit from a certification mark which requires that the SME's product or service conforms to prescribed standards which must be duly certified to have been met before the SME may use such a certification mark in advertising and marketing.

In hyper-competitive environments, successful enterprises, big or small, rely largely on knowledge assets. As a result, the market value and/or market capitalization of such enterprises is largely linked to their knowledge assets which are protected by using the IP system. Thus, to make new or improved quality products and effectively communicate with customers and consumers, SME managements would need to encourage their employ-ees and technocrats towards knowledge-based inventive activity to ensure necessary industrial diversification.

The IP system helps an owner of useful new knowledge to identify, record, measure, value and manage such knowledge assets for competitiveness of the enterprise and for constantly bringing forth new and better products in the marketplace. A new product may target an existing market or a new market. A new market may be an adaptation of an existing product or a radically new product that substitutes existing products or creates a new market. In either case, it is necessary to identify and protect all the IP assets of the SMEs concerned.

In the United Kingdom, a study[14] of SMEs in four sectors – computer services, design, electronics and mechanical engineering – undertaken for finding out whether SMEs possess IP and if so, whether they attempt to protect it or not, concluded that overall, small business owners placed greater emphasis on informal methods to protect IP. These methods were found to be more familiar, cheaper, less time-consuming and fre-quently as effective as the more formal rights. Under most circumstances, SME owners considered formal registrable rights such as patents less important. Even business owners

---

[14]    John Kitching and Robert Blackburn, 'Intellectual Property Management in the Small and Medium Enter-prises (SME)', *Journal of Small Business and Enterprises Development* 5, no. 4 (1998): 327-335.

Table 3. Adoption of Formal IP Right by Enterprises Size (%)[15]

|  | Micro-enterprises | SMEs | All enterprises |
|---|---|---|---|
| Any formal rights | 82.2 | 90.5 | 86.2 |
| Registrable rights | 43.8 | 61.6 | 52.5 |
| Trade or service marks | 28.8 | 51.8 | 39.8 |
| Registered designs | 17.1 | 31.4 | 23.9 |
| Patents | 17.1 | 29.9 | 23.6 |
| Other formal methods | 2.7 | 1.5 | 2.1 |

having formal rights generally avoided entering into legal battles against the infringers. Table 3 provides data on specific protection practices used by different business owners. It indicates that the formal IPRs were not equally important to all business owners and large differences were found in their reported use.

The figures quoted in Table 3 only indicate whether specific protection practices were used or not. They do not reflect the intensity with which the individual firms used the particular methods. Adoption of formal rights is dependent on the anticipated value of an innovation, owner's perceptions of the relative efficacy of formal and informal protection practices and the availability of, and willingness to use, resources for the acquisition and enforcement of formal rights. For example, a cheaper form of protection, i.e., prominent copyright notices, were widely used to assert ownership of the material. However, as regards the acquisition of registrable rights, the business owners were highly selective and acquired those rights only where the potential benefits outweighed the potential costs.

The under-utilization of the IP system by SMEs might be due to ignorance about IPRs and their benefits. It may also be due to the lack of confidence that their products are sufficiently innovative to merit IP protection. However, there are several ways in which SMEs operating in low-tech sectors may benefit from patent protection. For example, for adaptations to existing products or less significant innovations, primarily in the manufacturing industries, some sixty countries worldwide, including around thirty developing countries, offer 'utility model' protection, also referred to as 'utility certificates' or innovation patents.

Grasping the strategic business relevance of the modern IP system, and making effective business use of IP assets, are the keys to making an SME globally competitive and increasing its market value. Most SMEs lack information about whom to contact for in-depth advice in matters concerning acquisition of IP rights and IP assets management. SMEs should be made fully aware of the importance of capacity building, protecting and using IP

---

[15]    (1) SIDBI Report on SSI Sector 2000 (<www.sidbi.in/>), also (2) *Handbook on Foreign Direct Investment by Small & Medium Sized Enterprises: Lessons from Asia.* UNCTAD, Geneva, 1998.

assets for the benefit of their enterprise. For example, the owner and/or manager of an SME must be made aware of the necessity for developing and deploying an IP plan and strategy as part of its business strategy. It is essential to instil in the management of SMEs the feeling that they not only require an in-depth comprehension of different categories of IPRs and assets but also that they must learn to use these assets to strategically target commercially valued markets for their products and services.

SME support institutions, be they in the government, private sector or civil society, will therefore have to devote attention to development and training of IP professionals. This is so both in regular teaching and training programmes in universities and in specialized SME training institutions to help SMEs with every facet of the business plan. This would invariably require the assistance of qualified IP professionals.

Improved IP asset management by SMEs essentially means that SMEs consciously plan and strive to get the best results out of their IP assets in line with their business objectives. Identification of IP assets is the first step, followed by protection and effective management of IP assets. SMEs should also learn to use the IP system, especially the technical information disclosed in patent documents, for obtaining competitive intelligence on the business strategies of their competitors. Further, they need to learn to use the IP system for developing advertising and marketing proficiencies; for licensing, subcontracting, franchising; pinpointing deficiencies, if any, in their licensing relationships; and determining any further opportunities in respect to their own technology development that could help create new products and services and increase marketing possibilities. In other words, all key business activities may benefit from proper IP asset management.

SMEs not only need access to markets but also suitable network partners and joint ventures, management skills and credit guarantees. Many SMEs have integral links with foreign firms or with national exporting firms. These need technology transfer for quality improvement, skilled staff, industrial planning and inter- and intra-firm trade. Some SMEs manufacture for international trading activity. In each of these areas, the IP system has a beneficial role to play.

While protecting its inventions, an export-oriented SME should secure protection for the inventions concerned in all countries that are likely to be significant for its particular product. At present, patent protection can be obtained in more than 164 countries. While national filing costs of a patent are generally nominal, multiple foreign filings may be very expensive as costs increase on account of factors including translation charges and foreign agents' fees. It is, therefore, advisable to decide on foreign filing only after considering the likely demand, licensing possibilities and enforcement difficulties. But this decision should be made as early as possible so that the SME is able to take full advantage of the possibilities offered by the Patent Cooperative Treaty (PCT). This would enable the use of a single application to target some 138 countries which were members of the PCT as of 2007. For a relatively small fee for using the PCT, SMEs in all of the member countries can simplify the filing of a patent application. This can defer a lot of costs associated with multiple national filing of patent applications by over eighteen months, over and above the twelve months available for international filing under the Paris Convention for the Protection of Industrial Property.

Thus, making technocrats and staff of SMEs aware and informed of the costs and benefits of the use of the IP system, and through it, protection of new and original ideas, is essential for reaping the benefits of improved product quality in an increasingly competitive marketplace of the knowledge-driven global economy.

Such awareness promotion would also help SMEs to overcome many of the challenges in comparison with larger business firms and industries which generally have much better financial resources and technical knowledge.

### 6.7 ROLE OF INTERMEDIARIES FOR SMEs

SMEs play a key role in world economies. Globalization offers opportunities as well as threats to SME competitiveness; in particular, it widens the innovation and technology gap between countries. In order to bridge this gap, better access to financing, information and services that facilitate the innovation process has to be provided to SMEs through intermediaries. Value addition by enhancing SME competitiveness can be created by fostering the networking and integration of intermediaries as well as extending their networks at international and regional levels.

An intermediary can do a particularly good job of disseminating innovation and technology to its SME clients. Steinbeis-Stiftung from Germany is a good example of this. It aims at promoting and facilitating technology transfer from research centres and universities to the society and the business community, especially among small- and medium-sized companies, through different tools and interventions. This intermediary is very market oriented, is completely self-sustainable and works as a global player in the field of technology transfer. It provides services and consultancy in all technology areas and industrial sectors worldwide, through a network of partners in forty countries, including more than 500 centres and enterprises. About 4,000 professionals are involved. They combine research and technology transfer activities and are very strongly connected with universities and enterprises. They have developed a good internationalization strategy as well.

### 6.8 FOSTERING COOPERATION AMONG SMEs

At the same time, it is important that linkages are encouraged and strengthened between SMEs, R&D institutions as well as universities and the government institutions supporting the development of the SME sector. These linkages will help SMEs in becoming immediate end users of such institutional research in their respective production fields. At the same time, SMEs should be encouraged to plough greater funding into their own R&D activities so as to constantly improve their products and services to compete in an ever-changing, dynamic and increasingly competitive marketplace. Clustering is an important tool for SMEs to compensate for their material, technological and various other disadvantages. An important motive for SMEs to cluster and cooperate with large firms is for the sake of achieving economies of scale. Cooperation in the field of innovation is advantageous for participating firms. Today, clustering has become strategically important for the mainte-nance and enhancement of a small firm's competitiveness.

Creation of practical national guides for teaching and training entrepreneurs is another area that requires special attention. These should focus, amongst other things, on the practical problems faced by enterprises and on the contribution that the IP system can make in accessing new technologies, financing, markets, etc. These practical guides should present the IP system to the SMEs from the perspective of their day-to-day problems in order to help them substantially in improving their performance in the marketplace.

It might also be useful to gradually make available countrywide the teaching of, and training in, the use of the IP system. This can be done in the framework of a wider package of inputs provided by SME support institutions so as to emphasize the importance of the synergy in adopting a holistic and integrated approach in delivering SME support services.

In the national programmes on IP for SMEs, priority should be given to development of high-technology sectors. These could be, for instance, sectors such as information and communications technology, biotechnology, micro-technology and nanotechnology. Other high-growth sectors include the services sector and, most notably, the high-growth cultural industry sector as well as export orientation and agri-based sectors. These should be specifically targeted, depending on the policy priorities of the country concerned.

It would also be advisable for national ministries to systematically assess the true IP-related demands and needs of the SMEs. This could be achieved by undertaking in-depth studies, on a periodic but regular basis, of the challenges faced by the SMEs in their access to, and use of, the IP system. This is an important task and should be initiated in a systematic manner and continued on a regular basis. Without a time-series analysis and benchmark of the true state of affairs, it would not be possible to evaluate and measure progress in helping SMEs to use the IP system in order to improve their business performance. This analysis should be done on a sectoral basis in view of the heterogeneity of SMEs of different sectors. Apart from govern-mental initiatives at supra-national, national, regional, local and municipal levels, a number of initiatives by non-governmental and civil society organizations are noteworthy.

### 6.8.1 International Cooperation among SMEs

International cooperation in the SME sector in each of the G-15 countries has been growing steadily. The small-scale industry training institutions have already been working on improving the human resource development skills of the SME sector with various countries. For improving access to information, India offered to set up an interactive portal for trade, technology and investment information for use by G-15 members.

SMEs in developing countries need to cooperate with each other and set up joint projects in order to achieve excellence and to increase their share in world trade following the Uruguay Round. South-south cooperation was needed to expand trade among developing countries. The possibility of exploiting e-commerce as a means of enhancing competitive-ness also needs to be explored.

The Asia-Africa Investment and Technology Promotion Centre had been established to enhance business cooperation between Asian and African countries. The role of the Centre was to provide business information, assessment (identification, formulation and assessment of business opportunities), promotion and consulting services.

For example, the World Association of Small and Medium Enterprises[16] (WASME), which has members and associates in 112 countries, plays an important role in encouraging dialogue and cooperation amongst the private sector SME support institutions. WASME has its international headquarters in Noida near New Delhi, India. Its activities include promoting enterprise cooperation amongst small- and medium-sized businesses. This is done with a view to promoting joint ventures, business cooperation and technology transfers and enhancing market access. In response to specific requests received by WASME, a search process is initiated for locating suitable partners by utilizing WASME's network of partners, members and associates apart from relevant SME focal points in most countries.

Over recent years, WASME has organized more than a dozen international conferences in Europe, the Russian Federation, the US, Africa and Asia, including China and India. It regularly receives and disseminates information to its members on training programmers organized by institutions in various developed and developing countries for training entrepreneurs and SME personnel. WASME has also conducted several training programmes for SME entrepreneurs with particular emphasis on training women. The Economic Division of the said organization publishes research studies on various issues relating to SMEs including, among others, government policy formulation, international trade regimes, small businesses and sustainable development, and economic linkages of SMEs with the rest of the economy. Its bimonthly newsmagazine, which is circulated to members and associates in 112 countries, contains the latest information on SME matters and, directly or indirectly, targets some 2 million SMEs worldwide.

WASME also seeks to increasingly strengthen its cooperation with WIPO in spreading awareness amongst SMEs on the need to use the IP system for improving the competitiveness of their products and services. It has been distributing the WIPO'S CD-ROM on IP for SMEs to its member associates and at its conferences. WASME feels that a majority of SMEs need assistance and support for making use of the IPR system in solving day-to-day problems. For this, it works in close cooperation with WIPO and also organizes workshops, seminars and training programmes for end users as well as policy-makers. In view of its worldwide reach, WASME envisions its role to function as a coordinating agency between national industry associations and WIPO.

WIPO has also taken a commendable initiative by including proposals on IP protection amongst SMEs in its agenda for discussion at its General Assembly of Member States held in Geneva in September/October 2000. This was done upon some government requests that WIPO should play a larger role in enhancing competitiveness of SMEs by promoting the use of IPRs by these enterprises.

Following a decision by its Member States, WIPO augmented its role by establishing, in October 2000, a division to deal with the needs of SMEs and to create a substantial new programme of activities focussing on IP-related needs of SMEs

---

[16]    <www.wasmeinfo.org/>.

worldwide. The overall objective is to enhance competitiveness of SMEs through effective use of the IP system. For this, the first step is to create awareness amongst SMEs for using the said system to make informed decisions to exploit their innovative and creative capacities. At the same time, it seeks to improve the policy framework and business environment so as to make it conducive and easy for SMEs to access and effectively use the IP system.

The intention of the organization was, and is, to make SMEs aware that IP adds value at each stage of the value chain from creative and innovative ideas to producing a new, better and cheaper product for the marketplace. Also, WIPO wanted to promote the concept that IP strategy should be an integral part of an SME's overall business strategy.

It proposes, through the establishment of a division devoted to SMEs, to target a new audience, establish new partnerships, create SME-friendly publications, provide relevant information and support outreach activities of national and industrial property offices and copyright administrations in assisting SMEs to improve their competitive capabilities. New partnerships would mean better contracts with national focal points for SMEs in governments, SME associations and chambers of commerce, business consultants, etc. This would promote use of the IP system in existing business development services of such institutions; in the training programmes for their entrepreneurs; and in programmes aimed at encouraging innovation and creativity.

WIPO has set up a comprehensive and very user-friendly website on IP for SMEs in six languages (English, French, Spanish, Arabic, Chinese and Russian). The SME Division intends to focus on the cultural industries as well as on the IP needs of SMEs in specific sectors such as biotechnology, agriculture, handicrafts, machine tools and software.

This SME Division also provides assistance to IP offices and SME support institutions to develop SME-targeted IP services. Conscious of the fact that in most countries the availability of the Internet is still limited, the SME Division has produced a CD-ROM based on the content available on its website. This CD-ROM is also available in six languages (English, French, Spanish, Arabic, Chinese and Russian).

It is indeed a timely initiative by a United Nations Specialized Agency to strengthen its programme of activities for the benefit of SMEs. In particular, it will:

– advise governments to take into account the specific needs of SMEs in their IP policies;
– disseminate information on best practices on the use of IP by SMEs and of their exploitation of technological knowledge through the valorization and commercialization of IPRs; and
– make access to technological information easier and perhaps cheaper for SMEs on a global basis.

While all forward-looking industries and businesses can, and do, benefit from IP protection, SMEs stand to gain substantially through use of the IP system. In WIPO's[17] brochure on SME it is very aptly emphasized and worth quoting that while new products, brands and

---

[17]    <www.wipo.int/export/sites/www/sme/en/documents/pdf/brochure.pdf>.

creative designs appear constantly in the markets and are the result of continuous human innovation and creativity, it is often the SMEs that are the driving force behind such innovations. However, their inventive and creative capacity is not always fully exploited as many SMEs are not aware of the protection that the IP system can provide for their inventions, creativity, brands and designs.

In order to urge SMEs worldwide to make more effective use of the IP system, within months of setting up of its SMEs Division, WIPO, in collaboration with the Italian government's Ministry of Industry and Foreign Trade, organized a forum on IP and SMEs. It took place in February 2001 in Milan – the city described by its mayor as Italy's capital of innovation. It was attended by some three hundred participants from all over the world. The forum was organized to discuss specific challenges for SMEs in today's knowledge-based economies and to foster innovative activity in, and promote market potential of, SMEs, as well as the role of the trademark, industrial design system and copyright sector.

The forum discussed, among other topics, the core issue of enhancing competitiveness of small- and medium-sized enterprises though optimal use of the IP system. It adopted a course of action known as 'The Milan Plan of Action'. Some of the important points that emerged, and which have a specific relationship with IP issues, are:

– SMEs play a vital role in employment creation, investment and exports and significantly contribute to national economic growth;
– SMEs are proven innovators with great creative capacity and are the driving force behind many technological advances;
– Through adequate and effective management, commercialization of IP, SMEs can significantly enhance their competitiveness, export opportunities, market share and overall market value;
– SMEs could and should significantly benefit from the wealth of technological information available in patent databases, thus avoiding duplication of R&D efforts and use such information for the development of new products, processes and services and for the execution of license agreements;
– SMEs should, (particularly in developing and least-developed countries) exploit the potential of the IP system for increasing their competitiveness, innovative capacity and market access.

Inadequate utilization of the IP system may be largely due to lack of information on how to acquire and manage IP assets and technological information in an effective manner. The absence or shortage of IP-related services in SME support institutions as well as the perception that the IP system is time-consuming and expensive, makes it difficult for SMEs to acquire, maintain, enforce and use their IP rights effectively in trade whether domestically or internationally.

The International Forum at Milan recommended that in order to empower SMEs to fully benefit from the IP system, the following actions should be undertaken:

– Strengthen interaction amongst SMEs, SME support institutions and associations, national governments and IP offices, WIPO and other relevant intergovernmental and non-governmental organizations with a view to better identifying the needs of SMEs and facilitating the implementations of customized targeted activities addressing the specific IP needs of each sector, group or cluster.

– Support national and international efforts for further integration of IP issues in programs and policy initiatives aimed at fostering the technological and innovative capacity and export potential of SMEs.

– Increase awareness and understanding of IP issues within the SME business community, particularly through awareness-raising campaigns and targeted training programs with the optimal use of modern information and communication technologies, so as to enhance the capacity of SMEs to maximize their benefits from the use of the IP system.

– Encourage the creation of and strengthen IP-related services, particularly legal and technological information services, within and without SME support institutions such as chambers of commerce and industry, business incubators and science parks.

– Seek advice from WIPO and other relevant intergovernmental, non-governmental organization (NGO) and IP offices on the inclusion of IP issues in the relevant curricula of universities and institutions for technical and higher education and strengthen their links amongst SMEs, universities and R&D institutions through appropriate mechanisms for achieving greater synergy in joint research and higher rates of successful commercialization of research results.

– Promote the use of arbitration, mediation and other alternative dispute resolution mechanisms for more cost-effective enforcement of IP rights.

– Assist IP offices and SME support institutions in the development of SME-targeted IP services, including legal advice and IP information services based on the use of IP databases.

– Support efforts by national structures to reduce the cost of acquisition, maintenance and enforcement of IP rights while maintaining quality and reliability of rights.

– Strengthen WIPO's programmes of activities for the benefit of SMEs, in particular to:
   – advise governments to take into account the specific needs of SMEs in their IP policies;
   – disseminate information on best practices on the use of IP by SMEs and of their exploitation of technological knowledge through the valorization and commercialization of IP rights; and
   – make access to technological knowledge easier and cheaper for SMEs on a global basis.[18]

---

[18] Milan Plan of Action adopted at the Milan Forum on Intellectual Property and Small- and Medium-Sized Enterprises WIPO and the Ministry of Industry and Foreign Trade, Government of Italy, Feb. 2001. WIPO document (WIPO/IP/MIL/01/5 ): <www.wipo.int/edocs/mdocs/sme/en/wipo_ip_mil_01/wipo_ip_mil_01_5-main1.pdf>.

Given the recent focus on IP issues of SMEs, it will take long and hard work by governments, SME support institutions and the private sector and civil society worldwide to convert the oblivious majority of non-users of the IP system amongst the SMEs and to make them pragmatic users of the system for their enhanced competitiveness, greater profitability and prolonged business success in the hyper-competitive national and international markets. This alone is the surest way to expand the benefits of economic progress and enhance competition in the marketplace for the benefit of one and all.

# CHAPTER SEVEN

# ENCOURAGING RESEARCH AND DEVELOPMENT

- *Research and Development (R&D), Innovation & Patents*
- *Publicly funded R&D and Innovation*
- *Small- and Medium-Sized Enterprises (SMEs) and R&D*

## 7.1 R&D, INNOVATION AND PATENTS

The competitiveness of a nation today largely depends on how it is able to create, organize and disseminate knowledge as well as convert knowledge into economic and social good. The creation of this new knowledge primarily takes place in industry, universities and national laboratories; the latter two are largely funded publicly. We will examine the issue of innovation in such publicly funded institutions.

It is an established fact that modern economic growth has been inspired by a rapid generation of new scientific knowledge and new technology. Possession of knowledge alone is not sufficient. It is innovation that creates new knowledge from existing knowledge and also new products and services. An invention provides a new solution to a technical problem. An innovation is the practical application of an invention. Richard Langlois[1] in his paper described the views given by Schumpeter, who had considered innovation as the engine of development. He described 'invention' as the discovery of new techniques and 'innovation' as the practical application of an invention in production for the market. Innovation, indeed, is the key to competitiveness. Intellectual Property Rights (IPRs) play a crucial rule in fuelling technological innovation as well as creating a stream of revenues through which further innovation can be sustained.

The term 'innovation' in the context of developed countries is very often equated with the output of formal Research and Development (R&D). This is not the case with developing countries. Innovation, or 'incremental innovation' in the context of developing countries, results not only from R&D activities but also from a host of other technology activities such as the purchase of new vintages of capital goods or non-routine engineering. Innovation also takes place in informal systems.

Three discernible worldwide trends in industrial R&D are evident today. First, there is a high concentration of R&D activity in a few large companies. Secondly, there is the recent slowing down of investments in R&D worldwide. Thirdly, there is considerable globalization of R&D with a discerning trend of 'geography of science' shifting increasingly from

---

[1]  Richard N. Langlois, 'Schumpeter and the Obsolescence of the Entrepreneur', Paper presented at the History of Economics Society, Annual Meeting at Boston (1987): <http://langlois.uconn.edu/SCHUMPET.HTML>.

the US and Europe to Asia-Pacific.[2] Further as a consequence of the process of globalization of R&D, companies in the US and Europe are choosing to build R&D facilities where maximum value creation is possible.[3]

Innovation can be fostered actively through the instrument of Intellectual Property (IP) systems, mainly patents, in diverse ways:

– Patent licensing can lead to direct revenues.
– Patent information can be used as a strategic tool for:
– simulating technological changes within an enterprise;
– identifying as well comparatively evaluating technologies;
– monitoring global technological changes;
– avoiding infringement of existing patents;
– forecasting future technological developments and industrial cycles.

Patents can be used for protection of technological innovation, for creating a bargaining position as well as for building an image for an organization or an enterprise. Thus, patents are instruments of protection, bargaining and image building.

For protection:

– Proprietary product or process technology; and
– Creating retaliatory power against competitors.

For bargaining:

– Increasing the likelihood of selling licenses;
– Increasing the likelihood of accessing technology through cross-licensing;
– Facilitating R&D cooperation with others;
– Improving bargaining position in a standard-setting.

For image building:

– Improving the corporate image;
– Providing motivation for employees to invent;
– Benchmarking a firm's R&D productivity vis-à-vis those of its competitors.

## 7.2 GLOBALIZATION OF TECHNOLOGY: IMPACT OF TECHNOLOGY SPILLOVER FROM FDI

Let us examine the evidence of technology spillovers from foreign direct investment (FDI). Sunil Mani has provided a detailed discussion on this issue.[4] It is argued that when firms

---

2    R.A. Mashelkar, 'Indian Science, Technology, and Society: The changing landscape', *Technology in Society* 30 (2008): 299-308: <www.sciencedirect.com/science/journal/0160791X>.

3    Robert D. Atkinson 'The Globalisation of R&D & Innovation: How do Companies Choose Where to Build R&D Facilities': <www.itif.org/index.php?id=102>.

4    Sunil Mani, *Government, Innovation & Technology Policy*, (Cheltenham, UK: Edward Elgar Publishing, Dec. 2002).

establish affiliates abroad and become multinational, they are distinguishable from the already established firms in the host country for two reasons:

(1) they bring with them some amount of proprietary technology which constitutes their firm-specific advantage. This allows them to compete successfully with local firms that have superior knowledge of local markets, consumer preferences and business practices; and

(2) the entry of multinational companies' (MNC) affiliates disturbs the existing equilibrium in the market and forces local firms to take action to protect their market share and profits.

Both these changes cause various types of spillovers. These are also likely to lead to productivity increases in local firms.

One example of a spillover is the case where a local firm may improve its productivity by copying some technology used by MNC affiliates operating in the local market.

Another example is where the entry of an affiliate leads to more severe competition in the host economy, so that local firms are forced to use existing technology and resources more efficiently.

Competition may force local firms to search for new and more efficient technologies as the entry of a foreign affiliate may demonstrate the existence and profitability of new products and processes. This, in turn, may encourage local firms to adopt some of the new products and processes and these diffusion processes may even be repeated every time innovations are transferred.

In short, evidence of positive spillover from FDI from anywhere in the developing world is not easy to obtain. However, there are two developing countries, namely Singapore and Malaysia, which have benefited from FDI. Singapore has actually engineered spillovers from FDI by putting in place a host of target-oriented innovation and industrial policies such as the Local Industries Upgrading Programme. As a result, there has been a significant spurt in the number of local small- and medium-sized enterprises (SMEs). In a number of manufacturing industries, such as precision and transportation engineering and service industries, the R&D expenditure by local firms actually became higher in comparison to that of foreign firms.

For Malaysia, the impact of FDI was different. There was a spectacular expansion and structural changes in the composition of manufactured exports. Manufacturing in Malaysia is dominated today by a few industries, notably the electrical and electronic industries. This makes the economy vulnerable to global changes in demand. The industry dealing with electrical machinery, appliances and parts, in which foreign affiliates are prominent, is characterized by high import intensity. There is limited technology transfer and backward linkage. The share of value added is relatively low. It has even declined over the years. However, there are encouraging signs of foreign affiliates forging backward linkages and there are indications of technological deepening and upgrading. A principal constraint is the shortage of skilled manpower and substantial investments in R&D and this is the challenge facing the policy-makers in Malaysia.

## 7.3 ASYMMETRIES IN R&D

In 1998, the twenty-nine countries of the Organization of Economic Cooperation and Development (OECD) spent $520 billion on R&D – more than the combined output of thirty of the world's low-income group of developing countries. Also 91% of the 347,000 new patents issued in 1998 belonged to OECD countries, which represent just 19% of the world's population.[5] Some developing countries have greatly expanded the level of national resources that are devoted to civilian research efforts. The overall financial impact of their efforts is small, however, compared with those of the larger industrialized countries. For example, South Korea – a country that has made considerable strides in expanding its domestic R&D investment – spends about $7 billion annually, a figure equivalent to about 3% of the US total. The United States is the largest investor in industrial R&D.

Much of the world's industrial R&D expenditure is made by a few large MNCs. Among the various industrial sectors, the concentration of expenditure is highest in the automobile industry, followed by pharmaceuticals.

## 7.4 TECHNOLOGY DEVELOPMENT: ROLE OF GOVERNMENT

There is a renewed debate on the role of government with respect to technology development. In the industrialized world, industry invests in a major way in R&D. Should government, under such conditions, have any role at all? The best answer is provided by Stiglitz[6] (1998), who argued that:

Left to itself, the market under provides technology. Like investments in education, investments in technology cannot be used as collateral. Investments in R&D are also considerably riskier than other types of investment and there are much larger asymmetries of information that can impede the effective workings of the market. Technology also has enormous positive externalities that the market does not reward. Indeed, in some respects, knowledge is like a classical public good. The benefits to society of increased investment in technology far outweigh the benefits to individual entrepreneurs. As Thomas Jefferson said, ideas are like a candle, you can use them to light other candles without diminishing the original flame. Without government action, there will be too little investment in the production and adoption of new technology.

An important characteristic of R&D investment, distinguishing it from other types of investments, is that its output has the properties of public goods: non-excludable and non-rivalrous. It is now believed that if industrial R&D is left entirely to the market, then public good will be compromised.

---

[5]   Human Development Report (2001), UNDP: <http://hdr.undp.org/en/reports/global/hdr2001/>.

[6]   Joseph E. Stiglitz 'More Instruments and Broader Goals: Moving Toward the Post – Washington Consensus', The 1998 WIDER Annual Lecture (Helsinki, Finland): <www.ucm.es/info/eid/pb/Stiglitz98wider.pdf>.

## 7.4.1 Role of Fiscal Incentives in Technology Development

The financing of industrial R&D has been discussed repeatedly, especially with reference to the role of governments. There has been a significant slowdown in the financing of R&D by business enterprises, especially across the developed world. In addition, there have been significant reductions in the share of business enterprises R&D funded by governments. There has been little or no evidence of internationalization of corporate R&D, especially in the developing world.[7]

The 1990s witnessed another important event. Most developing countries across the world started reducing the role of their governments in most areas of economic activity. The opening up of the Indian economy in 1991 was one such example. Therefore, those instruments of innovation policy that imply the least amount of direction by governmental agencies or institutions need more attention.

The public innovation policies vary significantly across countries. Of the various policies, financial measures – among them tax incentives – have attracted much attention and analysis. Such tax incentives exist in one variant or another in both developed and developing countries. Another instrument of support is increasingly gaining in currency. Many governments provide direct grants for R&D, apart from providing tax incentives.

Tax incentives possess a number of attributes that policy-makers conceive as being useful during a phase of economic liberalization. The main attraction of the tax incentive system arises from the fact that it interferes less with the market mechanism.

Little is known about the efficacy of tax incentives to stimulate further investments in industrial R&D. Any type of subsidy is considered undesirable by governments. This is so for two reasons. First, governments are keen on cutting down their 'fiscal deficits'. Second, they wish to comply with the norms of the World Trade Organization (WTO) codes with respect to subsidies.

## 7.5 PUBLIC SUPPORT FOR R&D IN DEVELOPED COUNTRIES

Many leading OECD countries have recognized the importance of public funding for research and innovation. In the US, there is a widespread consensus on the value of increased support for publicly funded research. In 1999, the US Congress agreed to increase the support to publicly funded research by 5%. The US invested 10.4% of the science and technology (S&T) support fund in doing basic research that was largely done in universities. Subsequent US budgets have continued this pattern of support of university-based research. Canada, Japan, Finland, Denmark and Sweden have also increased their support for research in recent years. The mandates given to these public institutions in the developed and developing world have been, however, different. Whereas in the developed world public institutions have mainly done pre-competitive research and provided support for competitiveness of SMEs, in the developing world the focus has been on reverse engineering and social engineering. Distribution of government R&D budgets, in a few

---

[7] See fn. 4.

countries, as an example, based on selected socio-economic objectives (as a percentage of the total) is given below:

Table 4. Distribution of Government R&D Budgets

| Objective | India (1998) | US (1998) | Japan (1998) | Germany (1998) | France (1998) | UK (1998) | Russia (1998) |
|---|---|---|---|---|---|---|---|
| Advancement of knowledge | 4.9 | 6.0 | 49.5 | 54.7 | 40.3 | 32.1 | 15.2 |
| Agriculture, forestry and fishing | 21.2 | 2.1 | 3.5 | 2.6 | 3.0 | 4.5 | 5.2 |
| Space | 13.1 | 10.6 | 6.3 | 4.5 | 11.0 | 2.4 | 12.2 |
| Defense | 21.1 | 53.2 | 4.6 | 8.4 | 22.7 | 34.9 | 29.7 |
| Energy | 7.6 | 1.5 | 19.3 | 3.6 | 4.9 | 0.5 | 3.9 |
| Environmental protection | 3.3 | 0.7 | 0.7 | 3.5 | 1.6 | 2.6 | 1.8 |
| Health | 9.5 | 20.9 | 3.7 | 3.3 | 5.5 | 14.9 | 2.5 |
| Industrial development | 10.1 | 0.6 | 6.5 | 12.7 | 6.2 | 1.5 | 23.3 |
| Social development and services | 0.4 | 0.9 | 0.9 | 3.2 | 1.5 | 2.8 | 1.9 |
| Transport and telecommunications | 4.1 | 2.2 | 2.2 | 0.8 | N/A | 0.5 | N/A |

*Source*: National Science Foundation (NSF), US, 2002; Department of Science and Technology (DST), India, 2002

There is a clearly discernable change of emphasis between the developing and the developed countries.

In the United States, the federal government has encouraged and supported both basic and applied R&D over the years. Although the private sector has been an important source of innovation, it is increasingly felt that the federal government must encourage development, commercialization and use of technology. A major hallmark of the US technology policy since the 1980s is the existence of a number of key US partnership programmes between industry, government and the university system with the explicit aim of faster commercialization of innovations.

A report[8] by Fred Block & Mathew Keller entitled 'The Transformations in the US National Innovation System during the period 1970-2006' is most revealing of

---

[8]    Fred Block & M.R. Keller 'Where do innovations come from? Transformations in the U.S. National Innovation System, 1970-2006'. The Information Technology & Innovation Foundation (Jul. 2008): <www.itif.org/index.php?id=158>.

the changes that have occurred in the system over the years. The key lessons are as follows:

In the 1970s, approximately 80% of the award-winning US innovations were from large firms acting on their own. Today, approximately two-thirds of the award-winning US innovations involve some kind of inter-organizational collaboration – a situation that reflects the more collaborative nature of the innovation process and the greater role in private sector innovation by government agencies, federal laboratories and research universities.

The US innovation system today is much more collaborative than it was several decades ago and the federal government is playing a much more supportive and important role in innovation. Several factors explain this phenomenon:

– growing global competition is shrinking technology lifecycles;
– the complexity of emerging technologies is beyond the internal R&D capabilities of even the largest firms;
– the expansion of R&D capability in more industries is causing R&D investment to spread vertically in high-tech supply chains, which increases the potential for the loss of value-added from a single domestic economy; and
– a growing number of nations are responding to these trends by implementing new mechanisms that increase the efficiency of R&D.

## 7.6 GOVERNMENT SPENDING AND R&D IN DEVELOPING COUNTRIES

There is a relationship between government spending and spending by business enterprises. A reduction in the former often results in reduction in the latter. This had led to a renewed debate on the role of government in industrial R&D and it is interesting to note that this debate is taking place in the United States.

The main explanation for this so-called complementary relationship is that as government makes more contract R&D money available to industry, firms increase their own R&D spending in the hope of capturing more government funds. Industry spending may also follow federal spending patterns in order to take greater advantage of anticipated spin-offs from the government R&D programmes.

In the developing world, major investments in R&D are made in public institutions. For example, in India from 1980-1981, 84.1% of the investments in R&D were made by the government. This reduced to 77% in 1998-1999. In the advanced nations, these expenditures range from around 20% to 50%. The quality of output of national laboratories has varied in different countries. Measures have been taken to improve their effectiveness.

Most developing countries do not have a policy on innovation, as it is generally believed that developing countries do not engage in any such effort at all. At best, they are expected to undertake incremental innovations which are basically the adaptation of imported technologies to local conditions. But the recent growth experience of some of the developing countries, and especially those from East Asia, has shown that they have become generators of new technologies. Indeed, countries like India have launched programmes such as the 'New Millennium Indian Technology Leadership Initiative', indicating aspirations of technology leadership in the early part of the twenty-first century.

In addition to taking advantage of the large global stock of knowledge, the developing countries should develop capability to create knowledge at home. This capability to create knowledge at home must encompass not only strategies to develop knowledge locally but also policies and mechanisms that will eventually enhance the capability of the nation to absorb knowledge. Together these would constitute public innovation policies in the developing-country context.

The basic rationale behind public innovation policies is to combat private under-investment in R&D. Public innovation policies can be used in:

- The creation and maintenance of a legal environment conducive to private sector investment in innovative activities. This can be created by legal measures which enhance the power to appropriate the fruits of R&D. Patents and the relaxation of anti-trust activity are the primary means by which the government creates such a conducive environment; and
- The provision of sufficient stimuli to overcome the natural inclination of private agents to consider only their private benefits when choosing the level of innovative activity in which to engage. This takes a variety of forms ranging from governmental grants and contracts to targeted tax incentives.

Innovation policies will have to be changed according to the potential technological capability of a country. All developing countries can no longer be considered as a homogeneous group, especially in terms of their technological capability.

Recently, G.D. Graff[9] undertook an exhaustive survey of the Intellectual Property & Technology Transfer policies in emerging and developing economies by sampling eighteen countries, which represent an enormously broad cultural, social and economic landscape. Graff's study showed that availability of IPRs is determined by four important fundamentals. They comprise indigenous S&T capacity; level of economic development; history of IP laws within the country; and international agreements, such as Trade-Related Aspects of Intellectual Property Rights (TRIPS) and the International Convention for the Protection of New Varieties of Plants (UPOV).

Graff develops three tiers when gauging the robustness of domestic IP systems. Table 5 is a modified version focusing mainly on patents. The first tier comprises most innovative emerging economies such as Brazil, China, India and Russia. The second tier contains the bulk of the middle-income countries that have recently developed their IP policies but grant most of their patents to foreigners. These include countries like Argentina, Indonesia,

---

[9]    Graff G.D., 'Echoes of Bayh Dole? A survey of IP & Technology Transfer Policies in Emerging & Developing Economies', in *Intellectual Property Management in Health and Agricultural Innovation: A Hand book of Best Practices*, eds A. Krattiger, RT Mahoney, L. Nelson, J.A. Thomson, A.B. Bennett, K. Satyanarayana, G.D. Graff, C. Fernandez, and S.P. Kowalski, 2007 (UK:IHR & US: PIPRA, 2007): <www.iphandbook.org/>.

Table 5. Determinants and Indicators of the Status of National IP Systems

**A: Patent Applications Filed**

| | COUNTRY | PER CAPITA GDP BY PPP 2005 | DATE OF FIRST PATENT LAW | DATE JOINED TRIPS | DATE(S) PATENT LAW AMENDED FOR TRIPS COMPLIANCE | PATENTS TO RESIDENTS/PATENTS TO FOREIGNERS (YR) | RATIO OF RESIDENT TO RESIDENT TO FOREIGN |
|---|---|---|---|---|---|---|---|
| TIER 1 | United States | 41,399 | 1789 | 1995 | - | 84,271/80,020 (2004) | 1.05 |
| | Russia | 11,041 | 1812 | - | 2003 | 19,447/3,943 (2005) | 4.93 |
| | China | 7,198 | 1984 | 2001 | 1992, 2001 | 18,241/31,119 (2004) | 0.59 |
| | South Africa | 12,161 | 1925 | 1995 | 2002 | 5549A/5501A (1995) | 1.01 |
| | Poland | 12,994 | 1925 | 1995 | 2000 | 778/1,016 (2004) | 0.77 |
| | India | 3,320 | 1856 | 1995 | 1999, 2002 | 851/1,466 (2004) | 0.58 |
| | Brazil | 8,560 | 1809 | 1995 | 1996-1997 | 666/1,366 (2002) | 0.49 |
| TIER 2 | Argentina | 14,108 | 1875 | 1995 | 1996-2001 | 145/1,442 (2000) | 0.10 |
| | Mexico | 10,186 | 1850 | 1995 | 1997, 1999 | 162/6,677 (2004) | 0.02 |
| | Chile | 11,936 | 1850 | 1995 | 2005 | 32/569 (2000) | 0.06 |
| | Indonesia | 4,459 | 1989 | 1995 | 1997 | 16/615 (1996) | 0.03 |
| | Malaysia | 11,201 | 1983 | 1995 | 2000 | 31/1,542 (2003) | 0.02 |
| | Jordan | 5,095 | 1999 | 1999 | 1999, 2001 | 4/56 (2004) | 0.07 |
| | Vietnam | 3,025 | 1995 | 2006 | 2005 | 17/756 (2005) | 0.02 |
| | Philippines | 4,923 | 1947 | 1995 | 1998 | 16/1,437 (2004) | 0.01 |
| TIER 3 | Ethiopia | 823 | 1995 | - | - | 0/1 (2000) | 0.00 |
| | Kenya | 1,445 | 1914 | 1995 | 2001 | 0/33 (2001) | 0.00 |
| | Tanzania | 723 | 1931 | 1995 | - | 0/23 (1989) | 0.00 |
| | Uganda | 1,501 | 1950 | 1995 | - | 0/34 (2001) | 0.00 |

Malaysia and Mexico. The third tier consists of the lower-income countries in which there is no strong IP system in place nor are there a great number of patent applications. These include countries like Ethiopia, Kenya, Tanzania and Uganda. In Graff's survey, all of these countries are in Sub-Saharan Africa.

### 7.6.1 Supply and Demand Issue

The basic objective of all innovation policies is to increase the supply of technologies to local firms. But it is now well known that merely increasing the supply of technologies need not necessarily lead to positive or desirable outcomes for the economy as a whole. This is because increases in supply must be matched by increases in the demand for technology. Most developing countries are characterized by low levels of demand for technologies as a result of the high barriers to entry (both domestic and foreign) and, therefore, domestic firms have little or no real incentive to effect technological improvements.

### 7.6.2 Tax Incentives versus Direct Funding of Commercial R&D by the Government

Direct government funding is apt to be more effective than tax incentives when the aim of the policy is to enlarge the stock of basic knowledge available to domestic firms. Direct funding by the government is likely to raise total spending on basic research by more than the amount spent by the government. However, one unit of tax incentives is likely to yield significantly less than one unit of additional spending on basic research because of its relatively large spillover effects. But if the aim of the policy is to boost a country's rate of commercialization of new products, processes or services, then a tax incentive has some advantage over direct funding. Success in commercialization hinges on a sound understanding of the market; the tax incentives have the advantage of leaving the decisions of which projects to fund in the hands of private firms rather than government agencies. Even with the subsidies, firms will still be putting up most of the money for projects they pursue, which ensures that they, not the taxpayers, will bear most of the risks of failure. In contrast, direct funding of commercial R&D may possibly foster a misallocation of resources among major sectors of the economy.

Tax incentives also have a number of limitations of which the most important are:

- R&D tax subsidies tend to operate as an entitlement: all firms that qualify may claim a subsidy. In addition, a credit is easy to abuse by classifying routine research expenses as innovative;
- Tax incentives are blunt instruments. A tax incentive such as a credit cannot be targeted at R&D projects with large spillover effects, unlike direct funding programmes; and
- The propensity to relabel routine expenditures such as quality control and testing as R&D expenditure and then claim tax incentives is also very high, especially in the

developing-country context. For example, in India, such incentives were withdrawn in the mid-1980s due to these reasons, but they were reintroduced in the mid 1990s.

### 7.6.3 *Venture Capital and the Role of the Government*

Another fiscal instrument that is increasingly gaining currency is venture capital (VC), which is an equity form of investment in a technology-based firm at its early stage of development. In addition to providing the much-needed risk capital, the venture capitalist also renders a fair amount of value-added support to the investee. Thus, in a sense the VC institutions, theoretically speaking, are a solution to the financial barrier to innovations in both the developed and developing countries. It is interesting to note that even many of the OECD countries' governments have implemented their own programmes to mobilize VC in support of small, innovative firms. Direct measures refer to specific publicly funded schemes, which increase the supply of VC financing. The diverse forms of public policy instruments aimed at simulating the supply of VC on OECD countries can be grouped into three main categories: direct supply of VC to VC funds or small firms; financial incentives in VC funds or small firms; and investor regulations determining the types of investors in VC.

In contrast, most developing countries do not have any policies to address the financial barriers to innovation. Supply of risk capital must become an integral part of public innovation policies.

### 7.6.4 *Human Resource Development and the Role of the Government*

The importance of availability of a steady stream of highly trained personnel hardly needs to be emphasized. All successful countries, including the recent success stories from East Asia, had successful policies for increasing both the quality and quantity of technically trained personnel. Most developing countries, however, treat policies on human resource development separately from public innovation policies. Unless there is a critical mass of technically trained personnel, no amount of fiscal incentives can spur innovations. The number of tertiary students affects the number of research scientists and engineers. There is a very strong correlation between research scientists and engineers and the research intensity. But again, it is not merely the supply of technically trained personnel that matters. There has to be a match between the requirements of industry and the output of the higher education systems. Failure to recognize this can result in losing important markets.

### 7.6.5 *Government's Role in Industrial Standards*

Industrial standards are an integral component of public innovation policies. Many developing countries have not paid attention to the issue of industrial standards. If these countries want to emerge as manufacturers and exporters of manufactured products, especially to Western markets, then industrial standards become important. Standards confer both direct and indirect benefits.

The immediate impact of standardization is to reduce the transaction costs by providing clearly specified interface requirements for products. They can thus lower the barriers to market entry and speed up competition, and consequently, the demand for new technologies. Although it is a supply-side measure, it has the potential of stimulating demand for technological improvements as well. It fulfils a quality certification function, which is especially important for industrial components. In terms of indirect benefits, preparation of new standards and continuous revisions of the existing ones leads to a platform for exchange of technical information within the industry as well as its users and suppliers. It puts pressure on firms to upgrade their products, while providing them with the technical information required to do so.

For a credible presence in international markets, certification under ISO 9000 standards has become increasingly important for manufacturing and service sector units all over the world. ISO 9000 (first published in 1987 and revised in 1994) is primarily concerned with quality management. The definition of quality in ISO 9000 refers to all those features of a product or a service that are required by the customer. Although the share of developing countries in the ISO 9000 certification has shown an increase, there is considerable concentration of it within the East Asian countries (the traditional Asian 'tigers' plus China, Malaysia, Indonesia, Thailand and the Philippines). In fact, the number of ISO 9000 certifications secured by firms in developing countries excluding those in East Asia has actually increased very slowly and their share in the total also continues to be small.

## 7.7 ROLE OF PUBLIC AND PRIVATE SECTORS IN R&D AND INNOVATION

A nation needs to invest in innovation through both public and private sectors. Privately funded research is driven by the profit motivation of individual firms. The results of R&D are proprietary to the firm. Publicly funded research is generally done for public good and the knowledge is supposed to be in open domain. However, the specific issues of IP protection of such knowledge generated by public funding has been a contentious issue. As we will show later, different nations have adopted different strategies at different points in their history.

The main difference between public and private research incentives has been explained by David and Foray[10] as:

What fundamentally distinguishes various communities of scientific researchers is not so much their methods of inquiry, nor the nature of the knowledge they obtain, but the socio-political arrangements and the consequent reward structures under which they work. A crucial separation exists between 'open science' communities, and

---

[10]   P. David & D. Foray, 'Accessing and Expanding the Science and Technology Base', *STI Review OECD*, 16 (1995): 13-68.

proprietary research communities. . . . Loosely speaking, 'open science' may be associated with the world of academic research . . . conducted under university-like organizational norms affecting the autonomy of individual researchers with a reward structure that is based upon collegiate reputations, established through priority in publication of verifiable research findings.

In the private sector, the emphasis is on the economic returns from new knowledge. Presently, there is increasing pressure for industrial application in publicly funded research. As a result, the private sector and public institutions have come together to create proprietary knowledge that has the potential to create wealth that is proprietary.

Changes in government policy have a major influence on the nature of public and private knowledge. The US government has passed a law to encourage universities to patent their IP. Evidently, university patents have received significantly more first- and second-generation citations in patents than industrial patents. It is an indication that university research was important in the initial stages of a technology's development. It has also been observed that the differences between industrial and university patents have increased over time for a given patent indicating that university patents are important in the follow-up advances of a technology. The subsequent citations to university patents were spread over more technological areas than those for industrial patents, implying that those patents were more generic in their potential applications. University patents have a higher scientific content as they rely more on non-patent sources than do corporate patents. However, patents are only a partial measure of the output of university research. Upon being appropriated via patents, university knowledge is found to be basic and used in a wider number of technologies and firms than industry patents.

### 7.7.1 Commercialization of R&D in Public Institutions

Returns from public investment are obtained by commercial exploitation of research results from publicly funded research institutions. Different nations have adopted different approaches for achieving this goal. For example, the practice in the United States and Japan insists that:

– all publicly funded research activities envisage setting up clear guidelines for sharing IPRs;
– the management of research projects also include procedures for the management of the resulting IPRs and for the exploitation of their results;
– there are no restrictions on the rights of the owners of the IPRs from entering into commercial arrangements for the use of these rights by others, provided that existing laws and general policies regarding public procurement and contracting are complied with.

The prospects for commercialization of university research will be more successful if academics have access to the resources and freedom they need to conduct high quality research and are given the right mix of incentives to promote new ways of working with industry. Government policies should encourage collaboration and cooperation between academia, research institutions and industry and enterprises through licensing and other forms of technology transfer, collaborative research activities and sharing of expertise. In the long run, this will help industry and enterprises to become competitive in the present highly globalized market.

### 7.7.1.1 Technology Transfer from University to Industry

In order to enhance the contribution of university research for industrial & enterprise development, academia and industry need to work together. In order to obtain adequate returns from public investments, emphasis needs to be laid upon the following six key areas:

(1) An understanding of what the market needs is very crucial. Rather than being in 'supply' driven mode, demand-driven R&D – undertaken in anticipation of the potential market and the rescue process – has always led to better returns. Whether R&D is focused on current or future markets (pre-competitive research) depends upon the stage of the country's development.

(2) A technology-transfer supportive culture requires an incentive system. Different incentive and reward systems need to be put in place to promote such a culture.

(3) The internal management issue is strongly related to the effectiveness and efficiency of the transfer process. Knowledge management, improving operational efficiency through training in project management, quality systems, etc., are particularly important.

(4) Technology transfer from university and other R&D organizations to industrial organizations would be greatly facilitated if universities are able to patent and license the results of their publicly funded research to industry. The licensing of patents by universities provides an incentive for industries to get involved in the risky investments associated with the marketing of products from new unproven technologies. Strong incentives from private ownership are also essential for commercialization of new inventions.

(5) For facilitating the transfer of technology, a law was enacted in several countries allowing universities and public institutions to obtain patents and grant exclusive licenses to private firms. The Bayh-Dole Act of 1980 came into force allowing universities, non-profit corporations and small businesses to patent and commercialize their federally funded inventions. It allowed federal agencies to grant exclusive licenses for their technology so as to provide more incentives to business. A substantial enhancement in technology transfer between universities and industry was observed as a result of enforcement of the Bayh-Dole Act.

(6) Interaction between publicly funded research institutes, universities industrial firms and financial institutions is crucial. Different countries have created different models for this purpose.

### 7.7.1.2 *Facilitation of Technology Transfer from Public Institutions*

Transfer of technology generated in publicly funded R&D organizations to the private sector can be facilitated by:

- Providing the necessary incentives and rewards to the institutions and individuals who generate the inventions.
- Introducing new types of contractual arrangements that permit the organizations to capture the benefits from their inventions, e.g., taking equity in start-up companies as a form of royalties.
- Providing partial or exclusive licenses to firms interested in commercializing the technology.
- Focussing awareness by disseminating information to the private sector on the technological knowledge held in the form of IPRs.
- Promoting technology partnership arrangements with the private sector.
- Guaranteeing a clear definition of the IPRs that may result from research activities.
- And, where applicable and without compromising the public character of RTOs, learning from the private sector approach, orienting research at an early stage of development.

Mechanisms have to be developed to identify technologies with commercial impact, and IP protection for such technologies must be pursued and ensured.

### 7.7.1.3 *University: Industry Collaborative Research*

Over the last two decades, university/industry research collaboration is becoming more frequent and extensive. A number of collaborative mechanisms have been adopted, for example, university research sponsored by companies; agreements between individual companies and universities; industry consortia to support university research; university support for start-up companies, licensing of university-owned IP to existing companies; research centres to encourage university/industry collaboration; and government support for university/industry collaboration. But there are some barriers that produce hindrances in the progress of various ongoing collaborative programmes of universities and industries. These hindrances mainly relate to the following issues associated with such collaboration: publication, copyright and confidentiality; IPRs; regulation, liability and tax law; foreign access; infrastructure; and graduate student involvement.

Several interrelated issues in collaborative research may be categorized as:

*Issues of Culture, Management and Goal Alignment*

Sometimes collaborative partners lack understanding or trust as a result of ignorance about each other's fundamental interests. This kind of situation often results in slow decisions and insufficient resources. For creating mutual trust amongst partners, several solutions have been proposed from time to time. A few of these include:

- Expectation mapping in which the expected roles and contributions of partners are analyzed.
- Stakeholder mapping in which stakeholders in each organization are identified.
- Decision-making analysis in which the decision-making process of each organization is made explicit.

Similarly, one of the problems is the different time horizons of universities and industry. This problem may be resolved if industry managers understand that most of the sponsored research projects have certain fixed time limits and at the same time universities should avoid overselling in terms of potential accomplishments and timeliness.

## *Issues of Institutional Incentives and Integration of Research and Educational Missions*

In some cases the members of industries and universities are not given due recognition, either financial or intellectual, for their efforts, which may act as disincentive to the collaborative projects. Solutions to the problem may be found in the creation of innovative structures both in industry as well as universities.

Sometimes industries seek to stretch resources by not paying indirect costs and their faculty may pressure the concerned university to agree. Payment of indirect costs may create approaches to increase incentives.

## *Issues of Proprietary Rights*

The issue of proprietary rights in collaborative research is a much debated one. It has been observed that some universities take too restrictive an approach to licensing and put too high a value on their IP contributions. Technology-transfer activities are being taken more as a revenue source than as a public responsibility to assist in the commercialization of research results. To overcome this barrier, it is essential that the faculty as well as university management and industry leaders understand the role of IP in the innovation and valuation of IP.

Research institutions should consider the most appropriate way of exploiting the IP generated from publicly funded research. There is no single best approach for commercializing IP. Options include exclusive and non-exclusive licenses, research agreements or contracts through joint ventures or the establishment of spin-off companies.

In order to protect their IP, some steps need to be taken by research institutions, e.g.:

- research institutions must have policies approved by their governing body relating to the ownership, protection and exploitation of IP;
- research institutions must have procedures that provide support to publicly funded researchers so that they can recognize when their discoveries may have a potential

commercial value, and a review process may be taken up for identifying the IP that can be protected and/or exploited;

- staff of the institutes must be trained regarding IP protection so that premature public disclosure of research results may be avoided prior to obtaining IP protection;
- there should be a clear policy regarding the claim for ownership or associated rights by public funding agencies for IP generated from their supported research;
- research institutions must have policies for determining the subsequent ownership of IPRs;
- clear policies must be in place for the ownership of IP generated by students during their course of study and also for cases where IP impinges on the cultural, spiritual or other aspects of indigenous people;
- IP, associated commercial activities and outcome of publicly funded research must be reviewed regularly;
- provisions for sharing benefits by all stakeholders involved in the publicly funded research; and
- an annual report on the IP management of publicly funded research must be provided to government.

Thus, the organization must develop its own detailed IP management strategy within the framework of these principles to best suit its environment and needs.

The Bayh-Dole Act in 1980 opened up the doors to the use of federally supported US university research for enterprises. It created a uniform licensing system, reduced the steps needed to grant licenses and provided incentives for industry to invest risk capital in product commercialization. Its sizeable impact in measurable terms has been articulated in several studies.[11] Crowell[12] shows how US patents granted increased from around 250 (1980) to more than 4,000 (2004). It shows that 460 companies were created by the year 2004 as a result of university research, around 60%-80% of university spin-offs being in and around university campuses, thus creating jobs for university graduates.

## 7.8  SMEs and R&D

SMEs are an engine of economic growth and a major factor in promoting private sector development and partnership. Innovation has taken the centre stage for sustainable technological progress in the present technologically driven global economy. In this context, the development of SMEs must constitute the significant element in the growth strategy of national economies.

---

[11]  National Academy of Science 2001, Report of Committee on Intellectual Property Rights in the Knowledge-Based Economy: <www.nationalacademies.org/step/STEP_projects_Intellectual_Property-Rights.html>.

[12]  Wriston Mark Crowell, 'Bayh-Dole at 25 Years: Where have we been, and what can we expect?', International Patent Licensing Seminar (Tokyo, Japan, 2006): <www.ryutu.inpit.go.jp/pldb/seminar_a/2006/pdf/ps1_e.pdf>.

SMEs play a vital role in the national industrial system by providing most of the local industrial employment, production and value-added products generated in the global market. Fortunately, one-half to two-thirds of business the world over are SMEs, which traditionally have been known for the agility of their response to a changing environment. The industrial wealth of a nation is produced by SMEs and thus, they primarily contribute to real economic development and wealth creation. In fact, global surveys point to the fact that the giant Transnational Corporations (TNCs) account only for about 25% of all global production.

The growth of a nation is, to a considerable extent, linked with the growth of SMEs. Innovative R&D plays a crucial role in the growth of SMEs. Protection of the innovative research through IPR legislation has also been a key issue in the modern knowledge-based society.

Innovation for SMEs is imperative for their existence. Without innovation, businesses ultimately decline and cease to operate. R&D for SMEs is fundamentally different in focus and objectives from the research pursued by the large firms. The focus is often more on process than on product because process innovation matters more than product innovation in terms of reducing costs and cycle time. Also, for reducing risk, the objective is more related to design rather than totally new innovative products. In-house R&D also has a significant impact on competitiveness.

The technology frontier is constantly moving, so it is essential for SMEs to progress technologically or else they will become irrelevant.

Upgrading technology requires constant innovation through research & development. It requires multilateral and multi-layered inputs, many man-hours and much effort to continue to prove state-of-the-art technologies. Although only a small number of SMEs are engaged in formal R&D, (that, too, in a limited way), many make significant contributions to generating innovations as they are staffed by science professionals. Moreover, the fact that they are well represented in new, knowledge-based industries such as information technology and biotechnology enhances the totality of their contributions.

The technological performance of SMEs is emphasized to focus on what enterprises actually do technologically. An enterprise must bring together, at each productive point, people with the right technological knowledge and equipment with the right technological capabilities, suitable for the purposes and the techniques to be applied.

The development and growth of some of the smaller SMEs in certain countries is constrained due to certain factors. These include lack of experienced managerial capacity, inadequate technical skill levels amongst workers in order to keep pace with advancements in the technological field, limited access to financial capital, weak support services, industrial & social infrastructure and inadequate quality control. They also have limited access to export markets for providing quality products or services. Their marketing and distribution network is also not up to the mark.

These constraints of SMEs can be overcome through innovative R&D and understanding the IPR climate. This is particularly true for the SMEs of the developing world, which must remain in business in the highly competitive global and domestic market.

In the last ten years, there has been an unprecedented global upsurge in innovations and in patents granted in the growth of SMEs' competitiveness. Acquisition and exploitation of technological innovations have, therefore, become the key to guaranteeing competitiveness.

Innovations responsible for success of most SMEs need to be developed, turned into innovative products and commercialized successfully so that the enterprise is able to reap the benefits.

# CHAPTER EIGHT

# ROLE OF GOVERNMENT IN FOSTERING THE INTELLECTUAL PROPERTY SYSTEM

- *National System of Innovation (NSI) as Policy Framework*
- *Different Types of Technology Innovations*
- *National Innovation Policy: Nurturing the Innovation Base*
- *Venture Capital Financing*
- *Global Innovation Chains*
- *Support of Government in Fostering Development of High-Tech Enterprises through Incubators and Accelerators*
- *Expenditure on S&T*
- *Institutional Issues*
- *Role of Government in International Relations in IP*
- *Competition Law*
- *Intellectual Property Rights (IPRs) Institutions*
- *Role in Awareness Building and Effective Enforcement*
- *Enforcement Provisions in TRIPS Agreement*
- *Primacy of the Government Role*

## 8.1 NSI as a Policy Framework

Innovation is the key for the production as well as processing of knowledge. Indeed, a nation's ability to convert knowledge into wealth and social good through the process of innovation determines its future.

In the industrialized countries, and in a growing number of newly industrializing countries, policy-makers have found that the concept of a National System of Innovation (NSI) provides a useful framework for technology policy formulation. Such a policy helps define the necessary inputs, initiatives and incentives which produce a competitive economy in today's increasingly globalized markets. NSI can be thought of as a set of functioning institutions, organizations and policies which interact constructively in the pursuit of a common set of social and economic goals and objectives, and which use innovation as the key promoter of change.

## 8.2 Different Types of Technology Innovations

In a classical sense, we have three types of technology innovations. Firstly, there is a large system innovation (such as a man-on-the-moon mission); secondly, incremental

143

innovation (such as development of an improved fax machine); and finally radical break-throughs (such as an accidental breakthrough leading to the antibiotic industry). These invariably take place through formal systems of innovation such as universities, individual inventors and industrial R&D laboratories. Governments play a critical role in launching and managing large system innovations.

Out of these, radical breakthroughs are based on individual enterprise in which the government does not play a role. Government plays a key role in large system innovations and can be a facilitator in promoting incremental innovations.

Large system innovations require large funding and complex management techniques. They also require a total commitment by the government. They are driven by visionary leaders, who have faith in the ability of their people. Innovative blending of different tech-nologies and huge systems engineering problems are parts of such innovations. Many large-scale space, defense and atomic energy programmes run by different countries represent such large system innovations.

Incremental innovation is the 'nuts and bolts' innovation. This is essentially done in industrial enterprises. Firms try to displace their own products out of the fear that if they did not do it, their competitors will do it for them.

The entire chain of acquiring the know-how package, evaluating resources, formulating manufacturing methods, determining import contact, accumulating engineering experience, working out the design modification process, observing the product behaviour, using that experience to create new products, and finally, commercializing the product involve both learning and doing in an iterative manner.

An innovation strategy has to be effectively linked to need-based research for technol-ogy development. In this process, firms need to have a capacity to make an appropriate choice of technology, the sourcing and negotiation of processes most suited for acquisition, their adaptation to local materials and markets and their continuous improvement and dissemination. The governments can play an important role through many facilitating measures including fiscal measures (such as weighted tax deductions for investment in R&D), policy measures (such as provision of incentives for technology absorption) and so on. Essential to the national innovation system is a strong consultancy capability, whereby local engineers, scientists and managers take the prime responsibility for project design and implementation, with selective inputs from the best available international sources. Scientific research, technology development and industrial consultancy organizations are the troika which drive the process of knowledge-based enterprise creation.[1]

## 8.3 NATIONAL INNOVATION POLICY: NURTURING THE INNOVATION BASE

With increasing globalization, the question that is engaging attention with regard to the process of innovation is where the capabilities for innovation reside. Until recently, it was believed that they reside in nation states. Certain nation states were able to create the

---

[1]    Rustam Lalkaka, President, Business and Technology Development Strategies LLC, and Senior Advisor, United Nations Development Programme (UNDP), New York: <www.btds.biz/publications>.

climate and provide the necessary infrastructure, which could spur innovative genius; certain other states have failed to do so. This is how nations began building up an NSI and evolving a National Innovation Policy, which went beyond the National Science Policy or National Technology Policy. While the idea of the innovation system is still valid, the national part of it is diminishing in its importance as R&D becomes increasingly internationalized and the world becomes more and more integrated.

Different nations regard innovative capabilities as residing essentially in firms. It is the intertwining of scientific and technological capabilities of a firm with its organizational and management capabilities and strategies that determines its strength. It is also known that innovation flourishes in certain geographical regions with special attributes of history or talent, like in Silicon Valley in the US, or in Bangalore and Hyderabad in India. Some view global networks as the essential seat of innovative capabilities in the emerging R&D paradigm. These rival views are not necessarily mutually contradictory and they may be valid within their limited contexts. However, they do not point to the fact that while it may be appropriate to think in terms of 'technology systems' that encourage or inhibit a culture of innovation, it may be seen as artificial to seek such systems within the political boundaries of a nation.

For every nation, nurturing a strong innovation base through a balanced system of recognition and rewards is crucial. In the specific case of Intellectual Property Rights (IPRs), a liberal investment to enhance the skills and knowledge base of scientists, through structured in-house and external professional training programmes, becomes essential. Such programmes should be aimed at understanding, interpreting and analyzing the techno-legal and business information contained in Intellectual Property (IP) documents and in drafting claims and specifications for patent documents. As regards federally funded scientific institutions, the publication of R&D results in scientific papers is made contingent by many institutions upon prior clearance from an IP angle, by a careful consideration of the consequences of not obtaining IP rights. The scientifically advanced developing world is beginning to realize the loss of IP due to the inadvertent publication of new and commercially usable knowledge.

The government-funded R&D laboratories are becoming increasingly conscious of using patent information for decision-making prior to committing resources to apparently innovative new projects. Monitoring national and international patents and other IP through access to on-line databases is being used to ensure that wasteful investments are not made in duplicative R&D. The firms are also becoming careful before commercializing new products, which may inadvertently infringe IP rights of others. Forward-looking firms and institutions are analyzing and assessing techno-legal and business information and market intelligence to identify potential partners for strategic alliances and to exploit potential uncovered niche areas of opportunities themselves that could gives rise to some new knowledge-based business.

The governments in developing countries and countries in transition need to develop IP policy and strategies which will lead not only to encouraging more investment but also research and innovation from which they would benefit. Mere compliance with the World Trade Organization Trade-Related Aspects of Intellectual Property Rights (WTO TRIPS) Agreement, which sets out minimum standards of IP rights protection, will not suffice. In addition, precise details of national IPR regimes need to be proactively tailored to the particular circumstances of the individual countries concerned.

A few of the developing countries and countries in transition argue that offering greater protection for IP will not help expand their trade with other countries because they do not generally export original movies, books, records, computer programmes and the like. When they do create such works, those works will still be protected by the developed countries, even if the country of origin does not adequately enforce IP rights within its own borders. This mindset encourages free riding with no incentive to compete through superior products based on indigenous innovation and creativity. A well-designed and effectively functioning national IP system will complement other national initiatives to nurture an innovation base for developing internationally competitive goods and services.

Purely economic reasons will drive a country to protect IP through adequate laws and effective enforcement. If a country does not protect its IP, it is less likely that it will develop its own knowledge-based industries. The encouragement and development of local creators and inventors depends, to a great extent, on their ability to earn a living from their work. Without such protection, local IP is less likely to be created, and developing countries and countries in transition may be relegated to the role of net importers of new and useful knowledge and IP.

## 8.4 VENTURE CAPITAL FINANCING

Let us focus on government's role in creating and supporting venture capital (VC), which can encourage and fund innovations. VC is specifically defined as equity-linked investment in privately held companies. The venture capitalists provide equity investments in companies that are not mature enough to get access to capital markets but have high growth potential to compensate for the constraints inherent in such ventures. It is the availability of such VC that has led to the spectacular growth of technology-driven enterprises around the world.

Seventy five percent of all VC in the world is in the United States and about 75% of that can be found in six states. This is because of an environment in these regions that increases the probability for success. An encouraging business culture that is tolerant of failure and risk, the availability of intellectual capital from high-class research universities and access to financial capital are three critical factors attracting VC to these regions.

One of the crucial sources of value provided by venture investors is their ability to certify companies to other investors. For instance, venture-backed firms are much more likely to attract the interest of a reputable investment banker and complete an initial public offering. Similarly, corporate business development groups are much more likely to invest in new firms backed by venture investors. Thus, the financing contributed by the venture investor is often relatively modest compared to the total amount that the venture-backed firm finally raises.

How can governments encourage technopreneurship? They can provide an enabling environment in which the skilled entrepreneur gets easy access to capital, technology and infrastructural support.

In particular, governments can help:

- provide an educated talented and highly skilled workforce;
- provide funding for basic and translational research by using non-restrictive and win-win public-private partnership;

- enforce strong IP laws;
- encourage proactive technology transfer from universities and research laboratories by, e.g., using flexible licensing policies and funding proof of concept research;
- use a science-based transparent regulatory environment;
- provide financial incentives to investors and entrepreneurs such as tradable R&D tax rebates, deferred taxes, subsidized incubators and low- or no-interest loans. Providing sources of capital that match VC investments and tax offsets as enticements for investors can go a long way in reducing the overall risk to investors.

## 8.5 GLOBAL INNOVATION CHAINS

The innovation chains cross national boundaries today. Companies realize that to gain a competitive advantage they must leverage their technical assets and capabilities across the world; it would be rather unwise to attempt self-sufficiency in technology development, particularly in an era where R&D costs are increasing rapidly. With trade barriers between countries disappearing fast, companies have to provide the best technology globally to their customers. As a part of the global innovation strategy, several companies the world over are looking for new ideas and technologies, which the originator may have been unable to exploit for a variety of reasons.

Globalization of R&D is closely linked to globalization of business and consequently to global competition of knowledge and skills. The competitive advantage in high-technology business increasingly depends on knowledge management and technical skills of the business rather than on particular products. As product lifecycles become shorter, knowledge and skill lifecycles become longer. The product then is merely an intermediary between a company's knowledge and skills and the market it serves. Rather than being the focus of corporate activity, products are actually transient mechanisms by which the market derives value from a company's knowledge and skill base and the company derives value from the market. Many high-technology companies are, therefore, constantly assessing what knowledge, skills, capabilities and technologies they should build up, rather than asking stereotyped questions as to which markets they should enter and with which products.

## 8.6 INCUBATORS AND ACCELERATORS

It is generally recognized that the private sector is an effective medium for creating wealth, generating employment and promoting social well-being. In turn, entrepreneurial, knowledge-based small- and medium-sized enterprises (SMEs) are the backbone of the private sector as they help diversify the economy and offer a wide range of goods and services both to national and international markets. Most countries have formulated strategies for promoting innovation and assisting small enterprises in acquiring modern technological resources.[2]

---

[2]    See fn. 1.

Many countries have formulated strategies for promoting innovation and creating entrepreneurial ventures. In this context, business incubators and technology parks are now proving to be cost-effective in nurturing start-up technology-based enterprises. According to the National Business Incubation Association:[3]

> A business incubator is an economic development tool designed to accelerate the growth and success of entrepreneurial companies, through an array of business support resources and services. A business incubator's main goal is to produce successful forms that will leave the programme financially viable and freestanding.

These are workspaces managed in such a way that they provide and also improve access to a range of basic and specialized business services.

Technology incubators are useful vehicles for promoting R&D. An incubator is usually a non-profit entity that provides key advisory, informational, financial, managerial and infrastructure support to R&D and its commercialization. Countries like the US, Japan and Taiwan, among others, have been extremely successful in their use of incubators.

Technology parks are longer term, capital intensive and real estate driven investments. They take advantage of proximity to sources of intellectual capital (such as a university) and conducive infrastructure.

Incubators generally have a long payback period. In many countries, incubators are funded largely with government support. But in developing countries, governments may not be able to fund such incubators on the required scale due to budgetary constraints. Such countries would need incubators which are funded by the private sector or through suitable public-private partnership. Aside from providing a physical space and common facilities for companies to develop during their initial start-up phase, the main value-added provided by incubators to tenant firms are the support services that are generally provided on a wide range of issues that are important to start-up firms.

An interesting example of the services offered by incubators to their tenants is provided by the recent World Intellectual Propery Organization (WIPO) Survey of IP Services of European Technology Incubators. The survey reveals that the majority of surveyed incubators (60%) have staff responsible for IP assistance and consider IP ownership either very important or quite important at the time of selecting tenants for the incubator (57%). The survey also indicates that the types of IP services offered by incubators to tenant firms and the mode of provision varies significantly from incubator to incubator. Incubators often act as a first line of support for tenants, relying on the assistance of external service providers for more specialized support. Specific services such as assistance with patent searches and assistance for negotiating licensing agreements are provided (either in-house or with the assistance of external partners) by 90% and 84% of incubators, respectively.[4]

The infrastructure of incubators and parks has been built up gradually in industrialized countries during the last two decades. It seems that this movement has now reached maturity. In contrast, rapid growth is now occurring in industrializing developing

---

[3]  National Business Incubation Association: <www.nbia.org/resource_center/what_is/index.php>.

[4]  <www.wipo.int/sme/en/documents/pdf/incubator_survey.pdf>.

economies (such as Brazil, China, Egypt, India, Malaysia, the Republic of Korea, Taiwan) and in transitional economies (such as the Czech Republic, Hungary, Poland, Russia, Ukraine, Uzbekistan). Out of the total business incubators, which are estimated to be 2,500, these countries account for over 500 incubators.[5]

Technology parks, which require much larger investments and longer times to mature, have grown more slowly. But, again, these are proving to be vigorous, for example in certain Asian countries such as China, Japan, Singapore and Taiwan. In parallel, we observe the emergence of innovative enterprise support mechanisms and their convergence with parks and incubators.[6]

### 8.6.1 Business Incubators in Certain Countries

In the United States, for example, after two decades of growth, the number of incubators has grown to become a network of around 550, the largest in the world. These innovations have had a good record of job creation and catalyzing economic growth. Many incubators now take equity in tenant companies and operate programmes to serve affiliated companies outside the incubator. It is also the task of incubator managers to direct their graduates, that is, tenants of the incubator who move out of the incubator, to the work environments (technology parks, industrial estates, export processing zones or others) most suited to their needs and assist them in preparing for the transition from the incubator environment to the general business environment.

China has founded more than 130 high-tech business incubators since opening the first incubator in 1987. Most incubators provide companies with low-cost office space and strategic advice on issues such as management and financing, and most are government-owned. Some target rapidly growing industries such as biotechnology, microelectronics, software, and telecommunications and seek to attract Chinese students returning from overseas, as well as international investors.

The examples of the Czech Republic, Hungary and Poland show that business incubators linked to a research park or technical university appear to come closer to meeting the needs of their tenants. Indeed, three-quarters of all incubators in industrializing countries are generally located at universities or research parks.

Zablocki[7] analyzes business incubators as economic tools; and based on the fifteen-year experience of incubators in diverse countries summarizes the general factors that are critical to an incubator's success:

– On site business expertise
– Access to financing and capitalization

---

[5] See fn. 1.
[6] Ibid.
[7] Zablocki E. M., 'Formation of Business Incubator' in *Intellectual Property Management in Health and Agricultural Innovation: A Handbook of Best Practices* eds A. Krattiger et al. (UK: MIHR and US: PIPRA, 2007): <www.iphandbook.org>.

- In-kind financial support
- Community support
- Entrepreneurial networks
- Entrepreneurial education
- Perception of success
- Selection process for tenants
- Ties to a university
- Concise program milestones with clear policies and procedures.

## 8.7 EXPENDITURE ON S&T

Expenditure on S&T is a measure, however incomplete, of a nation's pursuit of innovation. As important are the uses of the funds, the productivity of research and the effectiveness of its utilization. Table 6, below, shows R&D spending by different nations for the year 2005.

Table 6. Comparison of Selected National R&D Spending, 2005[8]

|  | Total R&D Spending 2005 (billion PPP*$) | R&D spending as percent of GDP 2005 |
|---|---|---|
| China | 124.03 | 1.4 |
| France | 41.36 | 2.2 |
| Germany | 59.68 | 2.5 |
| India | 36.11 | 1.0 |
| Japan | 124.48 | 3.2 |
| Rep. of Korea | 27.33 | 2.6 |
| Russian Federation | 20.66 | 1.3 |
| United Kingdom | 36.72 | 1.9 |
| United States of America | 319.60 | 2.6 |
| (*PPP: purchasing power parity) | | |

In scientifically advanced developing nations – India, for example – a significant part of such investments is made by the government itself. In contrast, China has more contribution (57.6%) from industry.

The technology path that a nation follows depends very much on the state of technology prowess of the particular nation. A good example is post-World War II Japan, which spent

---

[8]  Global R&D Report, Sep. 2006: <www.rdmag.com/pdf/RD_GR2006.pdf>.

USD 6-7 billion in the period from 1960-1979 in buying the best technologies from the US and Europe, then spent eight times this amount on local research to improve them and finally began to export superior goods and technologies the world over. This requires competent scientists-managers and political vision. It does not preclude, but may indeed stimulate, good scientific research and, more importantly, shop-floor, incremental innovation. It does include learning by imitation through 'reverse engineering', a practice common among nations that are scientifically both rich and poor.[9]

## 8.8 INSTITUTIONAL ISSUES FOR DEVELOPING COUNTRIES AND COUNTRIES IN TRANSITION

The UK Commission on IPRs[10] has studied the issue of institutional capacity in terms of diverse aspects which include IP policy and legislation, IPR administration and institutions, introducing examination registration system, methods of meeting the costs of the IP system, enforcement and the issues of technical assistance and capacity building, especially with reference to new financing mechanisms and effective delivery of technical assistance. Some of the key recommendations which arise are summarized below.

The institutional capacity of developing countries and countries in transition for policy coordination across government and participatory processes for IP policy-making vary widely and may, in some countries, be one of the weakest areas of the IP system. In terms of participation in international rule-making, there exists a duality since some of these countries have no permanent representation. As a result, they are often little more than spectators at the meetings of WTO and WIPO, whilst others are active and influential participants in the international rule-making processes. Again, most countries face serious financial and human resource constraints in implementing new legislation and modernizing IP office procedures.

Such countries should, where possible, establish a single institution – preferably a semi-autonomous one – responsible for IPR administration, which should also endeavour to recover the cost of upgrading and modernizing its infrastructure through registration charges. They should ensure that their IP legislation and procedures emphasize, to the maximum possible extent, enforcement of IPRs through administrative action rather than through the judicial system. Their IPR administrations might also be encouraged to provide legal and policy advice to their governments.

Thus, developing countries and countries in transition should aim to make their IP offices financially self-supportive. To begin with, the aim should be to recover the full running/recurring costs of the national IP infrastructure through national IPR registration, IPR maintenance and value-added IPR service charges.

---

[9] See fn. 1.
[10] Report of the UK Commission on Intellectual Property Rights (CIPR), London, Sep. 2002: <www.iprcommission.org/graphic/documents/final_report.htm>.

Like-minded countries and donors should also redouble their efforts to support high-level dialogue on new regional and international cooperation initiatives in IPR administration, training and IPR statistical data collection involving developing countries. These countries should encourage policy research and analysis on IP subjects in the national interest (e.g., protection of plant varieties; traditional knowledge and folklore; technology transfer, etc.). To streamline donor coordination, the United Nations Development Programme (UNDP), the World Bank and UNCTAD should cooperate with the European Patent Office (EPO) and the Office for Harmonization in the Internal Market (OHIM), WIPO and agencies of the developed countries to implement IP-related programmes under an integrated framework.

## 8.9 Role of Governments in International Relations in IP

As mentioned in Chapter 3, it is advisable for governments to be parties to international treaties in respect of IPR protection administered by the concerned UN Specialized Agencies and Organizations. Examples include the TRIPS Agreement, the Paris Convention for the Protection of Industrial Property, the Berne Convention for the Protection of Literary and Artistic Works, the Patent Cooperation Treaty (PCT), the Madrid Agreement Concerning the International Registration of Marks, the Hague Agreement Concerning the International Deposit of Industrial Designs, the WIPO Copyright Treaty (WCT) and the WIPO Performance and Phonograms Treaty (WPPT) (known as the Internet Treaties). Adherence to these and other treaties by the maximum number of governments, especially from developing countries and countries in transition, would ensure their active participation as members and not observers in the deliberations concerning these treaties. Also, it is advisable for governments to consider membership in the International Convention for the Protection of New Varieties of Plants (UPOV). Membership in these treaties will help to ensure that any future addendums and amendments to these treaties would be settled with the broadest possible participation by the largest number of member nations.

## 8.10 Competition Law

Competition policy ought to aim at preserving and promoting competition by enforcing competition law against restrictive business and trade practices and by influencing the formulation and/or implementation of governmental policies or measures (state policies) affecting competition. Professor J.M. Clark describes, in his paper entitled 'Towards a Concept of Workable Competition',[11] the kind of market pressure that must be exerted to reward the enterprising creators, innovators and inventors in promoting economic growth.

There are roughly one hundred competition laws currently in force around the world providing different models of legislative drafting. There are, however, divergent views among various countries in regard to the objectives of their competition laws. In the United States, the statutes on competition law merely provide the broad objectives that enable

---

[11]   J.M. Clark, 'Towards a Concept of Workable Competition', *American Economic Review*, Jun. 1940.

antitrust agencies and courts to enunciate appropriate enforcement policies and statutory interpretations over time.[12]

The nature of competition law's objectives in different countries was examined by the WTO Secretariat in 1997, which noted that 'at the most basic level, a core objective of competition policy in most countries . . . is to maintain a healthy degree of rivalry among firms in markets for goods and services'. It also identified ten other, wider objectives that appear in some of the competition laws ranging from 'promoting trade and integration within an economic union or free-trade area' to 'protecting opportunities for small and medium-sized business'.

The scope and coverage of competition laws are also different in different countries. In the United States, for example, the laws apply to private conduct unless a particular economic sector or particular type of business conduct has been specifically exempted. The laws of certain countries provide for exemptions to particular transactions on either an individual or a block basis. Competition laws of some countries seek to ensure that they are effective competitive safeguards in today's global economy. Some countries, of late, have amended their competition laws to reflect the new economic scenario bringing them in conformity with those of other states. Some countries, like the United Kingdom, South Africa and the Netherlands, have substantially or entirely replaced their competition laws with new ones.[13] The Competition Act of 2002 of India passed by both houses of Parliament received assent on 12 January 2003. Certain sections of the Act have been brought into force through the government notification No. 340(E) dated 31 March 2003:

> The law of unfair competition basically comprises of torts that lead to losses in a business, through a deceptive or wrongful business practice. Unfair competition can be categorised in two main areas. First, the term 'unfair competition' is sometimes used to refer only to those torts that are meant to confuse consumers about the source of the product. The other category, 'unfair trade practices', comprises all other forms of unfair competition. In this context, unfair competition does not refer to the economic harms involving monopolies and antitrust legislation.

What constitutes an 'unfair' act depends on the context of the business, the action being examined and the facts of the individual case. The most familiar example of unfair competition is trademark infringement. Another common form of unfair competition is misappropriation. This involves the unauthorized use of an intangible asset not protected by trademark or copyright laws. Other practices that fall into the area of unfair competition include: false advertising, 'bait and switch' selling tactics, unauthorized substitution of one brand of goods for another, use of confidential information by a former employee to solicit customers, theft of trade secrets, breach of a restrictive covenant, trade libel and false representation of products or services.[14]

---

[12]  'Indian Competition Law on the Anvil', by S. Chakravarthy, RGICS Working Paper Series No. 22, 2001: <http://rgics.org/working_papers2.htm>.

[13]  See fn. 11.

[14]  <www.law.cornell.edu/topics/unfair_competition.html>.

## 8.11 IPR INSTITUTIONS

Governments are setting up special institutions to deal with IPR-related issues. As for the developed countries, there are the earlier established institutions such as the Max Planck Institute of Foreign and International Patent, Copyright and Competition Law, established in 1966 in Munich, Germany; the Centre for International Industrial Property Studies (CEIPI), established over thirty years ago in the University of Strasbourg, France, which was formed at the instance of industry and serves it in respect to related industrial property studies. Other institutions are the Common Law Institute of IP in London, and the Japan Institute for Invention and Innovation (JIII) in Tokyo. The latter has played an important role in the development of modern Japan through awareness building, spreading of patent information, research and training. The Institute of IP established in Tokyo in June 1989 focuses on research into various problems related to IP, systematic collection and distribution pertaining thereto, as well as promotion of international exchange.

The developing countries and the countries in transition are also responding to this challenge now. In the Republic of Korea, near Daeduk, some 160 kilometres South of Seoul, the government set up an International Intellectual Property Training Institute (IIPTI) in May 1991, which provides for training of personnel working in the patent sections of various industries. It has since played an important role in human resource development in the IP field by organizing quality training programmes to keep industry technocrats abreast of the demands in the context of rapid technological developments for IP and its protection. In China, the government has set up the China Intellectual Property Training Centre (CIPTC), which is under the Chinese Patent Office (CPO). It is a training institute for personnel specializing in the field of IP and undertakes systematic and professional training in this field. It is a national institute combining teaching, academic research and awareness building in the practice of IP. Internationally well-known experts and scholars of IP are also invited to lecture at the CIPTC.

There is also the Institute of Intellectual Property Development (IIPD) in India. It was established at the initiative of the Federation of Indian Chambers of Commerce and Industry (FICCI) and has as its chairman an outstanding entrepreneur and leader of a pharmaceutical industry and research foundation. The main objective was to set up a world-class institute to undertake research in IPRs issues and to establish, maintain, and manage a centre of excellence to promote the knowledge of IP law in India as well as IP systems of other countries. It has endeavoured to sensitize the public on various issues that directly impact technological competitiveness.

In Malaysia, an Intellectual Property Centre (IPTC) was established in May 1997 as a first step towards setting up a National Institute of Intellectual Property Training. The IPTC, managed in close cooperation with the IP Division of the Ministry of Domestic Trade and Consumer Affairs, aims at providing effective and quality training for developing national expertise in the field of IP. The programmes of the IPTC, which operate in connection with the Malaysian Intellectual Property Association (MIPA), are intended to benefit patent agents and lawyers dealing with IP, public sector officials involved with IP issues and enforcement, the judiciary, the industry and the private sector as well as academicians and researchers.

In particular, governments in the developing countries and countries in transition might help to encourage policy research and analysis on IP subjects in the national interest in their educational institutions, R&D organizations, the private sector and civil society organizations. Such subjects of national interest may include traditional knowledge and folklore; technology transfer; and protection of plant varieties.

## 8.12 ROLE IN AWARENESS-BUILDING AND EFFECTIVE ENFORCEMENT

Governments should help in creating a high level of literacy amongst a cross-section of people, particularly in the lesser developed or developing countries, about the IP system, its operation, costs and benefits as well as its value to society. Awareness-building programmes should be held at the national level periodically in order to help a progressive new awareness in business, research and development institutions, amongst public officials and in university circles. The Internet should also be fully exploited to create a greater awareness among the community. Awareness must be created about IPRs, not only among the technocrats in private industry, but also within universities and the public at large as well as the police, customs and the judiciary, which play an important part in enforcement. Knowledge about IP amongst lawyers and judges will become increasingly important.

A systematic and objective analysis of the IP system in every country should be a key priority of strategic planners and policy-makers at the national level. This analysis and study should be done in the framework of the national or global system of innovation, so as to deal with all related aspects that have a bearing on making the most effective and efficient use of the IP system for social, cultural, technological and economic development.

Harnessing the power of IP through its protection and strategic use should be included in the national economic agenda. IP policy should form an integral part of a country's economic policy, industrial policy, S&T policy and educational policy.

Likewise, the teaching of, and interdisciplinary research in, IP (from legal, economics, business and engineering perspectives), should become an essential part of the law faculties in colleges and universities as well as other institutions of higher learning such as institutes of engineering, management, business and scientific research.

Development of multidimensional perspectives in teaching/training and research in IP law needs to be encouraged particularly in developing countries and in the countries in transition. This should be done with improved teaching and training programmes and courses and improved design, development and application of the curricula on IP laws and practices. A business perspective on strategic use and management of IP assets needs to developed. Updating teaching and training materials; creating new structures for organized research in the fields of IP, law and economics; and establishing contacts between professors, businesspeople and researchers should assume priority. Links between universities, technical institutions and industry also need to be strengthened.

There is a dearth of teaching and training materials on IPRs that are especially suitable for use in the developing countries and the countries in transition. IP law professors in developing countries should be given necessary documentation from which they could build the desired teaching/training materials. That documentation could also include the laws, regulations and business case studies from other countries.

Preparations for introducing an IP course in the curriculum takes time. Much of the effort is directed in compiling teaching/training material and reference sources on the business aspects of the law of IP. Since some guidance or even some starting material was needed, WIPO published, in 1988, a book entitled *Background Reading Material on Intellectual Property*. This book consists of a collection of reading materials on various aspects of IP law and administration and is intended for students in courses of studies at universities, particularly in developing countries and countries in transition, which are most affected by the unavailability of suitable teaching literature on IP. While primarily intended for students, that book may also be of use as a reference work for government officials, attorneys and business executives concerned with IP law or its administration and management.

In this context, distance learning (e-learning) is becoming a practical alternative and a complement to traditional training methods in order to make course/training materials accessible to larger audiences worldwide, including those in developing countries and countries in transition. Very useful distance learning courses and professional training are given by WIPO's Worldwide Academy. They are delivered primarily via the Internet. They offer new teaching methodologies, specially designed course materials, evaluation tools and tailored means of delivery. Where appropriate, videoconferencing sessions are organized to stimulate an academic environment by linking remote sites. Courses are specifically adapted to allow student-teacher interaction, student tests, course monitoring and on-line registration and evaluation systems.

One of the advantages of WIPO's distance learning program is that it increases the number and range of beneficiaries of teaching and training programmes. The web-based teaching technique brings teachers specializing in IP issues closer to students and other interested parties worldwide.

Partnerships with universities around the world enable identification of core groups of experts to serve as authors and instructional designers and to adapt text-based teaching materials into distance learning courses. Other experts could serve as core faculty and tutors to teach, monitor course delivery and provide student-teacher communication.

Governments in developing countries and countries in transition also should consider helping to establish and support activities of a National Inventors' Association, and where such an organization or association already exists, help to strengthen its infrastructure by supporting invention and innovation promotion as well as providing advice and guidance to inventors in their work. Such an association could be based on models of similar associations in a number of countries (eighty or so, including more than forty-one developing countries). Such a national inventors' association should preferably be headed by an eminent scientist, inventor or researcher of repute and should be geared to help inventors particularly in commercializing their inventions, an important area in which national inventors need to be guided and assisted. Such an association should also be encouraged join the International Federation of Inventors' Associations (IFIA), so that it could interact with other, similar member associations and share their experience in invention promotion, as well as assist in commercialization of inventions at the national and international levels.

Governments, industry organizations and inventors' associations could consider encouraging clubs and societies at the state and/or district levels to tap individual inventive efforts among women and youth and promote useful ideas from technical and even non-technical staff of, inter alia, SMEs to improve existing products and processes.

Finally, developing countries and countries in transition might consider establishing a national or sub-regional IP institute if one does not already exist. Such an institute needs to be assisted by the government concerned, but should, preferably, be established and developed by the national chambers of commerce and industry. Initially the governments could help by providing suitable accommodation and funding to set them up.

Establishing a modern legislative framework, however, is just the beginning; implementation and enforcement are a major challenge. Assistance should be provided in creating and strengthening administrations and institutions which support the legal infrastructure, such as collective management societies, police and customs authorities and professional organizations. Efficient enforcement of IPRs, particularly against counterfeiting and digital piracy, also requires international cooperation.

While governments need to ensure that legislation concerning IPRs is constantly updated and modernized in order to keep in step with new technologies, it is obvious that even the best laws in the world, duly promulgated, are of no use unless they are efficiently administered and effectively enforced.

Piracy in the cultural industry, to take an example, has reached a significant magnitude and extends to many countries. Printing and distributing books without any authorization from the rights owners and unauthorized translations have resulted in revenue losses to the original copyright holders in the estimated amount of around USD 2 billion. Pirated music in respect to cassettes, tapes and audiovisual recordings was estimated as being more than 2 billion units, worth nearly USD 4.5 billion. Likewise, software piracy in regard to 'stolen' software downloaded from the Internet itself was reckoned as being USD 1 billion annually.[15]

It is important that legislation and procedures in developing countries and in countries in transition emphasize to the maximum extent the enforcement of IPRs and provide for stern penal provisions and adequate criminal penalties against infringement. Rights-holding organizations should be encouraged to help through increased cooperation with governmental enforcement agencies, including anti-counterfeiting operations and public awareness campaigns. The judiciary should also appreciate the need for imposing the maximum punishment in the case of IPR infringement. This will help in maintaining and enhancing the national inventive and creative activity as well as supporting the innovative spirit of the people.

It is important to promote a uniform and predictable application of law so that commercial stability is provided by a just and expeditious resolution of disputes that are inevitable in knowledge- and innovation-based competitive commerce. P. Newman,[16]

---

[15]   Shahid Alikhan, *Socio Economic Benefits of Intellectual Property Protection in Developing Countries,* published by WIPO, Mar. 2000, pp 167 and 168.

[16]   Newman P. 'The Courts and Innovation', *Intellectual Property Management in Health and Agricultural Innovation: A Handbook of Best Practices* eds. A. Krattiger et al. (UK: MIHR & US: PIPRA 2007): <www. iphandbook.org>.

a judge in the US Court of Appeals for the Federal Circuit, has provided a comprehensive view of the issues connected with the role of courts in IP issues.

It would be germane here to mention, as an example, that to ensure effective enforcement of IPRs, Thailand has created a separate IPR Court, designated as the Central Intellectual Property and International Trade Court. It was inaugurated on 1 December 1997, and established under the Act for Establishment of a Procedure for Intellectual Property and Trade Court (B.E. 2539: 1996). The judges of this court hear cases and issue rulings on IP matters. With the passage of time, this court has been taking much more severe action against offenders. With the growing complexities in respect of IPRs, it would be worthwhile to follow up on this experiment in other countries, to help it become an international trend.

The availability of appropriate legislative measures is an indispensable mechanism for enforcement of IPRs. The important objective of such measures is the prevention of acts of infringement and the seizure of infringing copies of reproducing equipment and other implements that could be used for further infringements and those that constitute essential evidence and could disappear if not brought under the control of the court.

Under such measures it should be possible for rights owners to obtain preliminary injunctions to prevent infringements. Also, the courts must be able to order search, seizure and temporary impounding of suspected unauthorized copies of works and other protected subject matter including packaging materials and implements for the making of such copies and documents relating to such copies.

Civil remedies are, however, not always sufficient deterrents. Where infringement has become a profitable business, the closing down of one plant with the assistance of courts and law enforcement authorities may only mean that the plant may reopen somewhere else.

Infringements committed wilfully and with profit-making purposes should be punished by criminal sanctions and the level of such sanctions must make it clear that such infringements are serious offences. The criminal sanctions could comprise both fines and imprisonment, and where merited by the case, courts should be able to impose both these sanctions on the infringer.

No amount of good legislative provisions can deliver results if penalty provisions are inadequate or if enforcement procedures are cumbersome, slow and costly; these latter need to be strengthened and modernized nationally. Enhanced penal provisions have been promulgated since the mid-1980s in a number of countries. It should, however, be clear that in the digital environment there is greater need to protect both creativity and investment.

The most important contribution governments can make to ensure the effectiveness of IPRs is to provide speedy and cheap methods of enforcing them. As Keith Maskus asserts,[17] 'firms with easily copyable products and technologies such as pharmaceuticals, chemicals, food additives and software are more concerned with the ability of the local IPRs system to deter imitation'. Sustained enforcement, increased and extended criminal sanctions, prompt and thorough prosecutions and the threat of imprisonment can and do

---

[17] The Role of Intellectual Property Rights in Encouraging Foreign Direct Investment and Technology Transfer', by Prof. Keith E. Maskus at a Conference on 'Public-Private Initiatives after TRIPS: Designing a Global Agenda', held in Brussels, July 16-19, 1977.

deter small operators from counterfeiting and piracy, especially if wide publicity can also be given to particular successful cases.

### 8.13 ENFORCEMENT PROVISIONS IN THE TRIPS AGREEMENT

The enforcement provisions of the TRIPS Agreement have enumerated, in some detail, the civil and administrative procedures and remedies that each Member State must make available in its national laws, to enable right holders to enforce the IPRs established in Part III of the TRIPS Agreement.

In addition, the Agreement establishes performance requirements against which each member's fulfilment of its obligations to effectively enforce IPRs will be measured. The link to Article XXII and XXIII of GATT, 1994, in Article 64 of the TRIPS Agreement raises the consequences for any nation which might be tempted not to give full effect to the provisions of the TRIPS Agreement as required by its Article 1.

Part III of the said Agreement, referred to above, in Articles 41 to 61 inclusive on enforcement contains five sections, i.e., General Obligations (Article 41); Civil and Administrative Procedures and Remedies (Articles 42-49); Provisional Measures (Article 50); Special Requirements Related to Border Measures (Articles 51-60); and Criminal Procedures (Article 61).

The importance of international trade is emphasized by the requirement that the procedures be applied in a manner which avoids the creation of barriers to legitimate trade. In other words, it should be a balanced enforcement approach that not only helps trade and free movement of legitimate goods, but also provides for effective enforcement.

The role of customs authorities, which is an important factor in effective enforcement of IPRs, has received formal recognition with the conclusion of the TRIPS Agreement, also because of the contributions that such authorities could make in tackling the illegal trade and its growing internationalization.

As with the police and the judiciary, customs authorities and administrations have an important role to play in enforcement of IPRs. In this context, it needs to be ensured that this department of government is helped to act in close conjunction with the police and other enforcement agencies as well as with business and trade. Most IPR authorities in the government, the public as well as the private sectors, would certainly welcome such an integrated approach, which should also be emphasized and encouraged through constant awareness-building programmes.

Even the customs services in advanced countries lack the expertise to identify goods and the sophisticated methods being used by pirates and counterfeiters. In addition, they have the responsibility not to unnecessarily impede or hinder the flow of legitimate trade. It is important, therefore, to encourage cooperation between right holders and customs officials, so that the former could provide the latter with information and intelligence about imports or exports of counterfeit or illegal goods. This would then enable the customs authorities to use the information in pursuing their enforcement efforts as effectively as possible. The necessary controls cannot be effectively enforced unless there is close and continuing cooperation between customs authorities and the right holders. Such cooperation is an integral element of successful border enforcement strategy against counterfeit and pirated goods. Such cooperation between right holders and customs authorities should be a continuing joint effort to ensure efficient enforcement. It is important particularly since, for example, modern print technology can make a pirated edition almost indistinguishable from the original.

In this connection, the World Customs Organization (WCO), with its headquarters in Brussels (earlier known as the Customs Cooperation Council), which is an intergovernmental organization with worldwide membership spanning more than 150 countries, has been building awareness through seminars in its member countries. At these seminars, expert customs officials could, together with trade representatives, explain by showing the real and infringing goods and elaborate on customs concern with the protection of IPRs.

WCO's approach is to have customs authorities given the necessary powers through legislation adaptable to national needs and commensurate with the TRIPS Agreement. The goal is to help ensure an active and effective role for customs authorities in combating counterfeiting and piracy in the context of IPRs' violations. Model legislation, which was adopted by the WCO Council in 1995 and was subsequently made available to all WCO members, is consistent with the TRIPS Agreement. While it could be adapted to suit specific national requirements in respect to differing practices and legal traditions, the intention was that the basic enforcement provisions required by the TRIPS Agreement must be provided. Beyond those specific provisions, individual countries could also legislate enhanced legal provisions.

Such initiatives by the government must be backed up by initiatives by the private sector. For example, the Business Software Alliance (BSA) – a trade association based in Washington, DC in the US – was formed by leading software publishers to eradicate illegal copying, sale, distribution and use of computer software. Since it was founded in 1988, it has been active in carrying out anti-piracy campaigns in respect to computer software in a number of countries, including through public awareness-building. The total losses due to piracy in the computer software industry in Latin America alone were recently estimated at nearly half a billion USD.

India's National Association of Software and Service Companies (NASSCOM), for example, is a kind of 'chamber of commerce' for the software industry in the country. It is also aggressively campaigning against software piracy by helping to create awareness about software piracy amongst individual users. NASSCOM feels that such awareness-building would further consolidate the country's development in computer software and encourage the creation of world-class products and packages for the global software market. NASSCOM has reached an understanding with Washington-based BSA whereby both entities have been jointly campaigning against software piracy in India since July 1994. Having started with a series of public-awareness seminars, they have stepped up the campaign by sending thousands of mailers to inform people on the risks of buying or using pirated software.

The anti-piracy hot line launched by NASSCOM in Delhi has successfully facilitated raids on private centres since July 1995. Future plans envisage launching additional anti-piracy hot lines in Delhi and proposed new hot lines in Mumbai, Bangalore and Hyderabad – search, seizure and prosecutions are facilitated through information received via the hot lines. NASSCOM is also planning toll-free lines which could be accessed from different parts of the country, including the smaller towns where piracy is, and has been, equally possible.

The ingenuity of commercial pirates is boundless. It must be remembered that technology is a double-edged weapon available to infringers as well. Pirated editions of new products can come to the market at almost the same time as the original. Thus, in reality, the lead-time is practically non-existent. A software-based society is burdened with the fate of decreasing lead-times, and if the legal system, which prohibits copying, is not strengthened, the incentive for creating new products is lost. Industry and enterprises in developing countries and countries in transition need to be helped with stringent enforcement, or else investments could be adversely affected.

The new WCT and WPPT 'obligate countries to make illegal the acts of circumvention as well as the manufacture, importation and trafficking in these circumvention devices. These laws will become critical components in the fight against on-line piracy. They must be incorporated into domestic law and enforced through imposition of meaningful sanctions, including criminal penalties for violations'.[18] Encryption and technological safeguards for protecting IPR holders and declaring illegal their circumvention technologies, services, devices, etc., would need to be effectively backed by determined government action. As also suggested by Eric Smith, President of the Intellectual Property Alliance, as referenced in footnote 18:

> [C]ountries must also have the means and the will to locate sources of one-line piracy, raid and shut down these locations, seize equipment involved in piratical activities, arrest those engaged in serious commercial piracy, and impose deterrent penalties. E-commerce holds great promise, particularly for developing countries, because it will provide greater and quicker access to technology, information and entertainment, and will enable quicker and cheaper transfer of technology. But without effective protection and strong enforcement, these benefits are unlikely to be realised.

## 8.14 PRIMACY OF THE GOVERNMENT ROLE IN ENFORCEMENT OF IPRs

In order to adhere to various international agreements or to join certain international and regional organizations, many developing countries have adopted highly sophisticated, 'state-of-the-art' IP laws. On one level, it would seem that all forms of IP are more than adequately protected in such a country. The reality can be quite different, because laws are not always adequately enforced. The adoption of such laws is certainly a first step towards protecting IP and does sometimes accomplish the immediate result of enabling the adopting country to adhere to or join in many key international agreements in the field of IP. However, the mere adoption of these laws without effective enforcement will not fool

---

[18]  Eric H. Smith, President, International Intellectual Property Alliance in his presentation at the Berlin Congress of ALAI, 18 Jun. 1999.

the IP community for long. Nor will their mere adoption give the country the long-term benefits of protecting IP.[19]

As mentioned above, Part III of the TRIPS Agreement requires that countries set up mechanisms for effective enforcement of IPRs. The enforcement mechanisms are important and useful. But it appears that many countries are unable to enforce their relatively new IP laws for a number of reasons.

The laws in many developing countries have been modelled on the laws of either the United States, the United Kingdom or Europe (primarily France). While these models differ in some aspects, one thing they share is that they depend almost entirely on private enforcement of the law by IPRs owners, and not by the government.

One of the basic reasons why private enforcement works in developed countries is that the law provides sufficient incentive to the IP owner to make enforcement economically justifiable, i.e., as a general proposition, enforcement should not cost more than can be recovered.

In many developing countries and the countries in transition, the judiciary (and often private lawyers) are not familiar with IP law. Indeed, there is much uncertainty as to how the laws are to be applied and enforced. Awareness-building is needed to explain that intangible rights are to be taken just as seriously as property rights for tangible objects.

These countries are often faced with a variety of challenges. In light of these challenges, enforcement of IPRs often becomes a low priority, particularly where such enforcement is viewed as benefiting only wealthy foreign corporations. But if governments focus on the long-term economic benefits to their own country – in terms of trade, techno-economic development and compliance with international obligations – it may be possible to make such enforcement efforts a higher priority.

In sum, it is in the long-term economic self-interest of developing countries, as well as countries in transition, to legislate balanced IP laws which will not only protect the national interest, but will also fulfil the obligation of respecting the IP generated by other nations. To achieve this goal, emphasis must be placed not only on enacting and updating IP laws, but also on making certain that those laws are effectively enforced.

---

[19]  Jonathan Zavin & Scott M. Martin, *Economic Perspectives*, Vol. 2, No. 3, Jun. 1997.

CHAPTER NINE

# ROLE OF THE PRIVATE SECTOR IN
# THE INTELLECTUAL PROPERTY SYSTEM

- *Invention to Innovation*
- *Private Societies/Associations as Protectors of Intellectual Property (IP)*
- *Patents as Tools for Encouraging Private Research and Development (R&D)*
- *Responsibilities of the Private Sector*

## 9.1 FROM INVENTION TO INNOVATION

Thinking about inventions brings to mind scientists and researchers, whereas innovations bring to mind entrepreneurs and enterprises. Patents add value to innovative laboratory results and in so doing, provide incentives for private sector investment. Thereafter, more than any other sector of a national economy, it is the private sector which makes practical use of the tools of the IP system. No wonder, the private sector has a decisive role in the evolution and fine-tuning of the IP system and it continues to contribute significantly to constantly improve, update and modernize the IP system. In most countries, this sector proactively helps and advises in legislative revision in response to market needs of constantly emerging new technologies, administrative reforms and enforcement of Intellectual Property Rights (IPRs). The profit motive in the private sector helps to harness creative expressions and inventions for bringing innovative new products to the market nationally and internationally and in the creation of economic value and wealth, which helps the overall economic growth and development.

Let us focus here on the distinction between an invention and an innovation. The former is the idea for a new product or method, the expression of new knowledge, while the latter is the translation of the idea into practice, the process of using the invention or knowledge in production. It is the innovator who develops the practical application of an idea, makes things happen and who helps bring a new or improved product or service into the marketplace. New and improved products and/or services based on continuous innovation are the defining traits of a successful enterprise. As has been well said, 'innovation without invention is a tree without roots'.

In envisioning the use of IP tools for competitive strategies in the twenty-first century, the inventive spirit of researchers and scientists should be combined with the innovative spirit of private sector enterprises. In most countries around the globe, it is generally the private enterprises that are known to be distinguished innovators of products, ranging from value-added packaged cereals for children to energy-efficient incandescent lamps to more effective and safer drugs and pharmaceuticals.

In the future, most new forms of IP are likely to be defined in response to the felt needs of the private sector, particularly since the current economy is increasingly market-driven and markets are best understood by the private sector. The private sector wields its influence through its various professional associations, by publishing/submitting white papers for influencing policy-makers in government as well as in international agencies and through public relations via the mass media.

Within a private enterprise, the regular and systematic documenting of R&D activities requires the same degree of care and discipline as in a scientific and/or technology R&D organization. Inventors working in private enterprises are also encouraged to keep a regular record of their R&D activities. Such documentation of their research-oriented activities, maintained with all relevant details and with regularity, helps the enterprises or organizations concerned in deciding questions of inventorship when drafting precise claims and specifications. For successful commercialization of patented inventions, keeping a regular documented record of detailed information of the inventive activities helps in preventing and/or resolving disputes concerning patent ownership and/or infringement of patents belonging to others.

The forward-looking private sector enterprises in most countries, whose scientists, researchers, technocrats, inventors and creators amongst them, understand the value of the IP and are keen on its effective protection. The system which stimulates inventive and innovative activity, through facilitating access to the latest technological information, helps them develop newer technologies and assists in keeping their products competitive in the marketplace. It also promotes investment by providing the requisite guarantee against unauthorized use of inventive or creative works. The creators or inventors, entrepreneurs and enterprises thus also have the opportunity of recovering their R&D costs, which helps the private sector industry, whether big, medium or small, in further risk-taking in the course of investment of their resources.

## 9.2 Private Societies/Associations as Protectors of IP

For creating new technologies and products, the private sector must constantly encourage R&D efforts and the commercialization of the resulting inventions. A well-remunerated inventor often finds his stake in the enterprise attractive enough to be an increasingly active part of it.

While invention and innovation are essential for active and successful participation in today's competitive marketplace, the private sector in countries where inventive and creative capability is increasingly available should, if one does not exist, help in setting up a national inventors' association. Such an association, preferably headed by an eminent scientist, could help, advise and guide inventors and assist them in commercializing their inventions. Such an association exists in more than eighty countries worldwide;

most of them are also members of the International Federation of Inventors' Associations[1] (IFIA). This helps each association to interact with other, similar associations with regard to their respective invention promotion activities.

The growing role of the private sector and some of its organizations in the protection and promotion of IP worldwide may be cited here as examples. There is, in respect of book publishing and the book publishing industry, the International Publishers Association[2] (IPA), established in Paris in 1896. With its headquarters presently in Geneva, Switzerland, it comprises national, regional and specialized associations. It has seventy-eight member organizations in sixty-five countries worldwide. The IPA, as a private sector non-governmental organization, has consultative relations with a number of United Nations agencies and upholds the rights of publishers in the publication and distribution of works of the mind, subject to their respecting all legal rights attached to these works, nationally and internationally. Importantly, the IPA helps to promote and protect the principles of copyright and to encourage authorship and dissemination of creative works; also to defend copyright against infringements which would restrict the rights of authors. It holds a copyright conference every four years. The IPA also publishes, inter alia, annual book title production in various countries, including new titles, new editions and reprints as well as final totals of titles.

To protect authors' rights worldwide, there is also the International Confederation of Societies of Authors and Composers (CISAC), with its headquarters in Paris and headed by a director general. It was initially established by eighteen societies in June 1926, and is yet another institution in the private sector playing an important role in IP protection. Today, it has as its members 203 authors' societies (also called performers' rights societies) in 105 countries including fifty-six developing countries. Each of these ensures the defense of moral interests of authors, as well as their material interests, and helps in the collection and distribution of copyright royalties.

It would be interesting here to recall that the first of the societies of authors was established in France. With Beaumerchais leading the legal confrontation with theatres which were not recognizing the authors' rights, *the Bureau de législation dramatique* was established in 1777; later, it became *the Société des auteurs et compositeurs dramatique* (SACD), the first collective administration society of authors' rights. Around sixty years later, towards the end of 1837, famous French writers Honoré de Balzac, Alexandre Dumas and Victor Hugo, among others, formed the *Société des gens de lettres* (SGDL). This was followed by the establishment in 1850 of a collecting agency that was soon to give place to the currently operating *Société des auteurs, compositeures et éditeurs de musique* (SACEM).

Such authors' societies, (referred to in Chapter 5), apart from SACEM in France, include in developed countries and in countries in transition, for example, MUSICAUTOR in Bulgaria; GEMA in the Federal Republic of Germany; ARTISJUS in Hungary; SIAE in Italy; ZAIKS in Poland; RAO in the Russian Federation; SGAE in Spain, SUISA in

---

[1]  <www.invention-ifia.ch/>.

[2]  <www.internationalpublishers.org/>.

Switzerland; PRS in the United Kingdom; as well as ASCAP, BMI and SESAC in the US. Authors' and performing rights societies also exist in a large number of developing countries, for example Algeria, Argentina, Brazil, Cameroon, China, Egypt, India, Jordan, Malaysia, Mauritius, Mexico, Morocco, Nigeria, the Republic of Korea, Senegal, Singapore, South Africa, Sri Lanka, Thailand and Tunisia, among others. These organizations assist in protection of copyright at both the national and international levels.

Mention should also be made here of an important London-based organization – the British Copyright Council[3] (BCC). It is an umbrella organization bringing together organizations that represent those who create or hold rights in literary and artistic works and those who perform such works. The BCC functions principally as a liaison committee for its member associations, providing them with a forum for the discussion of issues of copyright interest. It also acts as a pressure group for changes in copyright laws at the European and international level.

In respect to music, which itself is a universal language protected by copyright, the private sector has helped to develop legal conditions for the global music industry to prosper in the digital era and promote the value of music worldwide. It is through an international non-governmental organization, the London-based International Federation of the Phonographic Industry[4] (IFPI), that the creative and dynamic music and recording industry is represented worldwide. This organization represents, in the private sector, 1,400 recording companies in seventy-six countries, including major recording companies as well as small independent producers. It also has national groups in forty-six countries. While its International Secretariat is in London, it is linked with its regional offices in Brussels, Hong Kong, Miami and Moscow. The organization, which helps with market access, is geared towards fighting music piracy and, with the help of concerned international organizations, in promoting good and adequate copyright and IP laws.

The impact of technology, especially the Internet, in the context of the development of the digital music market is very much being kept in view. Again, since it is illegal to produce or sell copyrighted material without the permission of the rights holders, it is just as illegal to build a commercial business on the basis of industrial property and copyright infringement. Private sector recording companies are getting on with the job of providing legitimate content to consumers in new and creative ways in the online environment. While the online world is very much a part of the music industry's future, the industry's organization, the IFPI, is concentrating on tracking the legitimate market online as well as the growing volume and proliferating piracy levels on the Internet.

The IFPI is not only helping in protecting national copyright laws in the countries in which it operates and helping develop the legal conditions and technologies for the recording industry to prosper in the digital era, but it has also become a worldwide investor in local culture and in promoting the value of music. According to the IFPI's annual publication entitled, 'The Recording Industry in Numbers: 2001', (which is the most definitive source of global music market information), 68% of sales in the year 2000 were recordings

---

[3]    <www.britishcopyright.org/>.
[4]    <www.ifpi.org/>.

by local artists and local music, which is a sign of the industry's ability to thrive in all regions of the world.

The private sector throughout has had an important role to play in the promotion and protection of IP in respect to protecting individuals and enterprises in most sectors of the economy, including information technology, which now provides millions of jobs in a number of countries.

An important private sector organization, which is a coalition formed in 1984 consisting of seven trade associations representing an important segment of the US copyright industry, is also worth mentioning here. It is the International Intellectual Property Alliance[5] (IIPA) based in Washington, DC. Its associates are the AFMA (formerly known as the American Film Marketing Association); Association of American Publishers (AAP); Business Software Alliance (BSA); Interactive Digital Software Association (IDSA); Motion Picture Association (MPA); National Music Publishers' Association(NMPA); and Recording Industry Association of America (RIAA).

To briefly describe the supportive role of some of these organizations and their set-up, two examples are given below:

The Motion Picture Association of America (MPAA) and its international counterpart, the MPA, constitute the voice of the American motion picture, home video and television industries domestically through the MPAA and internationally through the MPA. Founded in 1922 as the trade association of the American Film Industry, MPAA has broadened its mandate over the years to reflect the diversity of an expanding industry. The MPA was formed in 1945 in the aftermath of World War II, to re-establish American films in the world market. The MPA conducts its activities from its headquarters in Los Angeles, California and from offices in Washington, DC; Brussels; New Delhi; Rio de Janeiro; Singapore; Mexico City; Toronto; and Jakarta.

Today, US films are shown in more than 150 countries worldwide and American television programs are broadcast in more than 125 international markets. The US film industry provides the majority of pre-recorded cassettes seen by millions throughout the world. This complex audiovisual industry is represented globally by the MPA.

Another important organization, which is an associate of the IIPA, dealing with an important sector protected by the IP – the software sector – is the BSA, founded in 1988 and based in Washington DC. It is a trade association concerned with promoting a safe and legal digital world; it is helping educate consumers on software management, copyright protection, cyber security, e-commerce and other Internet-related issues. It is assisting the world's commercial software industry with governments and in the international arena and has been active in carrying out anti-piracy campaigns in a number of countries, including through public awareness-building. Piracy of software, according to the BSA's estimates of software downloaded from the Internet itself, amounts to USD 1 billion annually, and indicates the enormous challenge of illegal software being made available on the Internet.

---

[5]   <www.iipa.com/>.

Having mentioned two of the private sector associates of the IIPA in the film and software areas, it may be worthwhile to go back to the film world to mention the Indian film industry. This important sector of the cultural industry is also very much concerned with the copyright protection against piracy.

The Indian Motion Picture Producers Association represents India's movie industry, which is the world's largest in terms of films produced annually. It is also an old industry with motion pictures having come to India in 1896, when the Lumière Brothers Cinematographe unveiled six soundless short films in Bombay (now Mumbai). This was just one year after the Lumière Brothers, inventors of cinematography, had set up their company in Paris. Indian technology in filmmaking is among the best in developing countries. According to unofficial estimates, the Indian film industry has an annual turnover of approximately over USD 1 billion. It employs more than 6 million people, most of whom are contract workers, not regular employees.

Now to come to another important area, broadcasting, a few words are necessary about an equally important, international non-governmental organization – the European Broadcasting Union[6] (EBU), which is the largest professional association of national broadcasters in the world. The Union has seventy-one active members in fifty-two countries of Europe, North Africa and the Middle East and forty-five associate members in twenty-eight other countries. The EBU was founded in February 1950 by Western European radio and television broadcasters. It merged with the International Radio and Television Organisation OIRT, its counterpart in Eastern Europe, in 1993. The EBU negotiates broadcasting rights, organizes programme exchanges, coordinates co-production and provides a full range of operational, commercial, technical and legal services. The EBU works in close collaboration with broadcasting unions in other continents and particularly helps in protection of IPRs of broadcasting organizations with WIPO, UNESCO, and the International Labour Organization (ILO).

## 9.3 PATENTS AS TOOLS FOR ENCOURAGING PRIVATE R&D

While it is universally admitted that patents have an important role in stimulating innovation and investment, it is equally felt that the IP and patent system should provide a balance between the necessity of suitable compensation for inventors and the public interest of enabling people to reap the benefits from new inventions. This balance is particularly important in order to prevent an adverse impact on health through any unreasonable increase in prices of drugs and pharmaceuticals with stronger IP protection.

Pharma and healthcare have become key sectors in the growth of economy of many developing countries. Consequent to the Trade-Related Aspects of Intellectual Property Rights (TRIPS) Agreement, a large number of countries (nearly fifty, including the

---

[6]  <www.ebu.ch/>.

developed and developing as well as those in transition), were required to update and strengthen their patent legislation and to revise their exclusion from patentability of pharmaceutical products. The transitional period for this was specified as no later than the year 2005 for developing countries while least developed countries need to transition before 2016. However, some countries legislated for the necessary revision and modified their patent legislation to provide for such protection well ahead of the TRIPS Agreement deadline. These countries include, inter alia, Brazil, China, Mexico, the Republic of Korea, and South Africa. Under the Indian law an invention included a new product or process involving an inventive step and capable of industrial application for all patents, except for agrochemicals and pharmaceuticals. The process of including product patents for agrochemicals and pharmaceuticals has been completed by the Indian government in the year 2005. For example, Indian patent laws now include products for pharmaceuticals, a major step towards maintaining Indian laws' compliance with TRIPS.

In view of the efforts of research-based pharmaceutical industry to generate, use and export their much cheaper drugs to various countries, such legislative revision in these and other countries constitutes a landmark that could also lead to reverse the tide of ideas and products coming from overseas. It was also expected to foster an innovative pharmaceutical industry committed to R&D, encouraging inventive activity and producing patent worthy molecules, especially of life-saving drugs which could, with their cheaper technocratic manpower, very effectively compete in the world markets. However, the time for producing such new molecules of life-saving and other drugs is estimated to be around ten to twelve years from synthesis to marketing, that is, from discovery to saleability or from the laboratory to the pharmacy.

It is also possible that after taking an innovative new drug on a ten-year plus evaluation in the process of its development, it may still fail commercially, or if it succeeds, could be copied or pirated unless protected by strong and effectively enforced IP legislation. Again, while R&D costs are common for all inventive activity, and are not special for drug research only, they are, perhaps in respect to the latter, a higher percentage of the total costs. R&D in the production of drugs is complex and expensive. It is claimed to cost around USD 700 million to 800 million to bring a molecule to the marketplace.[7] In developing countries, some of which have professionally very competent scientists and technocrats, this cost could be significantly reduced.

Consumer groups, however, argue that greed is largely to blame and that drug companies are making excessive profits. But those concerned in the industry consider that prices are largely high in order to cover the cost of R&D – a figure which runs into hundreds of millions of dollars. Particularly in the US, the 'big Pharma' industries ensure that the country's liberal pricing system stimulates globally dominant innovation, as firms spend their R&D dollars more freely in the hope of earning large profits to cover their R&D expenditure.

---

[7]   'Priorities for Global Research and Development of Interventions', Disease Control Priorities Project, 2006: <http://files.dcp2.org/pdf/expressbooks/researc.pdf>.

## 9.3.1 Importance of Product-Patents for Private R&D

Pharmaceutical companies understandably argue that to have an incentive to engage in R&D, and to recoup the large development expenditure involved, product patent protection is a must. That is, without product patents, the incentive to innovate would be lacking.

Since the IP system is a necessary policy planning instrument for encouraging invention and innovation, the main concern should be whether stronger IP protection could help in the long term in promoting innovation and commercialization of emerging new technologies. This, in turn, could generate gainful national employment as well as constantly provide newer and improved products at affordable prices for consumers, while allowing the industry to make a reasonable profit, enabling it to continue to do business.

Strong product patent protection also makes it possible for inventors to earn a reasonable return on their R&D investment. Newer products are costly to make and are the result of expensive research. They can be used by third parties at little cost, as imitation costs are much lower than the costs of creating an invention. Only product patent protection can provide the legal basis for the exclusive use of inventions. It also provides a guarantee for the inventor that his R&D efforts will not be nullified by much cheaper products, brought to the marketplace by competitors who have neither invested in the R&D nor in the invention. Strong patent protection enables innovation and creativity to become a legally protected item of trade and of international transaction. Thus, without legal safeguards, through constantly updated IP legislation and adequate protection against imitation, no investments could be expected in pharmaceutical research.

The focus on prices in relation to stronger IPRs has become more acute. Propelled by improved communications, lower transport costs, resulting in easier flow of products between countries (including those encouraging parallel imports), better information about product prices in other countries (which is of interest to parallel importers/consumers worldwide), the higher IP content in products, especially when traded between countries at different levels of techno-economic development, has been causing some concern.

The international norms and standards in respect to IP, such as those included in the TRIPS Agreement, require all World Trade Organization (WTO) member countries that had lower standards to raise their national standards of IP protection to conform to those of the Agreement. There is a feeling that prices of products that rely on such higher IP protection would tend to increase. Also, that the price increase would put common drugs out of reach for most people in the poorer developing countries. It is also argued that herbal medicines used for healthcare by the poorer segments of the population will also become unaffordable. The question asked is in the form of a quip, whether it is important to have patent rights or patient's rights. Patient's rights may be provided through good, efficient and prompt medical insurance services, which are, in many countries, very effectively operated by the private sector. Enhanced government spending on health services could also help.

However, the provision in the TRIPS Agreement allowing for compulsory licensing is important for developing countries, since they provide the necessary flexibility for addressing their public health needs. Compulsory licensing provisions allow governments to grant licenses to third parties to produce and distribute life-saving medicines, to ensure that these drugs are more readily available and more affordable for the general public. Although nothing in the TRIPS Agreement limits governments in issuing compulsory licenses, certain Member States of the WTO interpret the concerned provision rather narrowly, thus objecting to its broad-based use.

The factors responsible for increasing the availability of drugs at affordable prices for certain life threatening diseases such as HIV/AIDS with epidemic proportions makes an interesting study. Over the past decade, the emergence of competition from generic manufacturers,[8] direct negotiations with pharmaceutical companies,[9] activist pressure,[10] Compulsory licensing,[11,12] creation of international drug purchase facility such as UNITAIDS[13] have all helped in creating a dramatic drop in the prices of certain drugs to treat HIV/AIDS in resource poor countries.

### 9.3.2 The Patent versus Patient Debate

Since the TRIPS Agreement has considerably expanded the kind of products that could be protected by one or more forms of IPRs, there are fears that prices of some socially sensitive products, such as pharmaceuticals, or of the agricultural inputs to farmers in developing countries, could increase to unaffordable levels. The famous institution, Oxfam, which is campaigning to cut the cost of medicines for poor people, has produced the papers 'Cut the Cost'[14] and 'Patent Injustice : How the World Trade Rules Threaten the Health of Poor People'.[15] In its preface, Sir John Sulston, co-founder of the Human Genome Project, highlighted some points germane to the same argument. In brief, it was stated that when new technologies had such potential to contribute to human welfare and had emerged as an important determinant of competitiveness in the global markets, it is disturbing that monopoly rights of technology producers are being strengthened. It further stated how patent rules would affect the health of ordinary people, especially in poor countries. The pharmaceutical companies would, it is felt, as a result of lengthened patent protection (twenty years), be able to sell their new medicines at higher prices for a longer

---

[8]  'A matter of life and death: The role of patents in access to essential medicines', Medecins Sans Frontier (2001); <www.doctorswithoutborders.org/publications/reports/2001/doha_11-2001.pdf>.

[9]  <www.clintonfoundation.org/about-the-clinton-foundation>.

[10]  'A matter of life and death: The role of patents in access to essential medicines', Medecins Sans Frontier (2001); <www.doctorswithoutborders.org/publications/reports/2001/doha_11-2001.pdf>.

[11]  Implementation of paragraph 6 of the Doha Declaration on the TRIPS Agreement and public health, WTO (2003): <www.wto.org/english/tratop_e/trips_e/implem_para6_e.htm>.

[12]  'Thailand to issue compulsory license for efavirenz' Aidsmap (2006); <www.aidsmap.com/en/news/A774C0DF-0EB5-401B-A2DC-7E196831F8ED.asp>.

[13]  <www.unitaid.eu>.

[14]  'Cut the Cost – Fatal Side Effects: Medicine Patents Under the Microscope', published by the Policy Department of Oxfam (UK), Feb. 2001: <www.oxfam.org.uk/resources/policy/health/downloads/fatal_side_effects.rtf>.

[15]  'Patent Injustice : How World Trade Rules Threaten the Health of Poor People', published by Oxfam (UK): <www.oxfam.org.uk/resources/policy/health/downloads/patentinjustice.pdf>.

duration. The losers, it stated, were likely to be millions of people, and hard-pressed government health services, who will be unable to afford the vital new medicines. Interestingly, it also mentioned that patent protection has an important role in stimulating investment and innovation, but that any patent system should balance the need to reward the inventors with the greater public interest for people to benefit from such inventions.

There are others who argue that use of IPRs gives their holders a certain degree of what is termed market power, in the form of a right to exclude competitors for a limited period of time. The scope of this market power or right, however, is based not only on the IPRs owned by the rights holder, but also on a host of other factors affecting competition in the marketplace.

It is difficult, therefore, to single out strong IP protection as the main ingredient determining pricing. The latter is governed in different markets by their varying governmental controls on licensing, tax structures, extent of import controls, availability and prices of competing alternatives, price controls, purchasing power of consumers, and efficiency of distribution networks, among other factors. Thus, it is neither possible, nor perhaps correct, to pinpoint IP and patent protection as the single main factor determining pricing. In fact, the sale prices of drugs, like those for other commodities, are indeed regulated by the relevant producer companies in certain industrialized countries, in their own as well as other countries, on the basis of what the market can bear. Drug prices in developed country markets are steadily being regulated with reference to global pricing. It is, therefore, often quite misleading to make a cross-country comparison by simply multiplying pricing in certain developed countries by prevailing exchange rates. Prices in any market are influenced by several factors, including, in particular, the purchasing power in that market.

Again, the price premium, attributable to exclusivity, could be controlled through various checks and balances, such as the purchasing power of the patients or therapeutic competition from similar cheaper unpatented drugs. Importantly, government drug price control orders are available under permanent or reserve powers in a number of countries. These powers have been used to control drug prices by allowing cheaper, generic copies but should, however, be used to make sure that the national policies to obtain adequate supplies of essential drugs at moderate and/or competitive prices are not adversely affected. The Drug Price Control Order of the Indian government, for example, provides for public policy objectives of making drugs available at affordable prices, which is not, however, the main objective of the patent law. Their patent policy is not the prime policy instrument for control of pharmaceutical prices. For example, the National Pharmaceutical Pricing Authority (NPPA) of 2002 has taken into account new challenges posed by liberalization of the Indian economy, and has revised the Drug Policy of 1986. The revision will take care of public policy objectives of ensuring abundant availability at reasonable prices within the country, of good quality essential drugs of mass consumption, and simultaneously create an incentive framework for the pharmaceutical industry to channel high levels of investment into R&D and introduction of new technologies.

It is relevant here to quote from the United Nation Development Programme's (UNDP) report 'Cooperation South 2002' in the context of current issues in IPRs:

> Buying cheaper generic drugs rather than costly brand-names ones is now the policy of the U.N. disease fund created in 2001. The Global Fund for Fighting AIDS, Tuberculosis and Malaria, has a target of US$7 billion to 10 billion per year ... and has received requests from developing countries for US$ 8 billion worth of assistance ... The Fund's decision will encourage manufacturers of generic drugs in Brazil, India and other countries, to sell more in developing countries, in place of medications from patent-holders in the North. It may also prompt more price reductions by Northern manufacturers, as has already happened with some drugs for treating HIV-AIDS.[16]

In the US, attention has been focussed on the affordability of prescription drugs. The total retail spending on prescription drugs reached USD 154.5 billion (2001) according to the National Institute for Health Care Management. Some of the major drug makers were not in favour of efforts to accelerate the marketing of generic drugs, which usually cost less than brand-name drugs protected by patents. The goal, however, was to promote the lesser-priced generic drugs and it was proposed to bring new regulations aimed at speeding consumer access to lower-cost generic drugs.

Incidentally, governments can do everything to check prices, as price control is not prohibited under the TRIPS Agreement. Strict price regulation in two important countries in Europe has succeeded in controlling drug prices in other countries with freer pricing.

The WHO Commission on IPRs, Innovation and Public Health (CIPIH) has come out with a set of valuable recommendations that pertain to other actions that the developing and developed country governments can take. Some of these are:[17]

– Developed country governments could devote a growing proportion of their health R&D funding to the health needs of the developing countries, with an emphasis on upstream and translational research;
– Developed countries and the WTO could take actions to ensure compliance with Article 66.2 of the TRIPS Agreement and to facilitate the transfer of technology for the pharmaceutical production in accordance with paragraph 7 of the Doha Declaration;
– Encourage public funding bodies to introduce policies for sensible patenting and licensing practices from technologies arising from their funding to promote downstream innovation;

---

[16] UNDP Report 'Cooperation South 2002: Creativity, Innovation and Intellectual Property Rights,' <http://eric.ed.gov/ERICDocs/data/ericdocs2sql/content_storage_01/0000019b/80/1b/5f/40.pdf>.  &  'Current Issues in Intellectual Property Rights ... UN Global Disease Fund Encourages Use of Generic Drugs', <http://tcdc1.undp.org/CoopSouth/2002_dec/p66-69_in_the_news.pdf>.

[17] 'Public Health Innovation and Intellectual Property Rights' Report of the CIPIH, WHO, 2005: <www.who.int/intellectualproperty/en/>.

- Create practical initiatives that would motivate more scientists to contribute through 'open source' methods; and
- Create comprehensive and reliable databases of information about patents, which can remove barriers to the availability and access.


9.4 RESPONSIBILITIES OF THE PRIVATE SECTOR

The private sector in this field will also have to comply with the TRIPS provisions. Copying patented drugs will need to stop, in the industry's as well as in the larger national interests. Competition for advantage in the global trade and investment is not a new phenomenon. The industry would, in its own long-term future interests, need to seriously consider moving from a 'copying culture' to an 'innovation culture' or from 'breaking patents' to 'creating patents'. Also, greater emphasis will be needed on product development than on reverse engineering. New ideas should be helped to become new processes and new products.

Increased adaptation in the world market for innovative drugs by the concerned private sector would help meeting local requirements. The process should extend from increased R&D for new molecules to collaboration and joint ventures. National and international level mergers, as well as joint ventures, are now becoming a common feature. At the national level in a number of countries, smaller units are merging with larger companies, not only to benefit from economies of scale but also to upgrade their research facilities. Planning sales development of important drugs with co-marketing partners would help not only market penetration but also profits necessary for ploughing into further research.

It should not be overlooked that the techno-economic as well as the social purpose and objective of the patent system is to provide an incentive for R&D and in the context of healthcare, to ensure easier availability of life-saving drugs. This is especially so for the treatment of tropical and other diseases as well as AIDS, particularly in certain developing countries. This latter task is important because between 22 million and 23 million people are living with AIDS in Sub-Saharan Africa alone. Progress is not possible in this area without research (for example, in respect to vaccines or drugs for cancer, leukemia, malaria or AIDS), and research is expensive. Effective and strong patent protection is essential for financing such research and for promoting higher levels of national innovative activity.

As recommended by WHO CIPIH,[18] the private sector can do a lot to help improve accessibility of medicines to resource-poor people by adopting suitable patent and enforcement policies. It can avoid filing patents or enforcing them in ways that might inhibit access when it comes to low-income developing countries. It can grant voluntary licenses to such countries and accompany this with helpful technology transfer activities. Suitably developed corporate donation programs can also be of great value, if done in win-win partnerships with governments.

---

[18] See fn. 12.

While protection of inventive and creative research through use of the IP system is imperative, R&D promotion must also be an important aspect of private sector activities. At the same time, private enterprises producing easily pirated products in pharmaceuticals, chemicals or software should encourage and support their respective national IPR systems in deterring imitation.

In order to meet the twin objectives of growth with equity, knowledge must not remain the prerogative of the few in this twenty-first century. Members of each society should be given access to knowledge and should be helped to become knowledgeable workers. The private sector should devote increasing attention to achieving gains from stronger but judicious use of IPRs, and ensure that the IPR system is used advantageously, both for private as well as public good. Effective IP protection, supported by the private sector, can help encourage competition at all levels of economic development, and assist in promoting broad-based and sustainable growth.

# CHAPTER TEN

# CIVIL SOCIETY AND INTELLECTUAL PROPERTY

– *The Nature of Civil Society*
– *Flexibility in the TRIPS Agreement*
– *Civil Society and Biodiversity*

## 10.1 THE NATURE OF CIVIL SOCIETY

The current concept of civil society has grown during the last two and a half centuries. After the American and French Revolutions, like-minded sections of the population in the liberal world, with the gradually increasing competition in the marketplace, started associations or organizations around their respective common interests.

Civil society consists of many institutions, trade unions, charity organizations, neighbourhood groups, self-help organizations, etc. It includes a cross-section of voluntary organizations, social interest groups and cooperatives. It includes, importantly, non-governmental organizations (NGOs) as well as groups engaged in specific public interests such as checking and controlling crime, human rights and environmental improvements. During the last decade or so, such groups have emerged in the field of Intellectual Property Rights (IPRs) as well.

These networks evidently assist both the society and the economy. While they contribute the necessary checks and balances to the power of the state in their respective countries, they also encourage cooperative mutual support in societies and enhance social cohesion and economic development.

Civil society organizations, whether national or international, contribute their knowledge and expertise in monitoring activities that are concerned with sustainable development. They do have a kind of overlap with, or dependence on, the state or government sector as well as the private sector. The overlap could be on questions of public health, human rights, freedoms of speech and association or with regard to the rights of creators and inventors of intellectual works.

In particular, national NGOs in the Intellectual Property (IP) sector such as the local music industry, the software industry, the publishing sector, the collective management administrations as well as the national inventors' associations where they exist, not only contribute substantially towards an increasingly quality-conscious approach to economic management, but also help generate resources for different social programmes.

## 10.2 ROLE OF NGOs

For dialogue and transparency at every level, national, regional and international, these NGOs are represented in most United Nations agencies and participate actively in those agencies in giving their views for determining policy-making. Many of them have done original research and brought out position papers; they hold conferences on the subject of IPRs and their protection and these activities are conveyed through the press and on websites. The Internet has also given them an opportunity to reach out. For example, twenty-seven international NGOs took part in the third session of World Intellectual Property Organization's (WIPO) Intergovernmental Committee on Intellectual Property and Genetic Resources, Traditional Knowledge and Folklore, held in June 2002 at Geneva.

Important among these organizations were:

- International Literary and Artistic Association (ALAI);
- Centre for International Industrial Property Studies (CEIPI), which teaches the international IP system;
- International Chamber of Commerce (ICC);
- International Confederation of Music Publishers (ICMP);
- Crop Life International, a global federation representing the plant science industry;
- International Federation of Pharmaceutical Manufacturers Association (IFPMA), which represents the worldwide research-based pharmaceutical industry;
- International Federation of Industrial Property Attorneys (FICPI), an organization working for the interests of patent and trademark professionals worldwide;
- International Federation of Musicians (FIM);
- International Federation of Reproduction Rights Organizations (IFRRO), which links together all reproduction rights organizations and international associations of right holders;
- Genetic Resources Action International (GRAIN), which promotes the sustainable management and use of agriculture biodiversity based on people's control over genetic resources and local knowledge;
- World Self-Medication Industry (WSMI), a federation that aims to create and maintain an international environment intended to improve opportunities for people to manage their own health through effective self-medication products;
- Max-Planck-Institute for Foreign and International Patent, Copyright and Competition Law, a research institution devoted to the field of national, European and international IP law;
- Institute for Agriculture and Trade Policy (IATP), which promotes resilient family farms, rural communities and ecosystems around the world through research and education, science and technology and advocacy;
- International Environmental Law Research Centre (IELRC), an independent research organization focussing on international and comparative environmental law issues, with particular emphasis on India and East Africa;
- International Plant Genetic Resources Institute (IPGRI), which is devoted solely to the study and promotion of agricultural biodiversity;
- International Seed Federation (ISF), a non-governmental, non-profit organization representing the seed industry;

- International Publishers Association (IPA), which represents the publishing industry worldwide and is an accredited NGO enjoying consultative status in the United Nations; and
- World Conservation Union (IUCN), the mission of which is to influence, encourage and assist societies throughout the world to conserve the integrity and diversity of nature and to ensure that any use of natural resources is equitable and ecologically sustainable.

Similar organizations include:

- Aboriginal and Torres Strait Islander Commission (ATSIC), Australia's national policy-making and advocacy organization for indigenous people;
- Union of Industrial and Employers' Confederations of Europe (UNICE), which seeks to promote the common professional interests of the firms represented by its members;
- World Federation for Culture Collections (WFCC), a network of specialist microbiologists;
- Biotechnology Industry Organization (BIO), which takes up, among others, the issues and initiatives of IP;
- International Centre for Trade and Sustainable Development (ICTSD), which contributes to a better understanding of development and environmental concerns in the context of international trade;
- European Chemical Industry Council (CEFIC);
- International Association of Plant Breeders for the Protection of Plant Varieties;
- Association for Progressive Communications;
- International Cooperation for Development and Solidarity (CIDSE), an international coalition of fourteen Catholic development organizations working together with organizations and partners on various issues including trade-related IPRs;
- Indigenous Peoples Biodiversity Information Network (IBIN), a mechanism to exchange information about experiences and projects and to increase collaboration among indigenous groups working on common causes related to biodiversity use and conservation;
- Centre for Documentation, Research and Information of Indigenous Peoples (doCip), a Swiss NGO linking indigenous people and the United Nations; and
- International Association for the Protection of Intellectual Property (AIPPI), the world's leading NGO for research into, and formulation of, policy for laws relating to the protection of IP, which unites practitioners, academics and owners of IP.

Interestingly, civil society organizations worldwide and the concerned NGOs seem to share a common view, also emphasized above, that IPR is not an end in itself; rather it is a means to an end: the end being socio-economic welfare as well as techno-economic growth. Some of these organizations have been fostering participation through training and education of the elements in society who wish to engage in activities related to civic life. These civil societies and NGOs have increasingly been providing their respective technical expertise, through policy-makers, to governments with the aim of helping to shape policy.

Category-wise, civil society institutions and organizations fall into two categories, namely, those that are for effective IP protection and those that are against the developed world oriented IP protection. Amongst those who are for such protection are international NGOs including:

- Secretariat of the Convention on Biological Diversity (CBD); IPA;
- International Federation of the Phonographic Industry (IFPI);
- The International Confederation of Societies of Authors and Composers (CISAC);
- Motion Picture Associations and National Film Producers' Associations;
- National software companies and their associate, the Business Software Alliance (BSA);
- The International Intellectual Property Alliance (IIPA);
- The World Association of Small and Medium Enterprises (WASME);
- The Society for Research into Sustainable Technologies and Institutions (SRISTI), which is an organization set up to strengthen the creativity of grass roots inventors;
- Various chambers of commerce; patent agents and attorney associations;
- IP law firms;
- The large section of the press and journalists that are in favour of IP protection, among many others.

A few important associations of similar nature in the IP sector are:

- Asian Patent Attorneys Association (APAA) Hong Kong Group, an NGO consisting of IP practitioners who are patent attorneys or attorneys-at-law in the Asian region;
- National Association of Patent Practitioners (NAPP), a non-profit organization dedicated to supporting patent practitioners and those working in the field of patent law, its practice and technological advances;
- Association of Patent Attorneys in Swedish Industry (SIPF);
- Japan Patent Attorneys Association (JPAA);
- Nevada Inventors Association (NIA); and
- Inventors' Association of New England (IANE).

As regards those that are against developed world oriented IP protection, there are some national or regional associations of pharma generics and some other eminent institutions such as:

- Oxfam International, the CIDSE formally created in 1967 and earlier known as International Cooperation for Socio-Economic Development, whose seven founder members were Austria, Belgium, France, Germany, Netherlands, Switzerland and the United States;
- Certain consumer groups;

- Journalists and some sectors of the press which are against strong IP protection, especially concerning healthcare;
- Civil society groups representing people and consumers below the poverty line.

A few other organizations in the healthcare sectors are:

- The European Generic Medicines Association (EGA), the representative body for the European generic pharmaceutical industry which is in the forefront of providing high quality medicines at affordable prices for millions of Europeans;
- Health Global Access Project Coalition (Health GAP Coalition), which works to assure access to essential medicines by people with HIV/AIDS in the developing world; and
- Health Action International (HAI), a non-profit, global network of health, development, consumer and other public interest groups in more than seventy countries working for a more rational use of medicinal drugs.

The paradox is evident when some of the organizations that have most vigorously opposed globalization per se in this context have themselves often considerably benefited from the resultant improved technologies that have helped them in turn.

## 10.3 POINTS OF CONCERN

The points of concern of those in favour of strong IPR protection and those not in favour of such protection can best be seen in two statements in connection with public health concerns as quoted in the Commission on Intellectual Property Rights (CIPR) report[1] entitled 'Integrating Intellectual Property Rights and Development Policy'. First, Sir Richard Sykes, former Chairman of GlaxoSmithKline (GSK), at the Royal Institute of International Affairs in London on 14 March 2002, stated:

> Few would argue with the need for IP protection in the developed world, but some question whether it is appropriate to extend its coverage to the developing world, which the TRIPS Agreement is gradually doing. ... IP protection is not the cause of the present lack of access to medicines in developing countries. At Doha last November [2001], WTO members agreed to defer TRIPS implementation for the least developed countries until 2016. ... TRIPS will not prevent other developing countries like Brazil and India from obtaining access to the medicines they need. On the other hand ... these countries have the capacity to nurture research-based pharmaceutical industries of their own, as well as other innovative industries, but this will only happen when they provide the IP protection that is enshrined in TRIPS. TRIPS needs to be recognized as an important industrial development tool for developing countries.[2]

---

[1]  Report of the UK Commission on Intellectual Property Rights (CIPR), London, Sep. 2002: <www.iprcommission.org/graphic/documents/final_report.htm>.

[2]  Sir Richard Sykes' presentation at the Royal Institute of International Affairs, London, 14 Mar. 2002.

Secondly, Oxfam, on behalf of the NGOs, has argued the opposite:

> Why do developing countries object so strongly to TRIPS? Its essential flaw is to oblige all countries rich and poor, to grant at least twenty years' patent protection for new medicines, thereby delaying production of the inexpensive generic substitutes upon which developing country health services and poor people depend. And there is no upside: the increased profits harvested by international drug firms from developing world markets will not be ploughed back into extra research into poor people's diseases – a fact some companies will in private admit.[3]

Many groups are also concerned with biodiversity conservation and IPRs including the Trade-Related Aspects of Intellectual Property Rights (TRIPS) Agreement and farmers' rights; protection of specific resources of geographical origin (like those in the case of turmeric or basmati rice, for example); and the provision of IP protection for traditional knowledge and national folklore.

In one of its interesting policy papers,[4] Oxfam, an organization referred to previously, propounded its views on the impact of strong IP rules and regulations on, among other things, access to medicines, seeds and educational material and the ability of 'poor' countries to develop and participate in the international marketplace. In its view, the control of knowledge instead of largely being with the corporate interests for personal profit, should help in addressing issues of poverty and disease, healthcare and education.

While intellectual protection is a useful incentive for stimulating investment in inventive activity, strong IP protection as envisaged in the TRIPS Agreement tended, according to its view, to help the private interests of corporate IPRs holders more than the users of knowledge. It feels that the TRIPS regime would exclude poorer people from access to essential 'knowledge goods', for example medicines, seeds and educational material.

Although developing countries are rich in traditional knowledge and genetic resources, they are largely importers of high-technology produce protected by IP. Also, the developed countries account for more than 90% of the international spending on research and development and are the main exporters of IP products. For example, in 1998, the United States received a net surplus of more than USD 23 billion from its IP exports. Again, with just 10% of global expenditure on R&D and health research, the developing world has to cope with 90% of global diseases needing the necessary medicines, requiring large-scale funding and joint venture partnerships for research and development to be directed for their basic needs.

Oxfam's position in respect to access to patented medicines ('Cut the Cost' Campaign) and the focus in the future campaigning strategies of some civil society organizations raises the question of reform of the TRIPS Agreement. The short-term goal seems to be to strengthen public safeguards in the Agreement. Here, the concerned organizations felt that small gains during the interregnum could strengthen and not undermine the

---

[3] Oxfam (2001) 'Priced out of Reach: How WTO Patent Policies will Reduce Access to Medicines in the Developing World' Oxfam Briefing Paper No. 4, Oxfam International, Oxford: <www.oxfam.org.uk/resources/health/download/priced.rtf>.

[4] Oxfam Discussion Paper 12/01 'Intellectual Property and the Knowledge Gap'.

momentum through what was being termed 'reinterpretation', as at the WTO's Ministerial meeting in November 2001 and the Doha Declaration on TRIPS and Public Health.

While the civil society NGOs helped change the dialogue in bringing TRIPS and public health together in the aforementioned Doha Ministerial meeting, the ministers also clarified at that meeting that TRIPS should not prevent countries from taking the required measures to protect public health.

In the context of this campaign by certain civil society organizations concerning the cost of medicines, it is necessary to highlight two basic points. First, the TRIPS Agreement is a Paris Convention-plus, and a Berne Convention-plus, treaty. It has provided for strengthening of certain provisions in these conventions, such as protection of product patents and enforcement provisions in respect of IPR protection that did not exist in the said conventions. With the constantly progressive development of new technologies, national legislations as well as international conventions and treaties would require periodical updating.

So, for instance, the WIPO Internet Treaties – the WIPO Copyright Treaty (WCT) and the WIPO Performance and Phonograms Treaty (WPPT) referred to earlier in Chapter 3 – are, in fact, TRIPS-plus treaties in the field of copyright and related rights. Likewise, in the field of harmonization of patent legislation, TRIPS-plus treaties could certainly follow. So the first point to be stressed is that in respect to IPRs and the protection of creative activity, modernization of laws and treaties cannot, and will not, remain static.

It is interesting in this context to note that a number of developing countries, countries in transition and some developed countries which had to update their IP legislation, have incorporated into their national laws provision for levels of IP protection even beyond the provisions in the TRIPS Agreement.

The second point to stress is that while in the copyright field certain TRIPS-plus treaties have already been formulated, a TRIPS-minus situation is hardly likely to arise in the context of industrial property protection.

## 10.4 FLEXIBILITY IN THE TRIPS AGREEMENT

Some civil society groups have argued for an outright abolition of the TRIPS Agreement. This does not seem feasible. A much better alternative is to consider nearly two dozen 'flexibilities' in the TRIPS Agreement. It is important for civil society organizations, the private sector and governments to use these flexibilities to the fullest advantage in the process of implementing the Agreement provisions as well as national legislation. In fact, an awareness-building campaign in regard to the existence of these flexibilities in the TRIPS Agreement should be undertaken by the concerned civil society organizations with positive collaboration and assistance from governments. It should be stepped up, as it would greatly help, inter alia, in supporting access to medicines as well.

It is interesting to note here that, while addressing a seminar on 20 March 2001 at Brussels organized by Oxfam on 'What Future for WTO Agreement on Trade-Related Aspects of Intellectual Property Rights', the European Trade Commissioner made some very valid observations. Referring to the concerns of certain NGOs as regards the manner in which the WTO's Agreement concerning protection of IPRs would affect the developing countries, he emphasized that the TRIPS Agreement embodies the necessary flexibility that would permit developing and least-developed countries to adapt their IP laws to comply with their respective policy objectives.[5] He said that he also supported the Agreement because he believed that 'it provides the requisite flexibility to allow developing countries to reconcile specific policy objectives in areas such as public health and biodiversity with intellectual property rights laws'. He further added that, 'however, if it is felt that there are fundamental problems in implementing this flexibility, the European Union (EU) is prepared to promote discussion, within the WTO and other relevant organisations, to address and resolve these difficulties'.

The Commission's programme, it was stated, included working with WHO, WIPO and the WTO to consider the link between the TRIPS Agreement and health issues, as well as working constructively with the concerned NGOs and the civil society, in arriving at a global solution to the problem.

As regards the issues concerning biodiversity referred to in the previous paragraphs, it might be of interest here to mention very briefly that the conflicts and complementarities between the 1992 CBD on the one hand, and elements of the international IP regimes on the other hand, have been subjects of considerable debate over the past ten years.

During the last decade and a half, a number of significant developments related to IPRs and conservation of biodiversity have taken place. The two major international agreements that deal with these issues are the TRIPS Agreement and the CBD.

While CBD has already been discussed earlier in Chapter 4, it is germane here to point out that the CBD recognizes the sovereign right of countries to control access to their genetic resources and biodiversity. It also promotes the sharing of benefits that are derived from the use of genetic resources and biodiversity. It requires countries to respect and protect indigenous and local community knowledge. The TRIPS Agreement, on the other hand, contains no specific provision for the protection of community knowledge or for recognition of community rights. Further, it also does not provide for the need to equitably share in the benefits of knowledge related to biodiversity.

The CBD provides in its Article 16 that access to and transfer of technology, in particular to developing countries, should be provided for and facilitated under favourable terms, including concessional and preferential terms where mutually agreed. In the case of technology that is protected by patents and other IPRs, such access and transfer shall be on terms that recognize and are consistent with adequate and effective protection of IPRs.

Both Article 16(5) and Article 22 provide countries with some manoeuvrability with regard to IPRs. These articles specify that while recognizing that patents and other IPRs may have an influence on the implementation of the CBD, the states party to the Convention shall cooperate, subject to national legislation and international law, to ensure that such rights do not run counter to its objectives. Also, that provisions of the CBD 'shall not

---

[5]    Oxfam Discussion Paper 12/01 'Intellectual Property and the Knowledge Gap'.

affect the rights and obligations' of states party to it, 'deriving from any existing international agreement, except where the exercise of those rights and obligations would cause a serious damage or threat to biological diversity'.

Insofar as the TRIPS Agreement is concerned, Article 8 allows for legal measures by governments to protect public health and nutrition and to promote the public interest in sectors of vital importance to their socio-economic and technological development. Though environmental protection is not explicitly built into this, it could be justified as being in the 'public interest'.

Article 27(2) allows for exclusion from patentability, inventions whose commercial use needs to be prevented to safeguard against 'serious prejudice' to the environment. Article 27(3) allows countries to exclude plants and animals from patentability and also plant varieties, so long as there is some other 'effective' form of IPR for such varieties.

Article 22 allows for the protection of products which are geographically defined through 'geographical indications'. This could help protect some products which are known by the specific locations in which they have originated.

## 10.5 Civil Society and Biodiversity

The CBD has two interesting provisions relating to IPRs. First, Article 16.5 states that Contracting Parties shall cooperate to ensure that IPRs are 'supportive of and do not run counter to its [the CBD's] objectives'. However, this is 'subject to national legislation and international law'. Another provision in Article 22 states that the CBD's provisions 'shall not affect rights and obligations of any Contracting Party deriving from any existing international agreements, except where the exercise of those rights and obligations would cause a serious damage or threat to biological diversity'.[6] However, the actual impact of IPRs on biodiversity needs to be examined. Some civil society organizations are raising concerns about IP regimes encouraging loss of biodiversity through large-scale use of modern bio-technology resulting in genetically engineered varieties. The quest for new plants to create new products has resulted in a new 'gold rush', otherwise known as 'bioprospecting'.

The Environmental Forum of the Peoples Summit of the Americas for the Hemispheric Integration Process, held at Santiago, Chile, in April 1998, reiterated that the protection of biodiversity was a priority for the hemisphere, and indicated that the civil society's recommendations were that it was necessary to recognize the need for:

– Affirming the collective rights of local communities to biodiversity resources and knowledge;
– Food security as a right;
– Protection of agriculture, biodiversity and IP over genetic resources;
– Establishing bio-security standards which prevent the release of genetically manipulated organisms.

---

[6]   Convention on Biological Diversity (CBD) (1992): <www.cbd.int/doc/legal/cbd-un-en.pdf>.

Subsequent developments relating to issues of IPRs and genetic resources, traditional knowledge as well as expressions of folklore, are being discussed at the Intergovernmental Committee (IGC) of the WIPO. This committee is examining the concerns of developing countries with genetic resources and traditional knowledge that are valuable to them and also to the world at large and yet some of such countries do not have a strong enough technological base to benefit from them.

On the basis of the efforts made by various civil society organizations, the IGC is attempting to evolve a consensus on the issues related to IPRs vis-à-vis genetic resources, traditional knowledge and expressions of folklore.

The IGC in its first meeting held in April 2001 at Geneva had identified certain major issues of concern:

(i)  Genetic Resources:
   – Contractual agreement for access to these resources and benefit-sharing; legislative, administrative and policy measures to regulate access to such resources and benefit-sharing; and
   – Multilateral systems for facilitating access to genetic resources and benefit-sharing protection of biotechnological inventions.
(ii)  Traditional Knowledge:
   – Terminological and conceptual issues;
   – Standards concerning the availability, scope and use of IPRs in traditional knowledge;
   – Legal criteria for the definition of prior art; and
   – Enforcement of rights in traditional knowledge.

Similarly for expressions of folklore, a consensus is being attempted on protection of handicrafts and other tangible expressions of folklore in order to establish an international system of sui generis protection for expressions of folklore by moving forward from the earlier WIPO-UNESCO (1985) model.

The IGC has also been making concerted efforts to establish a relationship acceptable to the developing and the developed world, based on already well-defined and accepted instruments such as the TRIPS Agreement and the CBD. Thus, it is apparent that organizations of the Civil Society are extremely relevant and important for putting IPRs in an overall developmental context, and for evolving the necessary consensus on issues relating to both the developed and developing world, as well as to the countries in transition.

While, naturally, the interest of the producers and right holders, including inventors and creators of works, have dominated in the evolution of IP policy, that of the ultimate consumers and rights users need also to be heard and heeded. It is here that the organizations of civil societies have brought a certain focus to these issues at the international level. These organizations have also discussed the interests of the consumers in areas, among others, related to access to medicines needed by the poorer sections of society; systems for protecting plant varieties while safeguarding farmers' rights; and access to and benefit-sharing enshrined in the functions of biological diversity, traditional knowledge and genetic resources.

Again, civil society organizations have brought into focus the requirement of higher levels of IPR protection in the digital economy era. This has resulted in the formulation of treaties such as the WCT and WPPT (popularly known as the Internet Treaties). The role of civil society organizations is, and continues to be, extremely crucial in ensuring that IP systems are used for overall development, keeping in view that the interests of both the producers and the ultimate consumers in the developed or developing worlds must be balanced to their mutual satisfaction.

# CHAPTER ELEVEN

# CHALLENGES FOR THE INTELLECTUAL PROPERTY SYSTEM

- *Digital Economy*
- *E-Commerce*
- *Domain Names*
- *Biotechnology including Human Genome*
- *Nanotechnology*

## 11.1 THE NEW KNOWLEDGE-DRIVEN ENTERPRISES

Information and communication technology (ICT), biotechnology (BT) and nanotechnology (NT) are going to be the three defining technologies of the twenty-first century. Knowledge assets of high-tech enterprises in ICT, BT and NT very often represent almost 90% of their market capitalization. In each of these areas, the product or service is a piece of intellectual property (IP) – typical examples are a new connecting device to make routers and servers more efficient in ICT, or a new technique for rapid deoxyribonucleic acid (DNA) sequencing in BT. In this chapter, we look at the specific challenges connected with some of these technologies.

## 11.2 DIGITAL ECONOMY

Rapid developments in digital technology are changing the way we live, study, work, do business, communicate with each other and entertain ourselves. The changes are pervasive and far-reaching. Some of the technological changes have greatly affected the manner in which works can be created, used and disseminated. Some examples of these changes are satellite broadcasting and cable television and digital transmission systems, such as the Internet. The reach of such technologies is global and across borders.

### 11.2.1 Intellectual Property Rights Issues in Digital Technology

Digital technologies and the Internet, in particular, have far-reaching impact on IP and the international IP system.[1] Digital technology enables anyone to make perfect copies.

---

[1]   Eskedar Nega, 'Emerging IPR Issues in the Information Economy', Fourth Meeting of the Committee on Development Information (CODI-IV), (Ethiopia, 23-28 Apr. 2005): <www.uneca.org/codi/codi4/ICT/Day2-April26/EskedarNega.ppt>.

This can be done with speed, accuracy and in volumes that were not conceivable even a decade ago. Each copy in turn can be further reproduced and disseminated without any loss of quality. Works can be made available to the public in large numbers almost instantaneously. When, for instance, the Nobel Prizes are announced on the Internet, at a given date and time, millions of viewers across the globe discover who the winners are instantaneously. Digital networks allow dissemination to many individuals from a single point; each recipient on the network can engage in further dissemination of the work, causing the work to spread with exponential speed.

Previously, a user had difficulty in modifying work created by someone else. Not so today. Digital technology now makes it possible for users to alter the works with ease. Furthermore, equipment needed to do all this exists not only in commercial establishments but also in millions of private homes across the globe.

The ease with which works in digital form can be replicated or modified is good news for the user. But it poses difficulties for the law. There is a general perception that making copies for personal or private use is fair use and lawful. In the digital domain, 'perfect' multiple copies can be generated by the same technology, which is employed for making use of the digital product. Thus, it has become more difficult for copyright owners to exercise control over replication of their works and to obtain compensation for such replication. Although the copyright system in the print world has generally focused on sales of copies of copyrighted works, in the digital world, on the other hand, the trend is to reap financial rewards for creating and disseminating intellectual products by charging for access to, and use of, the digital mode and for limiting rights to use and copy these products.

Another challenge is created because of the fact that digital works can be transmitted and used by multiple users, compared to the paper versions of the same works. A pirated version of a digital work can be loaded into a large computer system with multiple user networks, each of which can have virtually simultaneous use of the same copy. These and other problems have led to the development of elaborate systems with access restrictions and regulations. The issues concerning who should regulate the types of rights to be controlled, and the kinds of access to information sources, have also sprung up.

Works in digital form are amenable to easy and quick modifications by users. Through digital sampling techniques, sound recordings can be mixed and combined with others to produce a new sound recording, different from the original works. Photographs and video recordings in digital form can be manipulated to add, delete and combine elements from different works. Computer programs can, by processing through some re-engineering tools, be transmuted into unrecognizable forms. The user can sell all these products as new works. Under the 'first sale rule', owners of copies of protected works have personal property rights which authorize them to exercise control over the derivative work. Now lawmakers will have to amend the copyright statutes to provide some authority for exercising suitable control over what users can do with a copyrighted work in digital form.

In multimedia works it is possible to combine text, sound, still and moving images into a single medium. Works protected by copyright will become less differentiated by type and more equivalent to one another because they will now be in the same medium. This equivalence of works in digital form will make it easier to create a difficult-to-classify work by combining what has previously been thought of as separate categories of works for copyright purposes. Therefore, another emerging challenge will be that of categorization.[2]

### 11.2.2 Technological-Cum-Legal Means of Intellectual Property Rights Protection

Digital economy will flourish only with safe and secure digital asset management methods. Protection of digital IP can be achieved by applying legal, administrative as well as technological measures.[3]

Insofar as technological measures are concerned, for protection of digital IP, these could be implemented through access control; control of certain users; integrity protection; usage metering; and electronic copyrights management. Password-based access control can be applied either at the level of service and contents or at the level of user or receiver. Subsequent access can be prevented by disintegration or shutting down of the program after a predefined period.

As concerns technologies for IP protection, these would need to, inter alia, also use encryption technology. 'Encryption' is almost as old as humanity; human beings have always tried to find ways to ensure that their communications are not understood by 'unintended recipients'. Businesses that need confidentiality (negotiations of a business agreement, protection of trade secrets, and the like) or want to restrict access to material (pay-television); or consumers and citizens who want to protect their privacy; also use this technology.

There are two main kinds of encryptions: symmetric and asymmetric. Symmetric encryption means that the same key that is used to encrypt a message is also used to decrypt a message. Encryption has so far used symmetric keys. The problem with symmetric encryption is that the parties to the transmission must have access to the key and must, therefore, find a secure way to exchange the key or password necessary to encrypt and then decrypt the file or message. Naturally, they must keep the key secret, and anyone gaining access to the key would be able to decrypt the message. While this risk exists in any form of encryption, it may be greater in the case of symmetric encryption, as parties might be tempted to use the same key for a long period of time. One of the most popularly used symmetric encryption algorithms is the Digital Encryption Standard (DES), which is used, inter alia, on bankcards for automated teller machines (ATMs).

Asymmetric cryptography came up in the 1970s. Asymmetric encryption makes it possible to divide an encryption key into two parts: one part that is private (or secret) and the other part that is public. In a way, it is a private key/public key encryption. A person can now send an encrypted message to another person without worrying about how the

---

[2]   A.S.A. Krishnan & A.K. Chakravarti, *Electronics Information and Planning* (Government of India, Department of Electronics, 1997), 618-625.

[3]   Urs Gasser, 'Legal Frameworks and Technological Protection of Digital Content: Moving Forward Towards a Best Practice Model', (Harvard Univ. – Berkman Center for Internet & Society, Univ. of St. Gallen, Jun. 2006): <http://papers.ssrn.com/sol3/papers.cfm?abstract_id=908998>.

other person will get the secret key. The sender uses the receiver's public key (which is freely available, for example in a key directory) and the receiver uses the private key that corresponds to the public key to decrypt the message.

A public key infrastructure (PKI) may be defined as the legal and technical structure necessary to issue digital certificates and License Certification Authorities (CAs). Digital certificates are the identity cards of those who buy and sell on networks. Issuance of a certificate is normally required before a CA will accept to register A's public key as belonging to A. The certificate might contain A's identity and the public key number(s) and algorithm used, since there are many in circulation. It might also have an expiry date and identification of the CA.

Another technology of IP protection is watermarking. Watermarking is the process of modifying image data for inserting codes for carrying information. Watermarking of contents is carried out to ensure: copyright protection; data authentication; and ownership identification.

Watermarking could be of several types, such as blind versus non-blind. Availability of original image is essential to detect a blind watermark, which helps in ownership identification. In the case of public/private watermarks, a private watermark can be read only by the owner, whereas public watermarks can be read by anyone. Similarly, watermarks may be readable and detectable. Watermarking along with Electronics Rights Management Systems (ERMs) enable enforcement of copyrights in digital networks.

An ERMs is essentially a database which contains information on rights and about right holders. 'Rights management information' means information which identifies the work, the author and the owner of the work or information about the terms and conditions for the use of the work. Such information may be attached to the copyrighted works electronically. At present, a number of technologies are being explored the world over. The components of the electronic copyright management may be:

– a registration and recordation system;
– a digital library system with affiliated repositories of copyrighted works;
– a rights management system; or
– a transaction monitoring system to check the illegal use of systems.

Such a system might be appropriate for applications like digital library, electronic commerce and for those projects for which copyright is likely to be an important consideration.

The need to tune the international treaties to address the impact of digital technologies was discussed in several fora during the early 1990s. The culmination of these discussions was the conclusion in December 1996 of two new World Intellectual Property Organization (WIPO) Treaties; namely the WIPO Copyright Treaty (WCT) and the WIPO Performances and Phonograms Treaty (WPPT). Among other things, these treaties and their interpretive statements require that right holders enjoy exclusive control over on-demand electronic disseminations of their works, and confirm that the reproduction right is fully applicable in the digital environment. They also require member countries to protect the technologies used to prevent infringement and the rights management information that right holders may choose to provide in digital form.

Article 11 of the WCT obliges Contracting States to provide adequate legal protection and effective legal remedies against the circumvention of effective technological measures that are used by authors in connection with the exercise of their rights under this Treaty.

Article 12 of the WCT obliges Contracting States to provide adequate and effective legal remedies against any person knowingly performing any of the following acts knowing, or with respect to civil remedies having reasonable grounds to know, that it will induce, enable, facilitate or conceal an infringement of any right covered by this Treaty; to remove or alter any electronic rights management information without authority; and to distribute, import for distribution, broadcast or communicate to the public, without authority, works or copies of works knowing that electronic rights management information has been removed or altered without authority.

National copyright laws in most countries incorporate exceptions for copying for personal use, research, education, newspaper reporting, etc., based on principles of 'fair dealing'. The scope and flexibility of these exceptions differ in different countries. Since the digital technology enables unauthorized creation of unlimited, perfect and costless copies as well as their distribution, the copyright industries are concerned about the impact of this on their business and profitability. They are responding by using digital technology, in the form of encryption technologies and anti-circumvention measures, supplemented by contract law and sui generis forms of data protection. It is a major challenge to see how the appropriate 'fair use' exception can be preserved in a digital context, especially for poorer developing nations.

## 11.3 E-Commerce

In the context of digital economy, one of the areas undergoing changes as a result of the technological advances is commerce. A new term used to describe this is 'electronic commerce' or 'e-commerce'. Electronic commerce is commerce conducted across electronic media, mainly through the Internet, which comprises electronic networks. This network, together with a global infrastructure of computer and telecommunication technologies, facilitates an array of activities including buying, selling, trading, advertising and transactions of all kinds, which are conducted by processing and transmission of digitized data. IP is important in e-commerce because the intangible products transacted on the Internet must be protected using IP laws or they can be stolen or pirated. Also, IP is involved in making e-commerce work because the systems that allow the Internet to function – software, networks, designs, chips, routers and switches, the user interface, and so on – are forms of IP and often protected by IP rights. Trademarks are also an essential part of e-commerce business, as is branding, customer recognition and good will. Essential elements of web-based businesses are protected by trademarks and unfair competition law.

With increasing global dimensions of the knowledge-based economy and the growth of knowledge-based products, several challenges are appearing in the administration and management of electronic commerce and trade:[4]

- Unauthorized copying of content has been a major problem causing the loss of millions of dollars in revenue for the owners of these rights because of the ease with which digital files can be downloaded;
- The global characteristic of e-commerce businesses affects IP in a number of ways. It makes it difficult to find the infringer and enforce IP rights that are violated on the Internet. It is unclear which courts will have jurisdiction over disputes relating to e-commerce and IP. Also, laws affecting IP vary from country to country, so levels of protection may be different.
- Difficulty in deciding which laws to apply is a common problem, especially if the laws of the countries of the parties involved are different. Finally, even if the lawsuit succeeds, it could be difficult to enforce a judgment in another country.

International arbitration is one way to deal with international e-commerce disputes, though generally participation is voluntary and cannot be forced. Arbitration clauses may be agreed to in contracts, in which case the parties are required to use arbitration. WIPO's Arbitration and Mediation Center specializes in international dispute settlement and is well suited to solving international IP problems arising in e-commerce.

## 11.4 DOMAIN NAMES

Domain names are simple and human-friendly forms of Internet addresses that enable users to easily locate and remember addresses. The domain name system (DNS) operates on the basis of a hierarchy of names. The top-level domain names are 'generic top-level domains' (gTLDs), such as .com, .org, .net, .biz, or .info and 'country code top-level domains' (ccTLDs), such as .ch (Switzerland), .fr (France) or .za (South Africa). The use of the DNS has grown rapidly over the last few years. By the end of first quarter of 2008, there were more than 162 million domain names registered across all of the top-level domain names, with more than 63 million of these names registered in the ccTLDs.[5] Because domain names are easy to remember and use, the DNS – the central system for routing traffic on the Internet – has assumed a key role in electronic commerce. On the one hand, it facilitates the ability of consumers to navigate the Internet to find the websites they are looking for, and on the other hand, it facilitates businesses' ability to promote an easy-to-remember name or word which may, at the same time, serve to identify and distinguish the business itself (or its goods or services) and to specify its corresponding online, Internet location.

The system of business identifiers that existed before the arrival of the Internet was trademarks and other rights of business identification such as geographical indications.

---

[4]  <www.wipo.int/sme/en/e_commerce/index.htm>.
[5]  The VeriSign Domain Report, 'The Domain Name Industry Brief', vol. 5, 2008: <www.verisign.com/static/043939.pdf>.

Domain names have now acquired increasing significance as business identifiers. The conflict between domain names and standard Intellectual Property Rights (IPRs) raise challenging policy questions. One system – the DNS – is largely privately administered. It gives rise to registrations that result in a global presence. The other system – the standard IPR system – is publicly administered on a territorial basis. It gives rise to rights that are exercisable only within the territory concerned.

This conflict has given rise to a number of predatory and parasitical practices that have been adopted by some parties to exploit the lack of connection between the purposes for which the DNS was designed and those for which IP protection exists. There have been many cases where domain names of well-known trademarks have been deliberately registered by entities with no connection to those trademark rights. The idea is to sell the domain names to the owners of those marks, or simply to take unfair advantage of the reputation attached to those marks.

The growing number of cybersquatting disputes (regarding the abusive registration of domain names that violate trademark rights) reflects the premium that businesses place on domain names and their potential for facilitating e-commerce. Cybersquatting is universally condemned as an indefensible activity. Keeping this problem in view, the US government sought international support to request that WIPO initiate a balanced and transparent process to:

– develop recommendations for a uniform approach to resolving trademark/domain name disputes involving cyber piracy;
– recommend a process for protecting famous trademarks in the gTLDs; and
– evaluate the effects of adding new gTLDs and related dispute resolution procedure on trademark and IP holders.

WIPO, in July 1998, commenced an extensive international process of consultations – 'the WIPO Internet Domain Name Process'. The purpose of the WIPO process was to make recommendations to the corporation established for the technical management of the DMS, the Internet Corporation for Assigned Names and Numbers (ICANN), on certain questions arising out of the interface between domain names and IPRs. WIPO came out with clear guidelines:[6]

– Adoption of a number of improved, minimum 'best practices' for registration authorities ('registrars') registering domain names in the gTLDs intended to reduce the conflict that exists between domain names and IPRs. In particular, a formalized agreement clearly setting forth the rights and obligations of the parties is important.
– The ICANN should adopt a uniform dispute-resolution policy under which an administrative dispute-resolution procedure is made available for domain name disputes in all gTLDs. The administrative procedure should be quick, efficient and cost-effective.

---

[6]  Guide to WIPO Domain Name Dispute Resolution: <www.wipo.int/freepublications/en/arbitration/892/wipo_pub_892.pdf>.

– Prior to the introduction of any new gTLDs, a procedure should be established whereby the owner of a famous or well-known mark can obtain exclusion in some or all gTLDs for the name of the mark where the mark is famous or well-known on a widespread geographical basis and across different classes of goods or services.

On 24 October 1999, the ICANN Interim Board approved a Uniform Domain Name Dispute Resolution Policy (UDRP), with accompanying procedural rules. Beginning in December 1999, the WIPO Arbitration and Mediation Center[7] has been providing dispute-resolution services under the UDRP. The Center is internationally recognized as the leading dispute-resolution service provider for challenges related to abusive registration and use of Internet domain names, commonly known as 'cybersquatting'. The dimension of the problem can be visualized from the fact that in the year 2007, a record 2,156 complaints alleging cybersquatting were filed with the WIPO Arbitration and Mediation Center, representing an 18% increase over 2006 and a 48% increase over 2005 in the number of generic and country code TLD disputes.[8] Since the launch UDRP in December 1999 through December 2007, 12,334 cases relating to gTLDs and ccTLDs have been filed from one hundred different countries, covering 22,301 separate domain names. So far, 85% of panel decisions have ordered transfer of the domain names in question to the complainant. The top five sectors for complainant business activity were BT and pharmaceuticals, banking and finance, Internet and IT, retail, and entertainment. The pharmaceutical manufacturers remained the top filers due to numerous permutations of protected names registered for websites offering or linking to online sales of medications and drugs. Considering an unprecedented number of cybersquatting cases in 2007, the evolving nature of DNS is causing growing concern for trademark owners around the world.

## 11.5 BIOTECHNOLOGY

BT deals with living systems, including plants, animals and microbes. BT derives its strength from harnessing biological processes that sustain life. It incorporates any technique which uses living organisms, parts of organisms and enzymes, proteins, etc., which are either naturally occurring or are derived from living systems. Emerging BT uses recombinant DNA, cell fusion and embryo manipulation, among others.

It is essential to realize the latent potential in the biotech sector. There is also a need to attract venture capital firms to this sector. Venture capital has played a critical role in the IT and software sectors. The same model should be replicated in the biotech sector.

The increasing economic importance of BT has made the IP issues connected with biotechnological inventions assume great importance. Manufactured living organisms do not fit in the existing systems for the protection of IPRs. The existing IPR system has been basically

---

7   <www.wipo.int/amc/en/>.
8   DNS Developments Feed Growing Cybersquatting Concerns, press release- PR/2008/544, 27 Mar. 2008: <www.wipo.int/pressroom/en/articles/2008/article_0015.html>.

designed for inanimate objects. Human intervention for the development of inventions employing living matter has its own complications.[9]

Except for plant varieties, living material was generally not within the purview of any IPR system until the 1970s. In many industrialized countries this situation changed with the extension of patent coverage to microorganisms, which by the beginning of the 1980s were major vehicles for pharmaceutical innovations. Patent protection of higher organisms, including plants, animals and human tissue and cell cultures followed. Ethical issues in biological inventions, distinction between discoveries and invention, farmers' privilege, researchers' rights, community rights, geographical indications and methods of sharing biological materials are some of the issues on which deep debates have taken place in the last few years.

An adequate description of the invention is a prerequisite to judging the novelty of an invention and its patentability. In a biological invention, it is not possible to adequately describe a living substance, nor is it possible to reproduce the invention without the biological material. Consequently, all biological materials have to be deposited in recognized international repositories. In accordance with the Budapest Treaty on the International Recognition of the Deposit of Microorganisms for the Purposes of Patent Procedure, microorganisms are required to be deposited by the inventors in designated repositories. Such provisions are required to be legislated by the states for all biological materials.

With reference to IP protection of biological substances, the issue of 'discovery' verses. 'invention' must be clearly distinguished.[10] All findings in biology – where a biological substance and its properties already existed in nature but were noticed for the first time individually or collectively by humans – should be termed as 'discovery'. This will apply to microbes, plants and animals including every substance in them in full or in part during their development in the natural form. Naturally occurring microbes, plants and animals, etc., should be termed as products of nature.

By the same token, all processes of multiplication and production of animals and plants by natural processes such as crossing or selection, should be considered as essentially biological processes and should not be considered as patentable inventions. Inventions require human intervention. If such an intervention leads to something that is new, if it involves inventive steps, and if it is useful then it can qualify for IP protection.

Some understanding is beginning to emerge regarding patentability of biological materials. For example, as regards public order and morality, Article 6(2) of the EC Directive 98/44 provides a non-exhaustive list of inventions which should be considered unpatentable. These are processes for cloning human beings, processes for modifying the germ line genetic identity of human beings, use of human embryos for industrial or commercial

---

[9] 'The Role of Biotechnology Intellectual Property Rights in the Bioeconomy of 2030', report by E. Richard Gold, Matthew Herder and Michel Trommetter, OECD, 2007: <www.oecd.org/dataoecd/11/58/40925999.pdf>.

[10] *The Patenting of Biotechnological Inventions Involving the Use of Biological Aterial of Human Origin,* German National Ethics Council, 2005: <www.ethikrat.org/_english/publications/Opinion_patenting-of-biotechnological-inventions.pdf>.

purposes and processes for modifying the genetic identity of animals which are likely to cause them suffering without any substantial medical benefit to man or animal, and also animals resulting from such processes.

A particular category of biotechnological inventions, namely, inventions concerning microorganisms, is governed by special provisions. In the Trade-Related Aspects of Intellectual Property Rights (TRIPS) Agreement, under Article 27.3(b) it is obligatory to provide patent protection for 'microorganisms' and 'microbiological processes'. The term 'microorganisms', however, is not defined in the Agreement. In the patent laws of most countries, the microorganisms have not been clearly defined. As a result, there is flexibility in determining what can be patented under microorganisms.

The patentable microorganisms could be considered to be those that have been produced by human interventions, where the interventions are non-obvious and do not involve an essentially biological process. Such microorganisms would no doubt satisfy the criteria of novelty, inventive steps and usefulness or industrial applications. Such patentable micro-organisms may include the transgenic viruses, sub-viral particles, plasmids, bacteria, actinomycetes, yeast, fungi and parasites.

Many countries have considered naturally occurring microorganisms as non-patentable. But presently the developed countries including the EU, Japan and the US have started sharing the view that if naturally occurring substances including microorganisms are iso-lated for the first time in a form or purity that did not occur in nature; if they were identified distinctly; and if they had industrial applications, then these could be the subject matter of patents.

The provisions of TRIPS require that plant varieties need to be protected either by patenting or by a sui generis method or by a combination of both, but countries could keep plants outside the purview of patenting. Patents on plants are obtainable in certain countries such as the US, Japan and Australia under certain conditions. But the patent laws in Europe exclude plant varieties from patenting; these are protected by the sui generis method.

In Europe, plant variety protection (PVP) has been given a separate legal system, com-monly known as Plant Variety Rights or Plant Breeders' Rights. Such rights originated from and through the enactment of the International Union for the Protection of New Varieties of Plants[11] (UPOV). TRIPS does not mention or refer to the provisions of UPOV, nor does it indicate the precise steps to be taken for protecting plant varieties, except that it promulgates that plant varieties are to be protected.

Developing countries are, therefore, free to enact their own PVP law that would be consistent with TRIPS. In the new law, farmers' rights as well as researchers' rights could be upheld in accordance with the traditional practices of the country. The research-ers' rights are consistent with the provisions of IP principles in any country that research could be carried out with any material, provided that the new material produced out of the utilized material (protected or unprotected) is not marketed. In order to market a new

---

[11]  <www.upov.int/index_en.html>.

material produced from a protected material, there may be a need to obtain the consent of the owner depending upon the IPR laws of the state. As regards farmers' rights of saving seeds, these have to be consistent with the traditional practices of the country.

Genetic resources are the properties of the sovereign states to which they are indigenous. Future accessions of such resources would require consent from the state. The Convention on Biological Diversity[12] (CBD) promulgates ensuring the conservation and sustainable use of biological diversity beyond fair and equitable sharing of benefits from their utilization. Supply and exchange of biological materials are, therefore, expected to move across the borders through the material transfer agreements on the basis of authorized, mutually agreed terms and subject to authorized prior informed consent. Consequently, authorities and legislation for the access of biological materials of states would be in the making for all the CBD member countries.

IPRs and their protection in BT through patenting or through other internationally acceptable laws have been discussed at the national and international levels.[13] Several issues are indeed complex. The laws of protection of biotechnological inventions in different countries are different and are not yet uniform. Member countries of World Trade Organization (WTO) are to amend their IPR laws to conform with the minimum provisions contained in the TRIPS Agreement within a specified period.

### 11.5.1 Human Genome and IPR

Genomic science poses new questions for the patent system.[14] For example, whether and under what conditions genes, or parts of them, are patentable. The application of computer-automated gene-sequencing techniques and issues relating to computer-assisted assessment of the patentability conditions are also under discussion.

Researchers have announced that they have completed a draft of the genetic master blueprint of a human being. They have completed preliminary sequence maps of the human genome, encompassing an estimated 3 billion DNA base pairs. Besides the question of ownership of the data, one of the most controversial aspects of patenting the human genome is the question of rights of the donor.

Patent law has also struggled with the question of relevance of the person who donates human genetic tissue to a study, which results in a patentable product. Developing countries would like to see the link institutionalized. This link is also the basis on which developing countries claim benefit sharing in collaborative human genetic research. The patent itself does not recognize the need for informed consent or benefit sharing, which are central points of contention between developing and developed countries.

---

12    <www.cbd.int/>.
13    'Keeping Science Open: The Effects of Intellectual Property Policy on the Conduct of Science', The Royal Society, 2003: <http://royalsociety.org/displaypagedoc.asp?id=11403>.
14    'The Ethics of Patenting DNA', Nuffield Council on Bioethics, 2002: <www.nuffieldbioethics.org/go/ourwork/patentingdna/introduction>.

There has been widespread concern that the full medical benefits that could flow from decoding the human genome will not be achieved if the genes become private IP and are exploited for profit. But the drug companies have argued in the past that without patenting, they cannot fund the expensive drug research required.

In fact, the idea of gene patents is still a matter of concern to some who regard patenting of genes per se as undesirable due to one of the following reasons:

– Genes are natural and therefore, should not be 'owned' by any individual or organization;
– Genes are discoveries and not inventions and therefore are not new; or
– Gene isolation and cloning is such a well-established technique that it is no longer inventive to do it.

It is important to note that the US Patent and Trademark Office (USPTO) has decided not to grant patents on a fundamental gene, expressed sequence tags (ESTs), or single nucleotide polymorphisms (SNPs) unless the research perceives their role in human health or if they have a potential commercial value.

The IP protection of human genome-based inventions in developed countries is also affecting people in the developing world. While most developed countries already allow patents on human gene sequences as part of genomic inventions, many developing countries face the prospect of changing their laws in order to allow patentability of such inventions.

Allowing multiple patents on different parts of the same genome sequence – say on a gene fragment, the gene, and the protein – adds undue costs to the researcher who wants to examine the sequence. In this case, a researcher has not only to pay each patent holder via licensing to study the sequence of his/her interest, but also must pay to search different patents and determine the applicable area. Even though the new rules call for 'specific and substantial utility that is credible', some still feel that the rules are too lax. The US National Institutes of Health, (NIH) has taken the position that patenting ESTs is not in the best interests of the public because the function and practical utility of these sequences are often unknown.

Patent applications for gene fragments have sparked controversy among scientists. Many have urged the USPTO not to grant broad patents at this early stage of human genome research to applicants who have neither characterized the genes nor determined their functions and uses. It is felt that patenting gene fragments stakes claims that extend beyond their actual achievements, i.e., on probable future discoveries. As stated, at the moment ESTs have limited value and non-obvious utility and the information is considered rudimentary in nature. A lot of effort is required to advance the utility of a gene fragment for mapping, tissue typing, identification, antibody production or locating the gene regions associated with diseases. Even if the utility of the fragment is known, several workers would be discouraged from use of the patented ESTs of great biological implications as the patent holder may claim the fruits of future utility. Several discoveries about HIV have evolved from sequence information, but have been made available to the public. It is also felt that the research tools should not be so broad as to block discoveries outside of the patent.

The Committee on Intellectual Property Rights in Genomic and Protein Research and Innovation of National Research Council studied granting and licensing of IPRs on discoveries relating to genetics and proteomics and the effects of these practices on research and innovation.[15] The committee concluded that IP restrictions rarely impose significant burdens on biomedical research, but there are reasons to be apprehensive about their future impact on scientific advances in this area. It recommended enacting a statutory exception from infringement liability for research on a patented invention and raising the bar somewhat to qualify for a patent on upstream research discoveries in BT. With respect to genetic diagnostic tests to detect patient mutations associated with certain diseases, the committee urged patent holders to allow others to perform the tests for purposes of verifying the results.

Amidst all controversies, gene patenting has grown significantly in the last ten years. More than 4,270 gene patents have been granted to nearly 1,156 assignees. Of the top ten gene patent assignees, nine are US-based organizations. Incyte Pharmaceuticals/Incyte Genomics, whose IP rights cover 2,000 human genes, tops the list. Some of the other organizations on the list include the University of California, Isis Pharmaceuticals, the former SmithKline Beecham, and Human Genome Sciences.[16]

## 11.6 NANOTECHNOLOGY

The term 'NT' has been variously defined. Without going into restrictive definitions, one can accept that the term is being used to represent a far broader arena, the deciding factor being that novel and differentiating properties and functions are developed at a critical length scale of matter, typically less than 100 nanometres (a nanometre is one billionth of a meter). The National Science and Technology Council of the US, in a report on the National Nanotechnology Initiative (NNI), defines NT as being in the range of one to 100 monometers.[17]

The domain of NT is not restricted only to the realm of materials and applications but extends even to life sciences. NT has been heralded as one of the key technologies of the twenty-first century. By manipulating particles 100 to 10,000 times smaller than the diameter of a human hair, materials with new properties can be created. Nanomaterials in the form of particulates as well as layers – both mono as well as composite – have been found to improve the characteristics of products.

Many new applications in this category are being developed that are likely to impact several industries. The unique chemical, electronic, magnetic, optical, and other properties of nanoscale particles have led to their evaluation and use in a broad range of industries such

---

[15]  'Reaping the Benefits of Genomic and Proteomic Research: Intellectual Property Rights, Innovation, and Public Health'. Committee on Intellectual Property Rights in Genomic and Protein Research and Innovation, National Research Council, 2006: <www.nap.edu/catalog.php?record_id=11487>.

[16]  Kyle Jensen and Fiona Murray, 'Intellectual Property Landscape of the Human Genome', *Science* 310 239, 2005: <www.sciencemag.org/cgi/content/summary/310/5746/239>.

[17]  <www.nano.gov/html/facts/The_scale_of_things.html>.

as those related to ceramics, chemicals, pharmaceuticals, BT, textiles, electronics, telecommunications, micro-electronic and aerospace. Some internationally known companies operating in various fields are utilizing NT to an increasing extent, for example, DuPont in respect to nanomaterials being used for improved semiconductors; Dow for improved automobile materials; Toyota for stronger and thinner bumpers; and BASF for scratch resistant paint.

NT involves research and technology development at the atomic, molecular or macro-molecular level. It helps to provide an understanding of materials at the nanoscale, and to originate and utilize structures and systems that have special novel properties and functions due to their small or intermediate size. R&D in nanotech includes manipulation under control of nanoscale structures and their merging into larger material components and systems. Again within such larger scale assemblies, the control of their structures remains at the nanometre scale.

NT not only helps in miniaturization but also renders useful the desired changes in physical properties of the concerned material, for example making thin polymers less permeable and enhancing heat and chemical resistance, transparency and reduced weight of concerned materials.

The fast-moving NT industry is busily acquiring patents on the material building blocks and processes that make everything from dams to DNA. The volume of NT patents filed worldwide has grown dramatically over the past few years. In 2000, patent offices in the US, Europe and Japan granted around 650 patents on NT. In 2006, that number had more than doubled, to over 1,800 NT patents in these countries.[18] By the end of 2006, the total number of NT patents granted by the US patent office has reached 7,406, which is about twice the number granted by European patent office (3,596) and more than six times the number granted by the Japanese patent office (1,150).

The majority of NT patents is assigned to the United States. Other leading countries in numbers of patents include Japan, Germany, France, South Korea, Switzerland, the United Kingdom, and the Netherlands. IBM tops the list of maximum number of patents in the area of NT. Other leading organizations on the list are the University of California, the US Navy, Eastman Kodak and MIT, which own maximum number of NT patents in the US. Within academic institutions, US universities and Japanese national laboratories contribute a large number of NT patents. Notably, the University of California and Japan Science and Technology Agency have shown significant growth in the numbers of NT patents since the start of this decade.

According to the inventory maintained by the Project on Emerging Nanotechnologies (PEN), every week three to four new NT consumer products are coming to the market.[19] By April 2008, the number of NT-based consumer products in the inventory had grown to more than 600. Twenty percent of the NT products in the inventory refer to the use of

---

[18]   Hsinchun Chen et al., 'Trends in Nanotechnology Patents', *Nature Nanotechnology* 3 (2008): 123.
[19]   The Project on Emerging Nanotechnologies, Woodrow Wilson-International Center for Scholars, Press Release No. 31-08, 24 Apr. 24, 2008: <www.nanotechproject.org/process/assets/files/6697/pen_press_release_080422.pdf>.

nanoscale silver. Other nanoscale materials referenced in the products are carbon nantotubes, fullerenes, zinc oxide, titanium oxide, silica and gold. NT was part of more than USD 88 billion worth of products sold in the year 2007. By 2014, Lux Research estimates USD 2.6 trillion in manufactured goods will incorporate NT – that is, about 15% of total global output.

ICT, BT and NT will continue to be 'defining' and 'transformational' technologies in the twenty-first century. Strategic positioning of institutions, enterprises and nations will very critically depend on the creation, valorization, and leveraging of IP portfolios evolving as we march further into the twenty-first century.

# CHAPTER TWELVE

# DEMYSTIFICATION AND DEPOLITICIZATION OF INTELLECTUAL PROPERTY

 – *Need for Public Awareness of Intellectual Property (IP)*
 – *Identification of IP*
 – *Depoliticization of IP*

## 12.1 NEED FOR PUBLIC AWARENESS OF IP: DEMYSTIFICATION OF IP

Precepts of Intellectual Property (IP) have become powerful drivers of economic growth. When linked to the development of human capital, these become a dynamic combination in terms of stimulating creativity and innovation, generating revenue, promoting investment, enhancing culture, preventing 'brain drain' and nurturing overall economic well-being. Yet, the evolution of the IP system has largely remained relegated, till almost the last quarter of the previous century, to the realm of legal and technical jargon, lending it an aura of complexity bordering on chaos for some and mystification for others.

The web-based file-sharing of 'peer-to-peer' applications, like Napster, have caused the disturbing phenomenon of illegal consumer behaviour by the tens of millions in P2P sharing and downloading of music, video games and films on the Internet. Therefore, the need for demystification of IP precepts and practices for wider public understanding and awareness is necessary. It should be done in simple language so that IP literacy can be encouraged at all levels. Similarly, much of the politicization of IP starts from incorrect or inadequate understanding of the basics of the IP system. Therefore, depoliticization of IP – a concept related to demystification – at various levels of the society, is equally important.

In appreciating the value of IP, and the potential positive impact that it can have on society if it is used as a proper tool of development, awareness of its relevance, importance and usefulness, should be spread among all sectors of society and all persons involved in the process. In a culture where IP is known to help in development, government officials and agencies act to increase the value and raise the standards of living by advocating an increased use of IP rights. The private sector, from multinational corporations down to small- and medium-sized enterprises (SMEs), recognizes the value of IP rights in knowledge-based industries and economies. The public understands the benefits of purchasing legitimate goods and services, thereby boosting local industries and economies and increasing the tax base. The absence of IP culture can conceivably result in a stagnant, receding economy, a lack of creativity and inventiveness and a business climate bereft of foreign direct investment (FDI), consistency or reliability. It is thus essential that creators and inventors be helped and supported in the protection of their work – the song, the film, the design, the painting, the book or other creative innovation – in order to ensure that the society as a whole benefits thereby.

However, in a number of countries there is still a lack of understanding in certain sectors of how IP could promote wealth creation. Although some businesses effectively wield the 'IP tool', others, especially the SMEs as a whole, do not have the information necessary to do so.

The creation of an appropriate IP culture which balances the interests of the creator of IP with those of society at large is particularly important in developing countries. The benefits of IP do not merely pertain to the developed countries. By promoting and pursuing appropriate and proactive IP policies, developing countries can also benefit. This, together with depoliticization, is particularly important in developing countries, since they have great IP assets as well, but should recognize this and exploit them, not simply take the attitude that IP belongs to the developed countries which then seek to maximize their rights in developing countries. Therefore, promoting and pursuing proactive policies is essential. Such policies may start with an IP audit and the preparation of a strategic IP plan integrated with scientific, cultural, trade, economic and educational policies. Incentives and awards can be given to inventors and authors, as well as to societies and collective organizations that develop and use IP assets.

Attention has to be paid to the total set of components that are required to get a proper perspective of growth of IP culture. It includes human resource that is properly educated in creation, valuation, marketing and exploitation of IP; also well-equipped, user-friendly and customer-oriented IP offices and administrations; purposeful involvement of civil society organizations; promotion of innovation culture and IP in national academic and educational institutions, universities and research centres; programmes to develop practical skills such as licensing; drafting good IP laws; and enforcement of IP rights.

Some countries have taken appropriate steps in a proactive manner. For example, Singapore recognizes the importance of IP as a national resource and in attracting foreign investments in its development as a knowledge-based economy. To develop IP as a strategic and competitive resource, Singapore has adopted an essentially proactive IP rights policy for the development of high value-added and creative-content industries. In November 2000, the Ministry of Law announced that the Intellectual Property Office of Singapore (IPOS) would be converted into a semi-autonomous statutory body charged, inter alia, with administration of the IP system in Singapore. One of the recent IPOS initiatives is the provision of IP information via the recently launched SurfIP (<www.surfip.com>), a one-stop IP portal for searches across multiple patent databases in various jurisdictions, as well as the provision of other technical and business resources. On the Intellectual Property Rights (IPRs) enforcement front, the agency primarily responsible for domestic enforcement is the IPR Branch, a specialized Crime Division of the Criminal Investigation Department, while border-specific enforcement is undertaken by the Customs and Excise Department. In the field of education, Singapore has public education campaigns led by IPOS and the National Science & Technology Board aimed at promoting greater public awareness of IP rights. Today, Singapore is one of the leading nations, in per capita terms, regarding patent filings and creation of other IP assets.

Likewise, Hong Kong, Australia, the UK and the US all have active and attractive outreach programmes for business and for young people. A start has also been made in Hungary, India, Malaysia, the Philippines, Sri Lanka, Thailand, Trinidad and Tobago and others.

There is a general lack of patent literacy in many developing countries. They need to have not only 'patent literacy' but also 'literacy about patents'. These needs extend from academia, on one hand, to the general public, on the other, to educate the masses in this context. There are several misconceptions that prevail today in regard, inter alia, to bio-resources. There is a common misunderstanding that protection will cover all the existing known materials, living or non-living. A good example of this pertains to India. The common perception among the public was that turmeric and neem were stolen. It was only when the Council of Scientific & Industrial Research of India managed the revocation of the patent on the wound-healing properties of turmeric that clarity emerged. The general public understood that it was not turmeric per se that was patented but its use as a wound-healing agent. It also became clear to the public that an appeal could be made against the wrong grant of a patent.

The key elements for mounting a public awareness campaign should be:

– A structured approach to public awareness programmes based on interactive and con-tinuous evaluation of user requirements;
– Development of specific, target-oriented awareness programmes; young people should also be involved in taking a participatory, inclusive approach, for example through invention clubs in schools;
– Wide dissemination of the usefulness of IP systems through optimal use of various means of communication;
– Promotion of a culture of respect for IPRs through appropriate educational policies.

Rather than asking a question as to 'what is it that we can do for IP', we must ask as too 'what is it that IP can do for everyone'. In other words, instead of looking at the rest of the world through IP, one has to look at IP through the practical needs of all those who could benefit from the IP system. One should explain IP to them in a language in which they are accustomed, and not in the normal legal terms. Inculcation of the basic concepts of IP should start at the earliest level, i.e., from schools and universities. Use of audiovisual methods to communicate the message would be most appropriate for demystification of IP. Moreover, demystification programmes should be closer to the geographical regions of the target groups. To illustrate to them the value of IP in the context of their business interest is particularly important. In the initial stages, use of the IP system seems to increase the costs with no tangible benefits in sight. Only after a period of time, which may be of considerable duration, tangible benefits may flow to the IP rights holder.

## 12.1.1 International Efforts in Demystification

Keeping in view the importance of IPRs, almost all countries are beginning to recognize the importance of systematically informing the public about the role of IP in their daily lives as well as in achieving economic goals and developmental aspirations. Furthermore, such public awareness is considered key to effective enforcement of IPRs. Activities designed to demystify IP and create a better understanding of its relevance to society are being undertaken through an array of programmes including National Focus Action Plans (NFAPs).

We need to set up courses to build awareness concerning different strategies in designing and executing public outreach programmes from the conceptualization of the message of IP, the identification of target audiences and ensuring delivery of the message using various tools and media, i.e., print, broadcast and the Internet.

Many countries have set up IP cells to provide relevant information about IPRs. For example, the European Commission (EC) established, in October 1998, the IPR Helpdesk, as the central reference point for IP inquiries and advice throughout the EU. In the US, a special website for independent inventors gives basic information on a number of frequently asked questions about IPRs. The Office of Independent Inventor Programs (OIPP) of the US Patent and Trademark Office (USPTO) established the site in March 1999. In India, for example, Technology Information & Forecasting Assessment Council (TIFAC), has set up a patent facilitation cell.

## 12.1.2 World Intellectual Property Organization Efforts

Initiation of a broader campaign for the demystification of IPRs was undertaken by World Intellectual Property Organization (WIPO) in late 1990s. This includes efforts to bring both the IP system and the organization closer to the people, to reach out to the grass roots level, to encourage and support inventors and research and development institutions and to protect industry, as well as to support SMEs in relation to their IP needs.

WIPO has launched a campaign to demystify IP and make it more accessible to all. It explains how IP works in practice, how it promotes investment and affects valuation, how inventions relate to research policies, how cultural industries can be supported by IP policies, how trademarks relate to branding and licensing, how incentives could be created for IP assets development, how IP assets are managed, how licensing operates to share knowledge and spread the value of IP, how IP can be protected, and other matters of interest to policy and business leaders.

Telling the story of IP and WIPO in an interesting and informative way and disseminating that story widely is being done through a combination of new products, new partners and new technologies. Using the Internet, contacts with the press, a wide variety of publications, multimedia products and exhibitions as well as working with partners in Member States, the organization has reached new audiences in its campaign to emphasize the key role IP plays in improving the quality of life and in acting as a tool for social, cultural and economic progress. Close cooperation with the media increased and improved the balance of reporting on its work and key IP issues, resulting in a greater understanding of both the organization and IP in general. New and updated publications and publicity materials for meetings and events targeting the general public as well as specialized audiences are increasing in scope and number every year. The organization has been working with some Member States and certain organizations, especially in regard to the cooperation for developing programmes in the area of public outreach.

WIPO believes that the human capital of developing countries is the key to those countries realizing the full benefits of the national and international IP systems. The WIPO Worldwide Academy helps to develop those human resources, setting up modern and tailor-made training programmes for policy advisers, development managers and other target groups.

Its activities include:

– new training and teaching techniques;
– a Distance Learning Centre based on Internet facilities;
– client-specific learning modules and materials; and
– use of modern public-access media to disseminate knowledge of IP.

These tailor-made programs have been accessed by more than 70,000 participants since its inception in 1999, benefiting large numbers of people from all walks of life.[1]

Today, WIPO has comprehensive education and training programmes at national and regional levels for officials dealing with IP, including those concerned with management of rights and enforcement and for traditional and new groups of users. These provide education and training on the value of IP and how to create their own economic assets through better use of the IP system. WIPO renovated its website in 2006, with improved navigational features with dedicated web pages on copyright, patents, trademarks, designs and geographical indications. This facilitates public access to the wealth of information regarding different forms of IPRs. A new webcasting area was launched on the website to show WIPO's outreach films. The latest film products in WIPO's creativity and copyright series include profiles of the music and film industries in Kenya and Nigeria. The web-based WIPO Outreach Guides were created to provide governments and organizations with a step-by-step guide for planning outreach campaigns. WIPO distributed some 185,000 free information products in 2006, in addition to 21,000 paid publications. The WIPO Awards program distributed more than 150 awards in 2006 to publicize the achievements of inventors and creators and their contributions to society.[2]

Initial responsibility for the implementation of this IP outreach program rests with the appropriate government authorities charged with overseeing IP issues in a given country. While the program is essentially designed for developing countries, where there may be more of a debate over the balance between producers' or owners' versus the public's rights to IP, parts of it can be applied to all countries, irrespective of their level of development,

---

[1]    <www.wipo.int/academy/en/>.
[2]    *World Intellectual Property Organization: An Overview*; 2007 Edition.

that are seeking to create broader awareness of IP issues in their society. Every government needs to promote IP issues and encourage invention and innovation.

A variety of informational materials are produced and tailored by WIPO to address the needs of specific target audiences, such as small businesses, artists, research institutions and young people. WIPO uses different means, starting from the web, film and television to publicity events, seminars and written publications to reach a diverse public. With the assistance of international news media, WIPO helps to disseminate factual information on new developments to encourage accurate and objective coverage of IP issues.[3]

SMEs form the backbone of most economies and are often the driving force behind innovations in the knowledge-driven economy. Their innovative and creative capacity, however, is not always fully exploited as SMEs under-utilize the IP system, partly due to their lack of awareness. With different programs, WIPO reinforces cooperation with governments in developing policies and strategies that meet the IP needs of SMEs.

## 12.1.3 Demystification of Biopiracy-Based Perceptions

Some of the conflicts have arisen from the perception that knowledge-rich companies and researchers from the developed world have been attracted to the wealth that the lesser-developed countries have in their biodiversity and in their traditional knowledge systems. The rich nations will argue that access to such biodiversity and community knowledge by the industrially developed nations is necessary for the larger welfare of mankind, as this advances knowledge and leads to new products, which in turn contribute to the well-being of global consumers. On the other hand, those who supposedly guard the interests of the lesser-developed argue that this access to resources of the lesser-developed does not benefit them in any way, while their natural resources and IP continues to be appropriated and exploited.

The conflicts further deepen when it is claimed that many researchers from the developed world have obtained knowledge about biodiversity and its uses from local innovators, communities and institutions, but they have not even acknowledged their contributions, let alone shared the benefits resulting from such knowledge. Many cases are cited as examples. For example, a new antibiotic was launched in the US based on a researcher's discovery of peptides in frog skin. The researcher had found three tribes in Africa and America that knew about the wound-healing capabilities of the frog skin and were using it for that purpose. However, no benefit was given to the concerned tribes.

It has been argued that communities have a storehouse of knowledge about their flora and fauna – their habits, their habitats, their seasonal behaviour and the like – and it is only logical and consonant with natural justice that these communities be given a greater say in all matters regarding the study, extraction and commercialization of their biodiversity. Conflicts will vanish only when a policy is developed that does not obstruct the advancement of knowledge and provides for valid and sustainable uses and IP protection with just benefit sharing.

---

[3]   *World Intellectual Property Organization: An Overview*; 2007 Edition.

We need to reach some understanding here. While it is true that many indigenous cultures appear to develop and transmit knowledge from generation to generation within a system, individuals in local or indigenous communities can distinguish themselves as informal creators or inventors, separate from the community. Furthermore, some indigenous or traditional societies are reported to recognize various types of IPRs over knowledge which may be held by individuals, families, lineages or communities. Discussion of IPRs and traditional knowledge should draw more on the diversity and creativity of indigenous approaches to IPR issues. In addition, there are power divisions as well as knowledge divisions among people in many communities, and sharing benefits with a community as a whole is no guarantee that the people who are really conserving traditional knowledge and associated biodiversity will gain the rewards they deserve for their efforts, since it provides much-needed financial support for the first time for such endeavours.

Conflict resolution and demystification can take place when it is recognized that there is a deep philosophical divide on the issue of IPRs that must be addressed. The existing IPR systems are oriented around the concept of private ownership and individual creativity or invention. They are at odds with indigenous cultures, which emphasize collective creation and ownership of knowledge. There is a concern that IPR systems encourage the appropriation of traditional knowledge for commercial use without the fair sharing of benefits, or that they violate indigenous cultural precepts by encouraging the commodification of such knowledge.

Whether one likes it or not, it is a hard fact that a mere focus on morally defined rights will not be successful because it is too difficult to build arguments to bridge the wide gap between general human rights and indigenous peoples' rights in the changing value systems of the modern world. It is generally difficult to attribute an objective economic value to the knowledge of local and indigenous communities and associated resources, for a number of reasons. One could be the absence of a market for genetic resources and the complexity of inputs going into the creation of new crop varieties. It will be more pragmatic to focus on the costs of conservation to indigenous and local communities as a guide to designing economic incentives that will help them gain adequate rewards. Different interest groups, such as industry, IP experts, and indigenous and local peoples' organizations need to cooperate in order to define mechanisms for more effective sharing of benefits with the providers of traditional knowledge and genetic resources.

## 12.2 DEPOLITICIZATION OF IP

Long considered a technical issue, IP policy has now entered the political arena and is often held up to public scrutiny, obliging its defenders to justify its raison d'être.

This is due in part to the increasing economic importance of IP, which has made it an important issue in trade relations between states.

Misunderstandings over the use of IPRs in connection with culturally and socially sensitive material previously assumed to be in the public domain can cause particularly severe difficulties. Companies, especially in the pharmaceutical and agro-food industries, are increasingly turning to new sources – such as genetic material, traditional remedies and little-known plants and animal species – in their search for new products. This has provoked emotional debates over the concept of 'ownership' of these resources and of products derived from them.

This increasing politicization of IP issues means that business has to focus on developing an effective communications strategy concerning IP issues, and on encouraging education about the importance of IP for society. This is essential if it is to garner the support of the public, and ensure that gains made to strengthen protection are not whittled away due to political opposition. Public support for IPRs would also greatly alleviate enforcement problems made more acute by new technologies and globalization.

In fact, as a result of inadequate understanding of the basics of IP, vested interests, politicians and the general public make misleading statements which are not based on the laws and practices of IP. The other element that influences the IP system is lack of balance when it comes to interests of different stakeholders, most often in relation to health, safety and agricultural security, i.e., pharmas and fear of genetically modified crops.

The increasing integration of IP issues and concerns with broader international issues and its emergence in many other fora as an issue of great interest also contribute to the increased politicization of IP. IP issues have been brought into debates on the protection and exploitation of biodiversity resources, on the development and transfer of technology for environmental protection, on the protection of folklore and indigenous culture and on other aspects of economic and social development.

Basically, IP is a techno-legal subject leading to the economic growth of the society. In a democracy, issues pertaining to technological and economic policies and the technocracy implementing these, should ideally remain a priority despite changes of ruling parties of the countries, whether developed, developing or those in transition. But this is an ideal which is always not practised.

In conclusion, it may be said that the need to continue efforts to build a greater awareness among all sectors of society – policy makers, government officials, the business community and the general public – about the relevance and role of IP with regard to economic, social and cultural activities in society is a must. The IP system is a sophisticated system with legal, technical, economic, social, cultural and administrative dimensions. A collective effort to demystify the system would make it integrate easily into development perspectives of both developing and developed countries.

# INDEX